Kungaloosh!

The Mythic Jungles of Walt Disney World

Jim Korkis

Theme Park Press
The Happiest Books on Earth
www.ThemeParkPress.com

Theme Park Press publishes its books in a variety of print and electronic formats. Some content that appears in one format may not appear in another.

Editor: Bob McLain
Layout: Artisanal Text

ISBN 979-8-89609-042-7
Printed in the United States of America

Theme Park Press | **www.ThemeParkPress.com**
Address queries to ben@themeparkpress.com

Dedicated to Ian A. Janosko, a former Jungle Cruise skipper, whose passion and knowledge of the Adventurers Club exceeds my own.

He first visited the club when he was six years old in 1989 and ended up proposing to his wife Kristin, another former Jungle Cruise skipper, at the Adventurers Club Hoopla on August 21, 2008. He continues to keep the magic of the club alive through Adventurers in Charity.

Contents

Introduction

Jambo! It's a jungle out there in Walt Disney World or, more accurately, several different jungles providing magical, memorable adventures.

The word "jungle" can refer to the lush vegetation of Africa, India, Asia, South America, the South Pacific or even an imaginary planet. All those different exotic locations appear in Disney live action and animated movies as well as at Walt Disney World.

To help pay my way through college, I worked as a tram driver at the Los Angeles Zoo for over two years. During summers, holidays, weekends and more, I maneuvered a tram full of passengers through twisting, narrow paths surrounded by overgrown foliage to several tram stops inside the zoo.

During my first week of training, I almost (accidentally) killed Mayor Tom Bradley who was riding in the back of his limousine for a special event because my route was unexpectedly switched to a different pattern from the one I had practiced. However, I eventually became so proficient that I was responsible for training other drivers and developing a spiel that contained not only facts but bad jokes.

"The Cheetah is the fastest land animal," I would say with authority into the microphone as we passed the appropriate animal enclosure. "But he was caught by man and that proves that cheetahs never prosper."

Even then I was a huge Disneyland fan and obviously my attitude about the jungle was strongly influenced by my experiences on the Jungle Cruise attraction. Despite the crackling of my microphone, my passengers could hear me clearly because my spiel was never obscured by any laughter.

There was already another tram driver named "Jim" who had been working there for years before I was hired so my supervisor thought that in an effort to distinguish between us that I would be named "Jungle Jim".

He thought it was a clever reference to the Alex Raymond comic strip character who later appeared in radio, comic books, as well as sixteen "B" movies and twenty-six television episodes with great white hunter Jim Bradley all portrayed by actor Johnny "Tarzan" Weismuller who foiled evil witch doctors, wild animals like gorillas and villains who were somehow threatening the jungle.

I still have that name tag along with the khaki pants, safari jacket and pith helmet that I wore and they served as my Halloween costume for several years. The clothes no longer fit but I still can't bear getting rid of them because they are filled with so many pleasant memories.

When I relocated to Orlando, I fell in love like so many others with the Adventurers Club on Pleasure Island. I came to know some of the performers and had the opportunity to interview many of the people involved in creating the beloved venue.

I was also able to spend hours researching material at the Walt Disney World Entertainment Library at Maingate that no longer exists with its holdings now either dispersed or destroyed. It had file folders overflowing with information, photos, video documentation tapes and more and I took volumes of notes.

The Adventurers Club appealed to my love of improvisational comedy, the mythology and romance of adventure from the 1930s and 1940s and the feeling of being immersed in an entirely different world where even the oddest person was warmly embraced.

I became so well versed in the history of the entertainment venue that I wrote several articles about it over the years as well as doing a lengthy presentation for the Disneyana Fan Club convention in 2008 and ones for the fan created "ConGaloosh Convention" in 2009 and 2010 as well as other venues. Disney put a stop to a third convention stating that it was a violation of their intellectual property.

Over the years as I continued to learn more and more, I debated about compiling all the information I had and writing an entire book about the Adventurers Club. I wanted to honor the many talented men and women, cast and guests, who over the years made the Adventurers Club such a beloved unique experience.

I was dissuaded by the fact that the book would have only a limited audience that was growing smaller and smaller each year since the venue closed permanently over a decade ago. A small but passionate group of fans still exist including one that held a one night evening event at Shipwreck Beach at Disney's Yacht and Beach Club Resort in 2019 introducing some newbies to the wonders of the club.

However, it occurred to me that if I could fill the rest of the book with the stories of the other jungle adventures at Walt Disney World I might be able to share some of the mystique of the Adventurers Club with a wider audience and keep its memory alive.

To get in the proper mood, I sat in front of my computer wearing my pith helmet and my unbuttoned and snug safari jacket with appropriate Hawaiian shirt underneath and cargo shorts. Somehow it made the always challenging task of writing about the jungle somewhat easier. Mahalo!

Jungle Jim Korkis
Disney Historian
January 2021

Jungle Cruise

"Welcome aboard! I'll be your skipper, guide, social director and dance instructor for the next three months. If we sink, I'll also be your swimming instructor. Everyone turn around and wave goodbye to the folks back on the dock... You may never see them again!"

The Jungle Cruise is one of the most loved and iconic attractions in Adventureland at four Disney theme parks worldwide although each version has its distinctive differences. The original version debuted at Disneyland in California on opening day July 17, 1955.

Inspired by the success of the Disney *True Life Adventures* documentary series (and in particular *The African Lion* installment that would appear in theaters that same year), the attraction was meant to share the delights, dangers and wonders found along the world's most exotic tropical rivers.

"At first (for Adventureland), we just talked about doing an outdoor garden attraction with exotic live plants and real birds perched in the branches, but when Walt would get an idea like that, he'd go pour right into it, full steam ahead," stated Dick Irvine, the former President of WED (Disney Imagineering).

Originally, the Disneyland version with narration written by Winston Hibler, who had co-written and narrated many of the documentaries, was intended to be a serious-minded trek into the jungles as a three-dimensional realization of the movie series for armchair adventurers who would never visit these locations.

However, this ride evolved over the years to feature more humor and create memorable phrases like "the backside of water" as well as include more sophisticated mechanical representations of wildlife. It became less of a nature travelogue and more of an amusing entertainment.

The 1955 Disneyland Guide Map described it as "(This) adventurous cruise in an explorer's boat, over the tropical rivers of the world is a highlight of Adventureland.

"On this exciting trip, you'll thrill to the life-like wild animals, reptiles, birds, monkeys and even native savages. Your boat ventures under a real waterfall as you admire the tropical plants and foliage gathered from all over the world. Truly an adventure to remember."

The Jungle Cruise Explorer Launches were designed by Imagineer Harper Goff to be reminiscent of the one used by actor Humphrey Bogart in the film *The African Queen* (1951). In addition, the movie also inspired the fact that the animals would never be fully seen by the guests but their presence just briefly glimpsed and heard.

The boats were among the first, and the biggest, to be built out of recently perfected fiberglass. The boats were constructed by the Wizard Boat Company in Costa Mesa, California.

Their striped canopies (red and white, blue and white, green and white) were not just to look pretty but served the purpose of narrowing the guests' vision so they could not fully see the tops of the still growing foliage or the buildings that the landscaping would eventually hide.

The river only averages a depth of about four to five feet and is dyed with color to hide that fact as well as the submerged track. The water is indeed clear as can be seen from the water flowing over the waterfall.

Since the boats are on a track, the captain's only real control of the craft is its speed so that it would not intrude on the boat in front of it. Basically, the Skippers are in charge of the forward, rear and holding motions of the boat although for dramatic effect they may spin the 'steering wheel' quite liberally even though it has no effect on the course of the boat.

"In the very early days," recalled Imagineer Herb Ryman," we thought the Jungle River ride was going to have live animals until they told Walt that every guest would see something different each time."

"Walt wanted every person who came through there to get a full show," Imagineer John Hench explained. "The only answer was mechanical animals. Walt's idea for the animals was really a form of his basic honesty — he wanted the audience to get a full performance every time."

In fact, a 1955 Disneyland postcard talks about animals lurking in the Adventureland bushes but the word "animals" is surrounded by quotation marks to hint that they are not real.

"Walt and I had both seen the film *The African Queen* and the animals were never completely visible," remembered Goff. "They were partially hidden in the underbrush on shore or just under the water. So we began to think of hippos and other animals whose mechanics and tracks could be hidden and still have animated elements.

"We brought in Bob Mattey who later created the shark for (the feature film) *Jaws* (1975) and had built the squid for *20,000 Leagues Under the Sea* (1954) to engineer the original animals."

Animal experts had also convinced Walt that using real animals was impractical since most of them would be sleeping or hiding during the daylight operating hours of the park as well as the added expenses for caring, feeding and offstage housing.

Harper Goff was in charge of developing the layout for the attraction including the impressive waterfall. As mentioned, Bob Mattey was in charge of what were then called "the electro-mechanical animals" (because of limited repetitive mechanical movements generated by electricity) that could be seen along the banks and in the water. Blaine Gibson did the sculpting of the figures. Bill Evans was in charge of the landscaping.

Evans told me in an interview in 1985: "I've traveled a great deal to tropic regions around the world and jungles can be endlessly monotonous. So I created a 'Hollywood' jungle', the type an armchair traveler who has never been to the tropics might visualize.

"What we were attempting in this jungle was to try to bring forth the illusion of a jungle. Turns out when you really plod through an authentic jungle you are apt to travel for a day or two and the scenery doesn't change much...maybe one or two species without interruption.

"In the Adventureland jungle, a lot of those trees are native to tropical Africa, India, South America but they are interspersed with things not truly tropical but they have a tropical aspect like that bamboo we use from China that grows forty feet high. You are not aware it isn't tropical but it fills a role conveniently.

"We picked material from Brazil, material from Africa, material from India and Asia and Malaysia. We pushed it all together. It's all quite compatible in the sense that it all has that lush, vigorous growth. Really strong growth. What we attempted to do in planting the jungle was to make it look as though we had nothing to do with it. We were working on a pretty tight budget."

Guests of all ages, sizes and health issues are welcomed onto the cruise without restriction. Even guests using a wheelchair or an ECV may remain in their seats.

Sign language and assistive listening devices are available upon request. Ears to the World, Disney's Show Translator, is capable of translating this experience into French, German, Japanese, Portuguese, or Spanish. The service is complimentary and devices can be picked up at the Guest Relations service counter at the Disney Parks.

Unlike the original in Disneyland, Walt Disney World's Jungle Cruise has remained fairly consistent with few changes except for some queue upgrades, new boats and changes in the skipper spiel.

It was an original opening day attraction at the Magic Kingdom in October 1971 and was once again instantly popular especially being the only E-Ticket attraction in Adventureland.

While there were intentions to make changes to the Magic Kingdom so it would not just be a duplicate of Disneyland, plans for including the Jungle Cruise were always part of the Phase One Master Plan. However, the ride would be enhanced because of additional space and because of what the Imagineers had learned during the last decade or so operating the Disneyland version.

Changes would be made to handle a larger number of guests including an additional two more boats as well as to increase the overall experience by an additional minute. The Jungle Cruise boats are twenty-seven feet long, and reach a top speed of 3.2 feet per second using a four-cylinder Chevrolet engine. .

Bill Evans would once again create the jungle landscaping, but had to make sure the plants could endure Florida's unique climate as well as having the appearance of tropical plants in an equatorial jungle.

The designer of the new storyline would be Marc Daviswho had been instrumental in transforming Disneyland's Jungle Cruise.

He told me in an interview in September 1998: "In the early 1960s Walt wanted me to add some more humor to the park. When I did the sketch of the trapped safari and the rhino, he saw that and he laughed like hell. So he put it inside as a major part of the attraction. With the Jungle ride we were trying to make it a little more interesting than just a boring travelogue.

"I also put in the elephant pool and I had done idea sketches of what the elephants would look like and what they would be doing. I made the headhunter at the end of the ride South American because that is the only place they shrink heads.

"We got marvelous sculpture done on the elephants. You can't compliment Blaine Gibson enough for supervising the sculpting of these audio-animatronics."

The Walt Disney World Jungle Cruise is themed to a Depression-era British outpost on the Amazon River that is operated by the fictional company, The Jungle Navigation Company.

The counter-clockwise voyage is familiar but still distinctly different from the Southern California inspiration.

After the boat leaves the dock, the guests find themselves on the Amazon River in South America with butterflies that have one-foot wingspans. Originally, the Amazon section was covered with an overhead canopy that was unique to this version of the attraction with both live and artificial plants.

Guests experienced a gentle mist from the overgrowth and heard some background music but it was removed in 2000. The boat then passes by the many cascades of the twelve foot high Inspiration Falls with the sound of all that constantly running water inspiring the guests to go.....further into the jungle. It then transitions into the Congo River of Africa.

Empty native canoes are a mystery until a giant twenty-five foot long python is revealed nearby. The skin color of the snake has changed over the decades so that it has become more realistic.

The three beached canoes have been re-designed so that the bows have impressionistic animal heads that resemble Mickey Mouse, Donald Duck, and Goofy. Donald is in the middle with the duck bill, Mickey is on the right end with the curved horns to resemble his round ears, and Goofy is on the left with the pointy horns to indicate his floppy dog ears.

Shortly afterwards, the boat comes upon an explorer's camp that has been overrun by gorillas who are enjoying themselves with the things they have found. Unlike at Disneyland, the gorillas are all grouped under the roof of the tent to provide some protection from the Florida weather like rain.

The cruise then transitions into the Nile River. The guests see two elephants and then pass by the African Veldt where a pride of lions are feasting on their kill of a zebra although the skippers may point out if there are young children aboard that the lions are just guarding the sleeping zebra because he is dead...tired.

After passing two enormous crocodiles, the fifteen foot long Old Smiley and his girlfriend Ginger who snaps, the boat encounters the wonders of Schweitzer Falls named after that famous explorer, Dr. Albert...Falls.

The waterfall doubles as a huge pump to keep the river's 1,750,000 gallons of water circulating. The dying agent in the water is distributed through Schweitzer Falls as a way to mix the dye throughout the entire attraction. When it is periodically injected it makes the waterfall look like Willy Wonka's chocolate waterfall.

Next, a lost safari finds itself trapped on a pole with an angry rhinoceros underneath threatening them with his horn. The lowest man on the pole has the same face as the grave digger in the Haunted Mansion and fabric from his shorts is wrapped around the tip of the horn of the rhino.

Not far away the boat passes under the rock overhang of the impressive Schweitzer Falls giving guests a view of the "back side of water" and discovers the remains of a plane crash that was added in 1994. Only the back half of the Lockheed Model 23 Electra Junior is visible. The front half was used in the *Casablanca* scene in The Great Movie Ride.

The boat is threatened by a pool of hippos who are preparing to charge until they are scared off by the sound of the skipper's warning gunfire.

Ominous drums alert the passengers that there are in savage Zulu native territory where the inhabitants are having a frantic celebratory dance while the remainder of the tribe is lurking in the nearby foliage for an ambush on unwary travelers.

The craft proceeds into the Mekong River (until the 1990s it was called the Irrawaddy River) and enters a flooded temple from the Khmer empire of Cambodia that has been destroyed by an earthquake.

Unique to this version of the attraction when it opened in 1971, this fiberglass and concrete recreation of carved stone features the vine-wrapped face of the Hindu God Vishnu with the interior filled with bas reliefs of Hindu mythology including a reproduction of the Hindu monkey god Hanuman.

Inside, it has become home to monkeys, cobras, huge spiders (similar to the ones that were in the Haunted Mansion attraction for over three decades) and a menacing tiger with reflective green eyes. Tree roots and vines seep down through the walls and ceiling, hanging into the river to indicate that nature is reclaiming the abandoned structure.

Safely maneuvering back outside, the passengers encounter an elephant bathing pool with many of the large pachyderms relaxing. It is okay to take photos because they are all wearing their trunks.

One elephant narrowly misses spraying the boat with its water-filled trunk. A final encounter with the shrunken head salesman of the jungle, Trader Sam, signals a return to the Amazon and eventually to civilization.

The fleet includes fifteen boats with usually nine in operation at any one time and after a long time nautical tradition, they are all named after females: Amazon Annie, Bomokandi Bertha (wheelchair lift equipped), Congo Connie, Ganges Gertie, Irrawaddy Irma, Mongala Millie, Nile Nellie, Orinoco Ida, Rutshuru Ruby, Sankuru Sadie, Senegal Sal, Ucyali Lolly, Volta Val, Wamba Wanda (wheelchair lift equipped), and Zambezi Zelda. At one time Kwango Kate was part of the fleet but retired in 2000.

Generally the boats are well maintained and were specifically designed to handle the rigors of the attraction. However, in 2004, Sankuru Sadie sank into the river but was repaired and put back in service.

On February 27, 2020 around 12:30pm, *Bomokandi Bertha* about mid-ride began to take on water, stranding guests in ankle-deep water. Everyone was evacuated safely out of the craft to the river bank and escorted back into the park after various guest recovery efforts.

Thanks to social media the incident went viral. The ride was shut down for roughly 105 minutes while the boat was towed away and Reedy Creek investigated. The boat was repaired and returned to service.

In Spring 1969, construction work began on the Florida version of the Jungle Cruise. The majority of the over one hundred animals were built by WED in Glendale, California while others were finished at a warehouse under the supervision of Bud Washo in the Dr. Phillips area in Orlando, Florida.

In 1971, Florida's version of the Jungle Cruise opened as an E-ticket attraction with a different geographic order and the addition of a finale to the ride inside a dark and foreboding flooded Cambodian temple. The ride lasted a minute longer than the adventure in Disneyland and there were two additional boats.

The original description to the press about the WDW version included descriptions that "around the last bend painted warriors continue the ritual of their ceremonial dances near burning skulls", "as the boat passes through the center of a huge elephant pool, passengers will be entertained by the 'shower singing' of an Indian elephant as he sits and soaks in the waterfalls of his jungle spa" and "in an exotic rain forest, guests will be treated to the croaking antics of giant frogs, as big as Boston bulldogs."

While the burning skulls did appear for the first few years but were removed no singing elephant was in the final attraction, but these items reveal how Walt Disney Imagineers wanted the WDW ride to be significantly different from Disneyland.

Actually, almost a dozen frogs did appear briefly for the first few months (until sometime at the very beginning of 1972), but were removed by WDW leader Dick Nunis who declared them too "hokey." They were located just past Inspiration Falls and before the abandoned canoes.

There were approximately a dozen frogs, both adults and juveniles. They opened their mouths and rocked back and forth while the adults distended their vocal sacs. They were actually a replacement for an earlier Marc Davis concept that would have featured man-eating plants. The sound of these audio-animatronics figures can still be heard.

Davis also proposed a scene just beyond the gorillas trashing an explorer's tent that would have shown a gorilla repeatedly smashing the head of a snapping crocodile.

Davis also proposed just after the elephant bathing pool a scene of angry crocodiles who have cornered a flightless parrot on top of a twiggy tree. One of the reasons for their aggression is that the parrot is supposedly taunting them with insults.

Later that scene was adapted for a segment seen from the train ride where alligators cornered a frog (one of the removed bullfrogs) on a stump.

The 1970 press material stated, "The 'Jungle Cruise' in Walt Disney World's Magic Kingdom theme park, like its namesake at Disneyland in California, is expected to be one of the most popular in the Magic Kingdom. The cruise will feature many new and different scenes and situations, however, including the ruins."

Imagineer Marc Davis was completely in charge of the Florida version of the ride, unlike his role in the Anaheim attraction, where he had merely added significant elements to an already existing template.

In Florida, most of the classic elements from the Disneyland attraction remained but a number of Florida exclusive (at that time) items were included — Inspiration Falls, giant butterflies, pygmy war canoes, gorillas ransacking a safari camp, a huge python, a Bengal tiger, cobras guarding ancient treasure and a family of prankster monkeys fooling around with it to the delight of guests. Some of these things were later added to the Disneyland version.

At Magic Kingdom, Trader Sam looked different than his Disneyland counterpart. He held an umbrella like a parasol, wore a black bowler hat, had a beer belly and wore a red and white striped skirt similar to the canopies on the boats. It is suspected he obtained the attire from a boat crash and unfortunate victims.

During part of the 1980s and 1990s, the Trader Sam figure wore a colorful tribal mask, though this was removed in 2005. For nearly two decades starting in 1991, he even had a different name: Chief Name (pronounced *Nah-Me*).

There are at least two versions of how that name originated. One story is that a revised script was incomplete. A Jungle Cruise skipper jokingly read "Chief (name)" in the script as "Chief Nah-Me" not realizing that the word in parenthesis was simply left temporarily blank so that skippers could improvise their own name and it proved to be a big hit.

Another version is that there was a contest to come up with a new name for the character and a skipper wrote "Name" in the blank, and "Name" won the vote as the best name since the skippers had an unusual sense of humor.

In 1991, there was a huge rehab to the attraction, especially in the queue area, with the addition of music and radio commentary provided by Albert Awol, a fictional Jungle Cruise boat captain and current disc jockey for the DBC (Disney Broadcasting Company) as part of the Global Brodcasting Service, serving remote outposts since 1928. Awol is a military acronym for "absent without leave".

He mentions being sponsored by *Aero-Casablanca*, an airline which apparently offers exotic vacations and tours and might be responsible for that crashed plane in the jungle. He is considered the "Voice of the Jungle" and broadcasts everything from news, quizzes, reminders, weather and more while he fills the queue area with authentic music from the 1930s. His empty office is in the center of the queue and open for guests to view.

His forty-seven minute background "loop" is specific to WDW. His spiel includes references to Imagineers connected with the attraction including Ted Sears, Winston Hibler and Harper Goff.

In addition, visual enhancements were made to the queue from wall murals to artifacts as well as crates addressed to "Dr. Winston HIbler, Special Arachnid Unit, Outpost #71755 (referencing the opening date of Disneyland's Jungle Cruise)" and "Goff's Crocodile Resistant Chest High Rubber Overpants."

Amusing permanent chalkboards hang in the queue. One announces that the Employee of the Month is E.L. O'Fevre (Yellow Fever).

Another has the following information: "Crew Mess Lunch Menu: Monday Fricasse of Giant Stag Beetle (taste a bit like chicken); Tuesday Barbecued Three-toed Skink (has a chicken flavor); Wednesday Consomme of River Basin Slug (poultry like); Thursday Filet of Rock Python (chickenesque); Friday Chicken (Really!)"

In addition another chalkboard documents "Missing Persons: Al Belaite, B.N. Eaton, Emma Boylen, C. M. Cooken, Ilene Dover, Ann Fellen, Seacum Yett, Albert Knot, Betty Dont.

"Missing Boats: Hapless Hortense, Lost Lucia, Unknown Usha, Sunken Sonya, Run Aground Sue, Burning Bianca, Missing Mele, Blown-Up Bonita, Nabbed Naoko, Fateless Fiona, Troubled Titania.

"Anyone with information concerning the above or anyone having made contact with survivors -- Please make your report to the Governor General's office immediately."

In 1993 during another rehab, the famous candy-cane-striped canopies disappeared from the boats and the hulls were "aged" to give the impression that these boats had voyaged through the jungle and had suffered as a result. The reason for this is that the boats at Disneyland had been re-themed to better match with the new Indiana Jones attraction so the WDW versions soon followed. A variety of props were added to each boat to give each an individual personality.

In 1995, the first women were trained as Jungle Cruise Skippers that had been a traditionally male only staffed role since 1971. The concept was that in literature and films a Great White Hunter or fearless jungle explorer like Jungle Jim were always men.

For a brief period between 1975 and1976 because of staffing issues, female cast members briefly filled the role of hostesses helping load and unload the boats. By 1996 as many women as men piloted the crafts.

One of the original gags, often unnoticed by WDW guests, in the Florida version was that actress Katherine Hepburn's shrunken head was dangling from the right hand of Trader Sam, the shrunken head dealer who will trade you two of his for one of yours, near the end of the ride. Hepburn was the star of The *African Queen* movie that had been an inspiration for the original attraction.

In 2013, both Disneyland and Walt Disney World introduced a limited time Christmas overlay called the Jingle Cruise.

The premise, according to the Walt Disney Company announcement, was that "the Skippers have grown homesick for the holidays, so they've added holiday cheer to the Jungle Cruise queue and boathouse with decorations that have been mailed to them from home (plus a few they've created themselves).

"The Skippers have also added a slew of new jokes to their tours that are the perfect way to get guests in the holiday spirit. Additionally, Jungle Cruise boats have been renamed with the holidays in mind, and if guests listen carefully, they may hear a holiday-themed radio broadcast playing in the background."

The addition of a few decorations in the queue, the temporary renaming of the ride vehicle boats with names like Garland Gertie, Icicle Irma, Poinsettia Sal, Yulelog Lolly, Candy Cane Connie, and Mistletoe Millie, some minor signage and Skippers wearing Santa hats and equipped with quips filled with holiday cheer did not necessitate the closing of the attraction for any significant period of time. It is one of the reasons Walt Disney World leadership decided to incorporate the changes since there was a minimal investment of time and money and no real downtime for the attraction.

Over the years, the overlay has become more elaborate with wrapped presents scattered throughout areas because of the crashed plane that was supposedly in a rush trying to deliver them.

Signs stating "Santa Stop Here" are scattered around as well as Santa's workshop elements and an actual North Pole where the lost safari group climbs out of the way of danger.

There are also costume additions including Trader Sam who is now attired as Trader "Sam-Ta" who might bring a shrunken head to stuff in a Christmas stocking.

Disney's *Jungle Cruise* movie inspired by the attraction was filmed in Hawaii and Atlanta, Georgia in the summer and fall of 2018. Due to the pandemic, its release was delayed until 2021. The film features Dwyane Johnson as Skipper Frank Wolff who pilots his riverboat through the jungle to help female scientist Emily Blunt and her brother on a mission to find the fabled Tree of Life.

Disney has announced that the classic park attraction will be re-imagined much like the Pirates of the Caribbean attraction was to include elements from the film franchise.

While there have been many changes to the attraction over the years, like changing the four black porters wearing red fez hats on the pole in the "Lost Safari" segment into frightened Caucasians around 1996 who are now a film crew rather than a hunting expedition explaining the camera platform at the top of the pole, it remains one of the most popular and iconic experiences at the Magic Kingdom.

"And now, probably the most dangerous part of our journey— the return to civilization! I certainly hope you've enjoyed our cruise. However, if your in-laws are still with you, you've missed a golden opportunity. However, bring them back later tonight for our 'in-law special'... halfway for half fare, no questions asked."

On January 25, 2021, Disney announced plans to update the classic *Jungle Cruise* both in California and Florida so that the experience would be more consistent in the two parks.

Concept art showed a re-imagined version of the Trapped Safari scene and an entirely new scene of chimpanzees who have taken over a wrecked *Jungle Cruise* boat.

Imagineer Kevin Lively explained, "As part of this story update, we'll get to follow a skipper and his passengers as their journey goes awry. For the first time ever, the skipper role will not only be that of a live experienced and witty guide, but also represented by a show figure within the attraction itself.

"In fact, the expedition will be up a tree literally after their sunken boat splits apart and chimps board the wreckage with monkey business ensuing.

"Fans of the Jungle Cruise attraction may recall some boats that used to make their way around the river but haven't been seen for a while—specifically the Mekong Maiden and the Kwango Kate. Ever wonder what happened to them? Well, you might go ape when you find out! Ultimately, the jungle gets the last laugh."

The Trapped Safari will feature five explorers — including two women and people of color representing a birdwatcher, an entomologist, a wildlife painter, a photographer, and the skipper, who will each have "their own story and cultural heritage" — escaping the horn of a rhino by climbing an aging tree. The figures are hauling equipment such as a camera, telescopes, painting supplies and butterfly nets.

A Disney publicity release stated "new adventures that stay true to the experience we know and love—more humor, wildlife and skipper heart—and also reflect and value the diversity of the world around us."

Chris Beatty, Creative Portfolio Executive at Walt Disney Imagineering, explained, "This is not a re-envisioning of the entire attraction. It's the *Jungle Cruise* you know and love, with the skippers still leading the way, and at the same time, we're addressing the negative depictions of 'natives'.

"Did you ever wonder who those explorers were or where they came from? What's their back story? As part of the enhanced storyline, each one of them will have their own story and cultural heritage. There's a birdwatcher, an entomologist, a wildlife painter, and a photographer, and each one will have a different reason for being on the expedition."

Beatty said in his interview "It's done in a way that celebrates diverse backgrounds and interests —that's part of the rich storytelling, not something you poke fun at it." They've been working with Carmen Smith, the executive for Creative Development and Inclusive Strategies, as well as Dr. Mark Penning at Disney's Animal Kingdom, to make sure that these additions are as accurate as possible.

Beatty shared that they want the plot to be cohesive on both coasts, "It's been fun to look at the nuances between the two attractions and what makes them slightly different, but the scenes that we're adjusting are the same.

"When we consider making changes to a classic attraction, we focus on ways to 'plus' the experience. The skippers of the Jungle Cruise bring humor to guests of all ages, and we're excited to be adding to that legacy along with a new animated skipper figure by celebrating their adventures and influence."

From Adventureland Veranda To Skipper Canteen

When guests cross over the bridge into Adventureland, on the right hand side is a large building with many different facades. It was meant to suggest the incursion of Western civilization on the edges of the jungle.

In 1971, this area was the home to shops like Tropic Toppers (Hats & Bags), Oriental Imports Ltd., The Magic Carpet, Tiki Tropic Shop and Traders of Timbuktu.

However the very first business that guests encountered on the right hand side was the Adventureland Veranda Restaurant.

It opened on October 1, 1971 as a counter service dining restaurant. It served mainly chicken and hot sandwiches. In 1976, the park's guide book described the location as offering "Polynesian entrees, hot sandwiches and soft drinks in a South Seas setting."

In 1977 the restaurant received sponsorship from Kikkoman known for its Japanese soy sauce and the menu changed to include Teriyaki hamburgers topped with a slice of pineapple, stir fry beef, and sweet and sour hot dogs.

The menu evolved over the years to include shrimp fried rice and egg roll, sweet and sour chicken, Lo Mein salad (Lo mein noodles with garden vegetables and pineapple in an Oriental dressing) and a "South Seas" fruit salad.

The tropical earth-colored floor tile patterns, hardwood latticework, dark wooden paneling, high ceiling with ornate rafters, French-colonial flowery brass lighting fixtures, and lazily turning fans made the restaurant a popular dining location.

In addition, inside there was an hour long background music loop of Hawaiian and Asian Pacific instrumental music (sometimes with the distinctive steel guitar sound) put together by Jack Wagner, who also arranged the other background music for the park, that was both soothing and romantic. Unlike other Magic Kingdom restaurants, there was an entirely different one hour music loop for guests who dined outside.

The restaurant had the hint of offering somewhat exotic entrees without straying too far from traditional American food tastes in what guests perceived as a relaxing and authentic tropical setting.

Imagineer Dorothea Redmond, who was responsible for some of the design of other Magic Kingdom buildings like the Columbia Harbor House as well as designing the Cinderella tile mural in the castle breezeway, tried to capture with the building the influence of British and French colonization that touched their holdings in the Caribbean, Polynesia, India, Africa and the Far East.

Redmond's initial designs directly referenced the architecture shown in photographs in the following two books: *The West Indies* by Life World Library (1967) and *Shadows From India* by Roderick Cameron (1958).

The Preview Edition Guide for Walt Disney World describes the Adventureland Veranda as an "old Caribbean village setting" while a 1971 mention in the *Orlando Sentinel* newspaper describes it as "South Seas food in a Tahitian setting".

Studying the architecture closely it seems most to represent a South Pacific French Colonial plantation house from the Victorian era that helps ease the transition from the Victorian architecture found on Main Street USA. It seems to be very similar in style to a house that was once in Port-au-Prince.

The restaurant went into a reduced operating schedule in 1993 before being closed in 1994. One of the restaurant's enclosed verandas is currently the home of The Aloha Isle and its famous Dole Whip.

It occasionally reopened as a restaurant when it needed to provide an option while other restaurants were going through remodeling or handle increased attendance in the park but when it did briefly re-open it did not offer its previous menu but just a generic offering of hamburgers and French fries and the like.

For years, the location mainly served as a character meet-and-greet location or a venue for internal meetings or special events like children's birthday parties or convention groups.

Over the decades, sections of the original layout have been truncated, altered, and removed.

Originally to the east of the restaurant was an outdoor dining area that was largely built up on piers that adjoined the canal offering a pleasant view of the waterway and the Swan boats.

To the west of the restaurant was another open-air circular dining area in the alcoves opposite the Swiss Family Treehouse called the South Seas Terrace. That area disappeared in late 2010 with the expansion of the restroom area.

In addition, there was another patio, a high, glass-ceilinged decagonal space with a brick floor. Much of this became the Mess Hall area of the Skipper Canteen.

However, for the majority of WDW guests it was a closed, abandoned location taking up a large piece of exterior real estate for nearly twenty years.

Over the years, there were rumors that the Adventureland Veranda was going to become Tortuga, a restaurant that was to be the pirate equivalent of the Royal Table complete with audio-animatronics pirates.

This rehab would have been just part of a total planned transformation of much of Adventureland to theme in with a *Pirates of the Caribbean* film franchise with the Swiss Family Robinson Treehouse becoming the *Black Pearl* pirate ship for guests to explore and the Enchanted Tiki Room having a pirate themed show.

In addition, a roller coaster attraction that tied in with the fourth movie in the movie franchise was being developed. Like many such proposals cost and changes in leadership and shifts in brand focus resulted in it never advancing beyond the general concept.

The restaurant was finally reformatted into the Skipper Canteen that opened in December 2015. The choice was made to be able to utilize the already existing restaurant infrastructure as well as offering a dining opportunity.

The new restaurant is named the Jungle Navigation Company Ltd. Skipper Canteen. The area was being used from 2011 to 2014 as a Pixie Hollow meet-and-greet area for Tinker Bell and her fairy friend characters. When the characters moved out, Imagineers considered several options for a themed Adventureland eatery including using Tarzan, Aladdin or pirates as possible themes.

Ever since the Jungle Cruise attraction debuted in Adventureland at Disneyland in July 1955, it was one of the most popular rides at the park and developed a special mystique and encouraged the creation of legends.

One of the oldest gags in the Jungle Cruise attraction at Disneyland for decades (besides the infamous "back side of water") was guides pointing out that the name of the dramatic waterfall that the boat narrowly misses is called Schweitzer Falls named after Dr. Albert... Falls rather than the expected Dr. Albert Schweitzer, noted for his humanitarian work in Africa.

Skipper Canteen is operated by Alberta Falls, the granddaughter of the fictitious Dr. Albert Falls. This 222-seat restaurant is home to "World Famous Jungle Cuisine". It opened December 16, 2015.

According to the Imagineering back story, the Jungle Navigation Co. Ltd. which operates the Jungle Cruise boats was started by Dr. Falls on April 8, 1911. His granddaughter Alberta who is the third generation owner has repurposed the company's tropical headquarters into a restaurant in order to generate additional revenue from the hungry cruise passengers.

Dr. Falls had a son who married a woman from India and they had a daughter who they named Alberta in honor of her grandfather. When she was eight years old, she was sent to live with him and learn the business.

The company was originally a tropical river cargo shipping venture ("and logistics services") but as business declined Alberta opened up sight-seeing cruises for passengers. A banner states that the inaugural cruise was October 1, 1931. That date is to reference the opening of the Magic Kingdom on October 1, 1971.

The restaurant includes three dining rooms. The Crew's Mess Hall (which servers point out is not actually messy at all) is the largest one and includes wall hangings of photos, documents, native musical instruments, and other expedition mementos gathered by the skippers on their travels.

The Jungle Room which was the family parlor is a more intimate location and features memorabilia culled from the Falls' family archives. It includes wood carvings of attraction scenes made from wood once used on the attraction's docks, stained glass chandeliers in the form of the Enchanted Tiki Room's birds, and one of the miniature boats from the Shrunken Ned's Junior Jungle Boats game that was once located next to the Jungle Cruise on display in a glass case.

The third dining area is behind a secret bookcase and was actually the private meeting place for the Society of Explorers and Adventurers (S.E.A.) an organization for which Falls was a founding member and features artifacts from the mysterious organization.

Several S.E.A. club fezes are on display in a glass case. In the room are large maps of mythological creatures discovered by the members referencing the films *20,000 Leagues Under the Sea* with the Nautilus and a giant squid and *The Island at the Top of the World* with the Hyperion Airship as well as the Epcot World of Motion attraction that featured a sea serpent now described as Horribus Sea Serpent and a mention of Kimballum referring to Imagineer Ward Kimball who worked on the attraction.

The room also has a display wall of butterfly specimens that once belonged to Walt Disney's wife Lillian, and a painting of Doctor Albert Falls discovering the Cambodian Temple seen in the Jungle Cruise attraction.

The menu features cuisine inspired by the rivers of the world locales on the attraction including Asia, South America and Africa.

Alberta has even enlisted the skippers to interact with the guests when they are not on a cruise. The servers are encouraged to share the same corny humor, quips and "groaners" that guests loved on the attraction.

A waiter will say, "I'd like to point out some of the highlights of the restaurant." He then points up to the overhead fixtures. "There's a light. There's another one. That one is pretty high." Another waiter might add, "I don't want to mention the elephant in the room" and then point at an elephant statue on a shelf.

In a typewritten letter affixed to the menu, Alberta briefly explains the history of the Jungle Navigation Company and the restaurant.

> Welcome to the Jungle Skipper Canteen!
>
> My name is Alberta and I'll be your owner, manager, bookkeeper, interior decorator, and sous chef for the next 3 courses (or as far as you get). My grandfather, Dr. Albert Falls, established the Jungle Navigation Company in 1911.
>
> His goal was to improve the way in which cargo moved up and down the jungle rivers for his fellow explorers and adventures. When I was eight years old my parents sent me here to live with my grandfather and the jungle boat skippers I call the jungle my home and the crew members are my family.
>
> That's why I turned to them when business began to decline soon after I inherited the company. Fewer and fewer full-fledged expeditions were seen in the jungle and Adventureland became more

of a destination for greenhorn globetrotters. Simply put, our cargo shipping business was dry docked. Then one of the skippers came to me with an idea. He suggested we use our vessels to offer guided tours to the visitors.

The rest is history! We have been offering Jungle Cruises for several years now and business has never been better. We've been so successful that I decided to open up our home offices to hungry travelers. The crew's mess hall, our old family room and even my grandfather's old meeting room are now open to our diners!

We enjoy having you and we hope you enjoy being had. Please relax and enjoy your meal, then get out.

Yours truly,

Alberta Falls

P.S. I'm sorry, that was rude...Please get out.

As a tribute to some of the Imagineers responsible for the original Jungle Cruise, there are three offices on the upper floor balcony for Skipper Marc (Davis), Skipper Harper (Goff) and Skipper Bill (Evans). Davis was responsible for the visual gags. Goff designed the waterway and the boats. Evans did the landscaping.

At the Skipper Canteen, the shelves are filled with books that reference Disney parks (*The Eyes of Mara* by Jones, obviously a reference to the Indiana Jones Disneyland attraction), Imagineers (*Crooning Flowers* by Sherman and Sherman referring to the Disney composers the Sherman Brothers and their songs for the Enchanted Tiki Room), as well as some books that are just silly wordplay (*Spotted Tigers* by G. Rowl or *Boat Evacuation Procedures* by Cap Size) or punny amusement (*Fleas Navidad and Other Winter Insects*) Some books have neither title nor author.

The secret meeting room of the Society of Explorers and Adventurers (S.E.A.) is behind the bookcase and is accessed by pulling on a volume of *The Jungle Book* by Rudyard Kipling.

Here are a handful of the many delightful titles:

- *In Search of the Yeti* by Harrison Hightower III. Hightower is not only a member of S.E.A. but was based on Imagineer Joe Rohde who was responsible for DAK's Expedition Everest and Aulani, Disney's Hawaiian resort hotel. Hightower has several different books on the shelves including *Treasures of the Animal Kingdom*.

- *A Manor of Fact* by Mystic is a reference to Henry Mystic and Mystic Manor in Hong Kong Disneyland. He is also represented by other books including *Treasures from the Manor and Primates as Shipmates* referring to his pet mischievous monkey Albert who causes trouble in the attraction.

- Captain Mary Oceaneer wrote *Parrots as Pets* referring to her diving companion parrot Salty. She also wrote *Charting Course* since she is an ocean traveler.

- *Leaders Throughout History* by Professor G. Kalogridis is George Kalogridis, the President of WDW when the restaurant opened.

- *Songs of the Tiki Bird* by Professor Boag honors performer Wally Boag who helped write the show and voiced the parrot Jose in The Enchanted Tiki Room.

- *Universus Arboribus* by B.M. Evans is tribute to Imagineer Morgan "Bill" Evans, who loved putting Latin names on the Disney park horticulture.

- *A Journey to the Stars* by Kimball references Imagineer Ward Kimball who wrote and directed the three Disneyland television Tomorrowland episodes about outer space.

- *Hamlet: A Lion's* Tale by Shakes Speare acknowledges that the Disney's animated feature film *The Lion King* was inspired by the Shakespeare classic play.

- *Native Orange Birds of the Southeastern United States* by Dr. Sidd Truss (pronounced "Citrus") is a nod to the Florida Orange Bird of the Florida Citrus Commission that was prominent for the first decade of Walt Disney World in Adventureland.

- *Banjos and Baboons* by Goff is a reference to Imagineer Harper Goff who was a banjo player but also the designer of the Jungle Cruise attraction.

- *Primates of the Caribbean* by Coats is Imagineer Claude Coats, who did set design for the Pirates of the Caribbean attraction.

- *Mission to the Stars* by Tom Morrow (the audio-animatronics operations director in the Flight to the Moon attraction who is still referenced by name in the audio track of the PeopleMover).

- *A Small Village With A Large Heart* and *Rockefeller, Hippo, Pet, Family* by Doctor Albert Falls

- *Married Into the Jungle* is written by Dr. Falls's wife Victoria Marie Falls, *Born Into the Jungle* is written by Albert Falls Jr., and *Married to Someone Born in the Jungle* is written by Sneh Falls, the wife of Falls Jr. and mother of Alberta.

- *Another New Year* and *Global Night Celebrations* by Merriweather Adam Pleasure the founder of the Adventurers Club on Pleasure Island where New Year's Eve was celebrated every night.

- *Illustrated Guide to Radio Broadcasting* by Albert Awol who broadcasts in the Jungle Cruise queue.

- *Friends for Dinner, Top Hats and Umbrellas,* and *The Missing Mask* by Trader Sam. In the original WDW Jungle Cruise Trader Sam was a cannibal called Chief Nah-Mee and wore a top hat and carried an umbrella. At one point the Trader Sam figure wore a witch doctor mask but it was removed.

- *Temple Tours*, a series by Paco from the Indiana Jones Adventure: Temple of the Crystal Skull attraction.

- *The Harambe Chronicles* by Wilson is a reference to a former fictional character on DAK's Kilimanjaro Safaris, reserve warden Wilson Matua, who warned guests about poaching and flew over the Harambe reserve to try to stop that illegal activity.

- *Birds of Song* by Tiki Kiki Serbano, a character from Disneyland's Adventure Trading Company event.

- *The Polar Voyage* by Captain Nemo referencing the moment in the 20,000 Leagues attraction when Nemo's submarine navigated under the North Pole.

- *A Flight Through Dreams* and *If You Had Wings You Could Fly* by B.L. references Buzz Lightyear's Space Ranger Spin and the two previous attractions in that location, DreamFlight and If You Had Wings.

- *Keel Boat of the Mississippi* by Fink refers to King of the River Mike Fink whose keel boat attraction was once in Frontierland.

- *The Mystery Castle* by Cindy Ella is a reference to Cinderella and the Cinderella Castle Mystery Tour that was once at Tokyo Disneyland.

- *The Wildest Ride* by J. T. Toad is a reference to the character J. Thaddeus Toad and Mr. Toad's Wild Ride attraction that was once in Fantasyland.

- *A View from Above* by S.W. Buckets refers the Skyway Buckets that once journeyed from Fantasyland to Tomorrowland.

- *Tiki, Tiki, Tikis of the South Pacific* by B. Baker refers to Disney composer Buddy Baker who supplied the waiting area music for the Disneyland Enchanted Tiki Room that was filled with Rolly Crump's clever Tiki statues.

- *Creatures From Space* by Clench refers to Chairman Clench of X.S. Tech whose teleportation technology brought an alien creature into the Alien Encounter attraction.

- *Keeping Time* by Williams refers to Robin Williams who was the Timekeeper in the Tomorrowland attraction of the same name.

- *A New Way to Manage Birds* from I & Z Management Publications is Iago and Zazu and their Under New Management approach to the Enchanted Tiki Room.

- *The Grace of a Swan* by Plaza refers to the Plaza Swan Boats that once journeyed into Adventureland.

- *Great Characters of World Literature* by J. Lasseter refers to John Lasseter, a former Jungle Cruise skipper as well as former chief creative officer of Walt Disney Animation Studios, Pixar and Disneytoon Studios as well as the Principal Creative Advisor for Walt Disney Imagineering.

- *Meeting Royalty* by Sklar refers to Imagineering legend Marty Sklar.

- *True Life Adventures* by W.E.D. refers to the True Life Adventures documentary series with W.E.D. being Walt Disney's intials as well as the former name for Imagineering.

- *A Small World of Traditional Wardrobe* by A. Davis refers to Imagineer Alice Davis, the wife of Marc, who costumed the figures in It's A Small World.

- *Profiles of Legendary Pirates of the Caribbean* by Gibson refers to Imagineer Blaine Gibson who sculpted the pirates in the attraction.

- *Treehouse Construction* by Mills refers to John Mills who played the role of the father in the 1960 Disney film *Swiss Family Robinson* who built a treehouse for his family.

- *The Stars Above Us* by Quill refers to the character of the space traveler Peter Quill in the *Guardians of the Galaxy* movies.

The Skipper Canteen is an imaginative and entertaining addition to the many legends of the Jungle Cruise with many "hidden" details yet to be discovered by enterprising explorers including the "Lost and Unfound" section with some items from the Adventurers Club.

Trader Sam:
Brandon Kleyla Interview

Brandon Kleyla was the Walt Disney Imagineer responsible for set dressing, writing, and giving life to Trader Sam's Enchanted Tiki Bar at the Disneyland Hotel (that opened May 2011) and Trader Sam's Grog Grotto (that opened April 2015) at Walt Disney World's Polynesian Village Resort.

In addition, he authored the hundred page 2018 book *The Field Guide to Tiki Decorating* that is only the first volume of a proposed series of books.

Kleyla joined Walt Disney Imagineering in 2009 and left in 2016 to become part of Universal Creative. During 2019, Kleyla was very gracious to answer some of my questions about himself and the location. Kleyla reviewed the final interview in November 2019.

Jim Korkis: It is my understanding that you worked for a time as a Jungle Cruise skipper.

Brendon Kleyla: I worked at Disneyland in 2005-2006 during the 50th anniversary. Having been an actor in my youth, I had done many commercials and print campaigns. When I moved to California, I realized that I had never worked at Disneyland. So I drove over there one day and applied for a job, telling the casting person I wanted Jungle Cruise.

They informed me that that's not how it works; you can't just pick a role. When I got called back into the office, the casting person had my IMDB page up on his computer, and he was confused as to why I wanted to work at Disneyland. But I told him I really wanted a role that I could do something with beyond just pushing a button if I was going to drive an hour and a half to work everyday from Camarillo.

JK: What was the training like for the role?

BK: Training was four days: two openings and two closings. I got signed off on the first try once I got thrown in a boat with guests.

I've always said that the jokes are good but it's the delivery that can make or break a trip. Some skippers like to get every joke in there and just bombard the guests, but I would do one joke per scene and let the delivery do the work for me.

I think my favorite part of the job was interacting with the guests. I used to reload my gun in an area where all the kids waiting in line could see, and I'd play it off very dramatic. I liked playing it off like we may not actually make it back. I miss working Jungle everyday! My least favorite memory was quitting. I loved it there.

I grew up in Florida, so I was always fond of the Magic Kingdom Jungle Cruise, and still am. I love the temple scene. The layout of the overall ride definitely messes with you once you've worked 70 hours a week for two years in Anaheim. My favorite Jungle Cruise attraction though is actually Hong Kong's. What an amazing ride, the layout, the scenes. Very well done.

My dad's aunt worked at the Aku Tiki in Daytona Beach in Florida. Their marquee has a giant Moai head so that was always fascinating to a little kid , probably my first real tiki memory so I naturally had to put a postcard from Aku Tiki into Trader Sam's Grog Grotto as well.

JK: How did you get assigned to the Disneyland Trader Sam's Enchanted Tiki Bar?

BK: I had been in the props department at Imagineering and had been assisting on several different projects at several different parks when the Disney Parks Blog had announced a new bar coming to the Disneyland Hotel that was going to be Jungle Cruise themed.

So I printed out the blog post, took it to my boss, threw it on his desk and said "I have to do this." He got me a meeting with the hotel team, and I listened to what they were presenting, and at the end what was originally designed for Sam's was not even close to what it ended up being.

The image I saw from them was white walls, three masks on them, and a hula girl clock. My skipper brain about exploded. So I asked if I could do a pass at the design, I took a couple of days, took my 4x4 board in and presented it to Tom Fitzgerald, and that's what we built in Anaheim.

The vision shifted from a posh Caribbean style bar to a fun, quirky, crazy Tiki bar, which was fun for me because I could buy a ton of things and have a lot of fun with coming up with things that you couldn't do in a nice classy Tiki bar. So it sort of became Adventurers Club meets Jungle Cruise meets Tiki Room.

When we started, Ray Spencer was the art director and Kevin Rafferty was the show writer. They are both great guys that I loved working with, and we worked together on multiple shows!

Ray became so busy getting Buena Vista Street developed at DCA that he basically handed Trader Sam's off to me, seeing that I was doing the right thing. So more or less I became the field Art Director.

Then Kevin and I would work on spiels and the story for the bar. I remember that I needed the back story for the bar so I could start buying props. I shopped for about a year on this. Swap meets, eBay, flea markets, antique stores, anything and everywhere. With a project like this you really can't plan it that much.

You just go "I need an anchor. I don't know what size anchor and I don't know what it'll look like." There's one outside chained to the palm tree at Anaheim. It was so big but so great looking.

Things were mix-and-matched and then we brainstormed gags. A lot of bars have house rules, so why wouldn't Trader Sam's have house rules? We came up with forty house rules and they were all great.

JK: The seven rules I saw posted were: (1) Blow Dart guns are not to be used as drinking straws. (2) Cannibals may not serve people!! (3) Rule three crossed out so it is completely illegible. (4) Do not provide alcohol to on-duty Jungle Cruise Skippers. No Exceptions!!! (5) Call Bartender if Schweitzer falls (6) No poison dart games (7) Management is not responsible (crossed out) under any circumstances!

BK: Three is painted out and to be honest, I don't remember rule # 3. And it was always intended to be scratched out. That was part of the gag. And of course we did different rules for Grog Grotto.

There are over 1600 individual items in the Enchanted Tiki Bar and about 1400 in Grog Grotto. That was how I could make the space feel lived-in and look like it had always been there.

Nothing is hung straight; nothing is perfect, it's a real breathing environment, with real genuine artifacts. Very little was fabricated. Almost everything is a found item from the real world.

I did a documentary called *Indy Fans and the Quest for Fortune and Glory* (2008) that focused on the fan base and culture of Indiana Jones. Through that I met Tony Baxter and other folks at Imagineering so I knew I wanted some Indiana Jones references in the bar.

I remember one executive saying he wanted to see Indy's fedora hanging on the wall "because it's iconic." But I said "no" and explained that the reason it's iconic is because he always with him. I'm always a stickler for story and staying true to the properties.

I knew I wanted to do the map from the Indiana Jones Adventure attraction. I went to the files of the Art Library at Imagineering and found that the map wasn't there at all! Turns out, the original map had been sitting in Indy's office on his desk in the queue for the last sixteen years, having been spit on, trash on top of it, you name it.

When I realized that I took the map, had it scanned by the Art Library team and made two copies. One came to Trader Sam's and the other went back into the queue. The original is now in the Art Library to be restored. But I always wanted the map in there because I was always a fan of that piece and you never get to really look at it in the Indy queue. So here you can really sit down and study the map.

Over on a wall there is a postcard from Marcus Brody asking if Sam has seen Indy. There's also the seltzer bottle from Marion's bar, picture of Trader Sam in front of the temple in Tokyo and the one in Anaheim.

JK: How did you end up becoming the show writer for the project?

BK: I would email Kevin, and he was far too slammed on Cars Land by that time. So I eventually said, "Hey I'm going to just write it and you tell me if it works for not".

We did that for a little bit, and then he said he was too busy to even read what I wrote, so then I became the show writer for Sam's and wrote all the bartender spiels and named most of the drink names.

When we were doing cast member training, I would install my props during the night, and then would come in and work with the cast during the day, writing material, reworking material.

I was doing about 18 hour days when working on Sam's, and then went every weekend for the first year to make sure it was all working. That the jokes worked and that the cast was having fun. This was way outside of many of their normal ways of doing a job, so if it didn't work, the whole place would suffer.

Kevin and I sat down, took the Jungle Cruise jokes and went through them figuring out which would work for this place. The bartenders have a few pages of spiel to know for each drink, certain props on the wall and the stories that go with them, the Aloha's when you come in the door, all that kind of fun stuff.

We knew early on that the cast would be off-duty or retired skippers helping out their pal Trader Sam. Working with Kevin was always so much fun. I miss working with that guy!

JK: How influenced were you by Disneyland's The Enchanted Tiki Room attraction?

BK: Well I think that was my first introduction to "Tiki" culture like so many people. So I knew we wanted to incorporate elements of the Tiki Room into Trader Sam's. Originally there was one of the flower boats from the attraction planned to hang over the bar, but I nixed that due to the fact that it would be full of dust all the time, over a food area. Bad idea.

But the tiki totems, the planters in the corner, and the drummers, we knew had to go in. Especially since the original Trader Sam's in Anaheim really plays into the 1930's Adventureland time period as opposed to Orlando's location. And then, of course, if you're recreating elements from the Tiki Room, they have to be perfect.

I remember when we had a producer on the project that was adamant about just painting the tiki columns just flat brown. And I kicked and screamed, ultimately choosing to bring in Kevin Kidney and Jody Daily to paint them for me. Those had to be right! They also painted the flower pots, and built the new ship in the ship in the bottle.

Kevin and Jody are well known for their Disney collectibles but are also huge Tiki experts so I asked them where I needed to go and what I needed to see. They pointed out all the good Tiki bars, the little places around town. So we went and they would have some drinks and I would just stare at everything, you know, because I don't drink.

I never looked at Sam's as a Tiki bar. It was a place where explorers and adventurers would come and hang out. I went to a few of the LA landmarks: Tiki Ti, Don the Beachcombers, even the horrible Trader Vics when it was open. But I didn't want to visit too many because I didn't want to copy any of them.

Kevin and Jody were helpful with their knowledge. Sven Kirstin was helpful as well, but I honestly designed a place where I wanted to spend time. I didn't want it to be based off of anything else. I just wanted it to be a dash of Adventureland, two dashes of Jungle Cruise, a sprinkling of Indiana Jones, and a little Tiki Room icing on top.

I didn't want to take from these places exactly because people come to Trader Sam's but they also go to the other bars. Being in Southern California, our clientele know the Tiki bar so we wanted to always go a little bit further in our approach and make both Disney fans and Tiki fans happy.

One of my biggest concerns was that we had to make sure people knew that this wasn't The Adventurers Club. A fun fact is that these are the only totems in the world that are three-sided. The ones in the Tiki Room are four-sided.

JK: How much did Walt Disney World's Polynesian Village Resort influence you?

BK: The Polynesian never really came up too much when doing Anaheim because it's a different time period. We leaned heavily on the Polynesian obviously for the location in Orlando. In Anaheim, we really just put the Polynesian logo on our doors, and then never talked about it.

JK: How had being a Jungle Cruise skipper influence Trader Sam's?

BK: It was always there, and I think certainly came through when I wrote the spiel books for the cast members, and always thinking of that Skipper sense of humor when purchasing props or creating things.

JK: How influenced were you by the Adventurers Club that was on Pleasure Island in Florida?

BK: I grew up in Florida and was always too young to get into the Adventurers Club. So I actually never got to go in ever! I was there for the night it was closing and didn't get in so I did not get a chance to experience The Adventurers Club. That being said, I certainly did my homework, talked to some of the original cast, and watched plenty of videos. Certainly there are references to the Club in both locations but we tried hard to differentiate ourselves.

JK: How did you envision the character of Trader Sam?

BK: Well in the Trader Sam's bar story, Anaheim Trader Sam is the true Trader Sam. This came up several times when we started working on the Florida Trader Sam's. At one point it came up to remove the Marc Davis Sam from the Jungle Cruise attraction and replace him with Anaheim Sam, which I think the majority of us opposed.

So I simply came up with the fact that the Florida Sam is Anaheim Sam's cousin, and he runs the east coast. Simple and we get the best of both. And I concreted that idea by creating a photo of the two of them standing together.

There's certainly a lot of mystery around who Sam is. I would certainly think he's a cannibal but he has some sort of arrangement with the Jungle Navigational Company. It's probably too dark for us to get into.

We had to establish "Who is Trader Sam?" Well, he's a trader and he's on the Jungle Cruise obviously. And then we asked, "What if he knew Indiana Jones? What if he knew Jack Sparrow, or Swiss Family Robinson?" You know, all those types of characters. Basically what it came down to is that he can know anyone live-action from pretty much anywhere in Disney's "Adventure" history.

There's the picture of Sam with Jack Sparrow on the wall; there's the note from Ned Land of *20,000 Leagues Under the Sea* to Sam; there's even a reference from *Castaway Cowboy*, the James Garner film that takes place in Hawaii. There's a lot of live action film reference and Disney park references as well including obviously Jungle Cruise, Walt Disney's Enchanted Tiki Room, Indiana Jones, and Adventurers Club.

JK: How was working with Kyle Barnes who was the Art Director for the overall rehab of the Polynesian Village Resort?

BK: Kyle was a great partner and trusted me to do what I did. We would often share the same outlook on most decisions and we had a great time working together on Sam's in Florida. You can't ask for a better partner than that! I do miss the days of running into his office to name a drink or share thoughts on an upcoming mug design. Those are great memories! We were a great team!

JK: Imagineer Rolly Crump used the reference book *Voices on the Wind* by Katharine Luomala for his work on the original Enchanted Tiki Room.

BK: I certainly read that same book during my research phase, and have a copy here at home. Rolly is great, and if I had to pick any of his work that inspired Sam's the most, it would actually be the South Seas Traders in Disneyland, a small store in Adventureland that has stuff all over, nets hanging from the ceiling, mismatched doors, I really loved that space at the time when we were putting Sam's together. And someone told me that Rolly designed that space. It's since changed from the original design sadly, but just such a cool place.

JK: What are the differences between the two Trader Sam's Tiki bars?

BK: Enchanted Tiki Bar is set 1930-1950, it plays off of the Adventureland look and stories. Every photo is sepia or black and white; the walls are dark; it's more of your classic aesthetic. It is really a love letter to Adventureland.

Grog Grotto picks up as a different adventure and takes us 1950-1970. Kyle and I agreed that each bar should be different and should have a different tagline. So in Grog Grotto, all photos are in color or colorized. It's a Technicolor adventure. I hand colored almost every photo in the place. That was fun! There's much more color in the space, beta tapes, cassettes. It's a later time.

One of the truly unique elements about Sam's is everything he's collected is one-of-a-kind discoveries, so you won't find two props that match on either coast. That was certainly challenging, but very exciting to accomplish. Even the drinks/mugs are different.

JK: I am especially fond of the sinking ship in a bottle at the Enchanted Tiki Bar because it came from Florida's Adventurers Club.

BK: The Ship in the Bottle was actually designed by Yale Gracey for the Haunted Mansion but never used there! But there are drawings for it in the WDI Art Library that I showed at the first Mahaloween show in Anaheim. It was later dusted off and finally built for the Adventurers Club. It's a beautifully simple effect and I'm certainly honored to have a Yale Gracey effect in Sam's!

That bottle is the original bottle. We built a new ship for it. I had Kevin and Jody build us an amazing one-of-a-kind *Wicked Wench* for the bottle. The *Wicked Wench* of course being the ship that is attacking the fort in Pirates of the Caribbean.

Very few other things came from the Adventurers Club: a couple framed images. Zeus' fishing pole is in Anaheim. When it came to salvage the Club, most of the stuff was in such bad shape from just being in there so long, that you really couldn't get much more use out of it. That and the fact that people were stealing things right off the walls before the club closed. A lot of the stuff from the Club actually got picked over and taken to Mystic Manor in Hong Kong.

JK: Grog Grotto has some unique items from extinct attractions as well.

BK: Yes, Grog Grotto has a couple of extinct attraction items like a life ring from Maelstrom at Epcot for instance. I actually found the statue of UhOa from WDW's Enchanted Tiki Room Under New Management in the Animation building in Glendale one day. She was leaning up against the wall, some months after the fire in the attraction. And I freaked out, ran down to Kyle and said we have to get this. The animation department let us have her, so then we had to redesign the wall where she sits now, because it was never planned to have her there.

JK: Who came up with the idea of ordering a particular drink triggering an effect?

BK: I believe that was a Kyle idea, and a great one. I did name a good portion of the drinks, but some of them just wrote themselves like HippopotoMai-Tai.

I like a lot of the effects we did at Grog Grotto, because we had a budget to really have fun. I love the Shrunken Zombie Head effect in Orlando. The drink doesn't have any effect in Anaheim. As a non-drinker, I usually have an off-menu Gorilla Grog.

JK: The only complaint I have heard is that the locations seem too small to accommodate everyone who wants to go there.

BK: I think this complaint falls into an overall thought that we as Disney were introducing people to Tiki Bars. The majority of people who came through Sam's doors had never been in a Tiki bar in their life, and they've told me this. So I think the complaint of size comes from the fact that nobody is used to Disney building a tiny space.

We did that because we had no choice. The space in Anaheim came out of a corner of Hook's Pointe, the restaurant there before. We didn't build a new space; it was repurposed.

Same thing in Orlando. I was there one day and noticed an empty arcade, so I took photos and sent it to Kyle and said here's the Florida location. So again, we didn't build something new; we repurposed the Arcade space.

On the flip side of that, Tiki Bars are small; they always have been. Look at Tiki Ti in Los Angeles. Even some of the more recent "big" locations are still small and tight. It is an intimate experience and that is what we created.

Part of the magic is that it literally looks like a tucked away, hole-in-the-wall Tiki bar. The size I think is fun and when you're in, the camaraderie and inclusion is a lot like Adventurers Club and everyone belongs.

JK: Did working on these two Tiki bars change your life?

BK: Well the biggest change was I met my wife working on Grog Grotto! My wife and I had Tiki Tony carve our wedding cake topper; we had custom mugs for everyone at the reception, and we built a Tiki backyard with a lagoon (pool) and bar.

Aside from that, yeah, Tiki had certainly become a part of my life. I love going to Tiki events and talking about Sam's and hearing peoples' stories about their experiences there. It's still surreal as I was just building a place I wanted to hang out in. I never thought other people would want to certainly not to the extent it has.

I can echo George Lucas when he says he's sad he never got to see *Star Wars* as the audience. There's a part of me that's sad that I never got to experience Sam's by just opening the door and discovering it.

But I do love going there and just sitting and watching peoples reactions, listening to their conversations, watching what they take photos of. And it's nice because nobody knows who I am. Occasionally someone will recognize me, but for the most part, I can get their genuine responses.

JK: Why did you write a book about Tiki decorating?

BK: The book all started because I would get so many people wanting me to write a book about Sam's, which obviously I can't do, as much as I'd love to because of my agreement with Disney. There are trademark restrictions, intellectual property restrictions, non disclosure clauses and more.

So I thought about it and ended up writing a "How to" book on how to make your own home Tiki bar. So it's full of ideas of how to build things, things to think about while you're out shopping, etc. The reactions have been great. We've sold over 3000 copies.

Volume two is roughly outlined, but it's so hard to find time in the schedules to actually do it. In the second volume, we wanted to take it a step further, some of the next steps, so things like foam carving, hard-coating, more things with power tools.

JK: I'm surprised Tokyo DisneySea hasn't asked for a Trader Sam's.

BK: We offered one to the Explorers Hotel in Hong Kong, but they said "no", and having been to Hong Kong now, I understand why. The locals don't seem to sit and enjoy themselves, they drink and leave. I went to a few local Tiki bars that were gorgeous, and I was the only person in there that was sitting and enjoying himself.

Designing bars is a really great time! I would love to design more Tiki bars, but with a full time job, that's hard to do now. You need to walk in and immediately be right at home and never want to leave. It needs to be fun.

As a designer, I always appreciate the décor, especially the traditional designs. Trader Sam's are actually what I would call "explorer bars" and that allows for so much imagination. I've never thought of them as Tiki bars.

JK: Mahalo! Thanks for taking the time to answer my questions.

Extinct Adventureland Adventures

Like the jungle itself, Walt Disney World is continually changing to adapt. In that process, some things are simply changed while others are completely removed.

Here are three things that went missing from the Adventureland jungle over the decades.

The Enchanted Tiki Room Under New Management

Disneyland, of course, was partly responsible for the revival of Tiki Culture in the 1960s. Stouffer's sponsored the Plaza Pavilion and the Tahitian Terrace restaurants at Disneyland and had contracted to sponsor the new "adventure in eating and dining" called The Enchanted Tiki Room which would share the kitchen for those two dining locations. Posters were printed up and guests alerted.

Reservations (the first ever restaurant at Disneyland to have reservations) were to be spaced at one hour intervals and after the main course had been completed the performing audio-animatronics tropical birds would spring to life in dozens of overhead bird cages.

Walt soon realized that guests would be so enchanted that they stopped eating and didn't finish in time for the next seating. In addition, it was so small that it would have limited capacity as a restaurant.

The Enchanted Tiki Room where all the birds sing words and the flowers croon opened June 23, 1963 at Disneyland and it was the first to feature audio-animatronics technology developed by WED (Imagineering) from recently declassified military mechanics.

The building was the first fully air-conditioned building at the park, in order to make sure the computers in the basement of the attraction did not overheat. Since the attraction was owned by WED rather than Disneyland, guests paid an extra seventy-five cents (cost of an "E" Ticket) to experience it.

It was immediately hugely popular and became an iconic Disney park attraction.

Walt Disney Productions entered into negotiations with the Florida Citrus Commission (FCC) for a Florida Citrus Growers sponsored Magic Kingdom attraction in 1967. A contract was signed on October 22, 1969, formalizing the FCC's underwriting of a "tropical bird show" at a cost of three million dollars.

The following year, 1970, WED Enterprises created the Orange Bird character to serve as the FCC's official mascot in promotional campaigns. When the Tropical Serenade show (a duplicate of Disneyland's Enchanted Tiki Room show) finished, guests exited by the Sunshine Tree Terrace for drinks, slushes, Orange sippers and the Citrus Orange Swirl.

The figureheads of water buffalo on top of the Sunshine Tree Terrace were chosen because the building was so tall that it could be seen in Frontierland. It was felt that the long horns on the stylized figures might be mistaken by guests as Wild West long horn cattle when viewed from that other land.

Unlike Disneyland where the attraction was housed in a space originally intended to be an American Tiki restaurant and then reformatted into an attraction, the Walt Disney World version was housed in a Balinese Temple, a location that was supposedly home to the native gods.

The birds and flowers speak and sing because they have been blessed by the power of the gods who demonstrate some of that power when they show their anger by creating a storm at the end of the show.

During the show, the Tiki figures sing a song known variously as the *Hawaiian War Chant* or *Kaua i ka Huahua'i*. The song was composed in 1860 by Prince William Pitt Leleiohoku II and described a romantic encounter. In 1929, composer Johnny Noble borrowed the tune and titled it *Hawaiian War Chant*. In 1939 Tommy Dorsey's big band turned the song into a hit.

The original show ran from 1971 to 1997 but attendance kept dropping. The Enchanted Tiki Room Under New Management debuted after a seven month transformation of the original version from April 1998 to January 2011.

"The new management" were audio-animatronics figures of Iago (voiced by Gilbert Gottfried) from the animated feature *Aladdin* and Zazu (voiced by Michael Gough rather than the film's Rowan Atkinson) from the animated feature *The Lion King* who had "been given the deed to the WDW Tiki Room as part of their bonuses for starring in hit movies as negotiated by their bird agents William and Morris (voiced by Don Rickles and Phil Hartman)".

William and Morris were two toucan audio-animatronics added to the queue pre-show in a cylinder shaped tube behind the waterfall that spun around.

The two bickered back and forth while establishing the premise that they represented the two new owners of the Tiki Room and that their new wise-cracking approach would be representative of the new show and not be the traditional one of years past.

Morris claims he just signed Donald Duck while William claims he just signed former Disney property and NHL Team, The Mighty Ducks.

> **Morris:** I just flew in from Hollywood. My client's the new owner of this birdcage.
>
> **William:** What? Are you cuckoo? My client's the new owner. Disney gave me an exclusive.
>
> **Morris:** Co-exclusive. Didn't you read your contract?
>
> **William:** I gave it a bird's eye glance.
>
> **Morris:** And you call yourself a talent agent! I negotiated my tail feathers off for this deal.
>
> **William:** Well, my client does not share credit. He's a very big bird.
>
> **Morris:** Your client is Big Bird?
>
> **William:** Not Big Bird. A big bird, you bird brain.
>
> **Morris:** Well, your dim little star is now half owner of *The Enchanted Tiki Room* with my superstar.

As one astute Disney travel writer wrote, it was possible to hear all the dialog clearly because it was not obscured by the audience's laughter. The Don Rickles character even referred to the other bird as a "hockey puck", a standard Rickles' insult.

It was hoped that a new, fast-moving approach to the show would increase attendance.

In particular, Iago sought to update the show and make it more hip for a modern audience but his approach is cynical and jarring and angers Uh-Oa, the green audio-animatronics "Tiki Goddess of Disaster" (voiced by Armelia Audrey McQueen) who emerges in smoke from the center fountain to punish him.

Iago later appears at the end of the show bandaged, burnt and with a crutch but not humbled by the experience. The revamped show was done by senior concept designer Jeff Burke and senior concept writer Kevin Rafferty.

"It was kind of demoralizing to see guests leave in the middle of the (original) show," said Burke. "So we wanted to infuse new life into it. We wanted to bring out the Disney magic that current audiences would relate to. People who have seen the show before will wonder 'What is going on around here?'"

For the recording session, three of the four original voices for the Tiki Bird hosts were brought back: Wally Boag (Jose), Fulton Burley (Michael), and Thurl Ravenscroft (Fritz). Ernie Newton who did Pierre had passed away in 1996 and was replaced by Jerry Orbach who had done a French accent as the character Lumiere in the animated feature *Beauty and the Beast* (1991).

Associate show producer Kate Zovich took pride in the creation of the two new audio-animatronics characters, "The work that (Imagineering in) Tujunga (California) did on the A-A figures is absolutely amazing. To fit all of that wiring and mechanics inside these teeny birds is an incredible accomplishment and they were very successful at making these figures more like cartoon characters."

Most guests were appalled that the lighthearted original show had been replaced by the newer snarkier version that eliminated familiar songs and had too many in-jokes like Iago commenting at the end of the show, "Boy, I'm tired! I think I'll head over to the Hall of Presidents and take a nap."

While curious enough to visit, guests were generally displeased with the misguided attempts at humor so they didn't revisit, defeating the purpose for the drastic changes.

On January 12, 2011, a small fire broke out in the attic of the attraction, damaging the figure of Iago as well as other show elements when the automatic sprinkler system went off to extinguish the flames.

The decision was made to replace the show with a newly shortened version of the original show now dubbed Walt Disney's Enchanted Tiki Room that opened August 15, 2011.

However, a reminder of the ill-fated new management attraction exists at Trader Sam's Grog Grotto in the Polynesian Village Resort. One of its signature drinks is the Uh-Oa. Above the bar is the Uh-Oa goddess figure from the attraction. If a guest orders the drink, a storm begins outside with winds and heavy rains.

The bartenders lead guests in the chant of "Uh-Oa, Uh-Oa, Uh Oa-aaaa!" and the Krakatoa volcano erupts and ligthning flashes illuminate the goddess figure who opens her eyes to reveal their glowing redness and she cackles, just as she did in the attraction.

Safari Club Arcade

In Disneyland's Adventureland from 1962 to 1982 was the Big Game Safari Shooting Game. It was the largest of the three shooting galleries at Disneyland.

This gallery used MacGlashan air guns and fired .22 caliber lead pellets that were still powerful and dangerous. The lead pellets were so abrasive that they caused severe dings on the targets and the surrounding artwork. As a result, the attraction required new hand painting every night using roughly forty gallons of paint every week.

When Walt Disney World opened, there was a similar shooting attraction in Adventurland called the Safari Club. It would be the first attraction at WDW to close in spring 1972 after roughly seven months of operation.

Basically it was felt the location would be more valuable to sell merchandise since it was directly across from the Swiss Family Treehouse and that the Frontierland Shootin' Gallery was close enough to handle any guest who might want enjoy such an amusement.

It wasn't actually an arcade but more of a game room like the Caribbean Arcade that opened in 1974 with a mounted rifle on an individual wooden cabinet. The shooting games in the rectangular room gave guests the opportunity to shoot at a variety of African wildlife like lions, zebras and tigers in custom sculpted cabinets.

Roughly twenty-four one player such games were in the location that was not specifically themed except as a generic African outpost look. The entrance was through large arched doorways. At the back was a room that also connected to the Frontierland Shootin' Gallery that served as the operations room.

The location would become Colonel Hathi's Safari Club and later Island Supply Company because merchandise wanted another location in Adventureland.

Shrunken Ned's Junior Jungle Boats

Shrunken Ned's Junior Jungle Boats, a remote control miniature boat experience, existed next to the Jungle Cruise attraction from 1997 to 2012. It occupied an area between the Jungle Cruise and the Swiss Family Treehouse and was eventually replaced in spring 2013 by stations for the interactive game, A Pirate's Adventure: Treasures of the Seven Seas.

A sign identified the game as the "Jungle Expedition Skipper Training School, established 1854". Named for and apparently owned by Shrunken Ned, the attraction gave guests a way to experience manuevering the famous Jungle Cruise launches through a variety of obstacles.

The game cost two tokens (with a nearby machine exchanging one dollar for one token so it cost two dollars) and featured sixteen control stations featuring a steering wheel and throttle. Each station was numbered and corresponded to the same numbered boat.

Guests could attempt to navigate through an obstacle course containing such features as: a volcano, spears, Tiki God statues, an Elephant Shrine, ancient ruins and Headhunters. A path to guide the boats was lined with the spears sticking out of the water. Guests could steer the boat in any direction along the designated path.

It was so popular that a similar experience (Safari Adventure) was operated at the Disneyland Hotel from 1999 to 2010.

The boats were named Amazon Annie, Congo Connie, Bomokandi Bertha, Mongala Millie, Ganges Gertie, Kwango Kate, Volta Val, Nile Nellie, Orinoco Ida, Ucyali Lolly, Sankuru Sadie, Rutshuru Ruby, Irrawaddy Irma, Senegal Sal, Wamba Wanda and Zambesi Zelda.

Shrunken Ned was meant to be play on the words "shrunken head" that also referenced that guests were playing with shrunken boats but the WDW attraction sparked a mythology behind just such a character.

Colonel Nedley Lostmore was a British colonist reportedly from the late 1800s/early 1900s who had some connection to the company that ran the Jungle Cruise. It is surmised that it had something to do with the training and possible hiring of new skippers. He had a distinctively huge white mustache and wore a monocle.

At some unknown point in time, Ned was decapitated and had his head shrunk but in an unusual supernatural process. His sentient but preserved shrunken head was mounted in the South Seas Traders shop at Disneyland's Adventureland.

Apparently the experience somehow helped him to become a fortune-teller and witch doctor. He identifies himself as "The Jungle's Only Self-Service Witch Doctor", diagnosing guests with strange jungle diseases and offering equally strange solutions.

He might diagnose a guest with some type of fever and claim the guest is hallucinating that he was in Disneyland when he is just lost in the jungle and sleepwalking. He is one of four fortune telling machines found in Disneyland park and his voice is provided by Imagineer Eddie Sotto.

Dropping two quarters into his "office," Ned prompts the guest to place their hand on a carved hand-shaped plaque in front of the glass. Guests will feel an eerie pulsing heartbeat and then be told to take the prescription card that is produced. There are twelve different versions.

One one side is the face of Ned and on the other the advice on twelve different "prescription cards". A totem of Ned's head is hung in Trader Sam's Grog Grotto in Disney's Polynesian Village Resort where his voice is provided by Imagineer Brandon Kleyla.

SHRUNKEN NED'S TWELVE PRESCRIPTION CARDS:

1. Be careful of following the advice in health books. You could die of a misprint.

2. Shrunken Ned's Sure-Fire Insomnia Cure: (1) Get plenty of sleep (2) See #1.

3. Boil one eye of newt, sprinkle on a thick paste of Yak fur, spread on saltine crackers and take twice a day until you get better (or your Yak runs out of fur).

4.
A) Take Your Best Shot

B) Get A Clue

C) Shake It But Don't Break It, Wrap It Up and Take It

D) It's Your Thing, Do Whatcha Want To Do (I Can't Tell You Who To Sock It To)

E) Discontinue If Itching Persists

5. Shrunken Ned's Rules for Good Health:

a) Never eat anything bigger than your head
b) Get Plenty of Sleep, Especially at Work
c) Run Only If Chased.

6. How to make Shrunken Ned's "Jungle Juice" Longevity Cocktail:

1 Shot Zambezi River Water
1 Gallon Pomegranate Juice
1 Tsp. Emu Toenails
1 Dash Rhino Eyelid Dandruff

Blend for 6 hours, or until clear. Drink over ice 10 times a day.
(Notice: This product has no therapeutic value whatsoever. Its value comes from the exercise you'll receive from chasing a rhino to get his eyelid dandruff.)

7. Shrunken Ned's Philosophy for Total Health:

"For a long, happy life, eat whatever you want and don't worry about it. A waist is a terrible thing to mind."

8. Shrunken Ned Prescribes:

Indecipherable scrible, scrible, scrible signed Col. Nedley Lostmore, D.J.M. Esq.

9. Shrunken Ned's Life Extension Formula:

A) Eat only celery for 6 weeks. After 6 weeks, eliminate celery.
B) Give up all bad habits, hobbies, television, friends and forms of amusement.
C) Move to the Aleutian Islands and Sell Refrigerators.
(None of this will make your life longer—it will just seem longer. . .)

10. "Nothing in Excess, Including Moderation"

11. Shrunken Ned's Sure-Fire Guide to Tell If You Learned All of Life's Lessons:

1) Hold mirror up to mouth.
2) Fog mirror.
3) If you succeed you must have learned something, because you're still alive!
4) Continue to learn life's lessons.

12. Shurnken Ned's Balanced Diet:

1) While holding a double chili cheesburger in each hand, balance a pepperoni pizza on your head, and a bowl of chocolate chip cookie dough ice cream on your nose.

2) Eat everything you can balance.

The Secret of S.E.A.

Despite the closure of the Adventurers Club on Pleasure Island, the concept of a group of high-spirited adventurers and explorers with colorful histories remained so beloved that some of the original performers recreated their characters for special Walt Disney World convention events for a few years after the club disappeared.

Avid fans created a "ConGalooshConvention" that was held in Orlando, Florida for several years trying to keep the memories alive. Various sites on the internet tried to do the same including the "Society for Explorers and Adventurers" and "The Congaloosh Society" on Facebook.

Walt Disney Imagineering Creative Entertainment itself briefly tried to recapture lightning in a bottle by creating a different form of a distinctly American adventurer group for conventions and special dinners that never seemed to capture the same magic, even though the group was composed of some of the same performers from the Adventurers Club.

It was called PSHHAA! (Preservation of the Secret Society of Historical American Adventurers). The characters were Abigail Adams, Clementine Darling, Professor Beauregard Jackson, Edison Jersey Brown, Ace Spitfire, Bitsie and Ragtime Rags. The focus was on American adventuring but featured the same wild improvisational interactions, archaic costumes as well as a pseudo-history of the organization.

The group's motto was: "We re-enact the stories just to say that we've been there. We charge the hill and wave the flag living history from our chair. From the wide open prairies to the purple mountains hue, we salute the eagle feather as we stuff the gobbler true. We're obsessive, faithful, loyal and with patriotic pride, we preserve our country's history but we never go outside!"

When this attempt failed, according to Imagineering, there was yet another group of fearless adventurers with somewhat tentative connections to the Adventurers Club. Formed on August 12, 1538, the Society of Explorers and Adventurers

(S.E.A.) began attracting the attention of Disney fans in 2001 with the opening of Tokyo DisneySea.

The organization began in the 1500s with the founding members being Ferdinand Magellan, Leonardo Da Vinci, Sir Frances Drake, Tycho Brahe, Vasco Da Gama, and Cristova Colom.

The Society was first founded in Italy at Porto Paradiso. Consisting of scientists, explorers, researchers, artists, travelers and adventurers from around the globe, S.E.A. is dedicated to the continued exploration ("Exploration Continua") of the world's oceans and exotic lands.

Its four guiding concepts are represented on SEA's original Fortress Explorations crest: Adventure (represented as a Galleon), Romance (an Armillary Sphere), Discovery (a Compass), and Innovation (Artist Tools), selected as the best ways to represent the original charter and mission statement, which simply read: "We the Society of Explorers and Adventurers shall acquire knowledge through exploration".

In the Fortress Explorations area, designed by Imagineer Scott Chase, a type of museum of fanciful items enchants guests including a seismic recording station embedded in Mount Prometheus where S.E.A. members tracked and recorded the volcano's activities.

Fortress Explorations is the home base of S.E.A and a bronze plaque near the water's edge touts: "We, the members of the Society of Explorers and Adventurers, herewith establish Explorers' Landing in order to promote the sharing of nautical and scientific knowledge for world exploration."

A more detailed version of its mission statement can be found at Mystic Manor and the Oceaneer Lab:

"The mission of the Society of Explorers and Adventurers is to collect, conserve, and curate valuable cultural and artistic artifacts from around the world and make them available to the public in an artistically pleasing and sensitive manner. It is furthermore the mission of the organization to equip and mount socio-cultural expeditions to discover, explore, chronicle and protect the artistic achievements of human society, past and present, exalted and forgotten."

However, as the legend and popularity of S.E.A. started to expand to other Disney parks and literature, under the direction of Imagineer Joe Lanzisero the story started to be revised and expanded. Henry Mystic and Barnabas T. Bullion first appeared in 2013 and were followed by Mary Oceaneer in 2014.

At the D23 Destination D 2016: Amazing Adventurers event, Imagineers and Disney Parks and Resorts president Bob Chapek said that the incorporation of more references to S.E.A. would take place in parks around the globe.

The story now seemed to be that the organization, as Disney guests now know it, was actually founded in the late 1800s by Captain Mary Oceaneer, Harrison Hightower III, Dr. Albert Falls, Barnabas T. Bullion, Lord Henry Mystic, and Jason Chandler.

Captain Mary Oceaneer is a treasure-hunting heroine and world-famous oceanographer who was accompanied on her travels by her parrot companion, Salty. The Oceaneer Labs on the Disney Cruise Line on the *Disney Magic* and *Disney Wonder* were supposedly inspired by Mary and her high-seas exploits to enhance the voyages for children.

Her back story is that she and her parrot found pirate treasure on and below Castaway Cay and established the first Pirate Party onboard the ship. The amazing Miss Adventures Falls attraction at Disney's Typhoon Lagoon Water Park is a notable tribute to Captain Mary.

Her goal was to sail the seven seas and collect treasures from numerous ports of call to share with the rest of the world. Unfortunately, during her travels, her ship was caught in an unexpected storm and swept to Typhoon Lagoon where her deep-sea artifacts were scattered throughout the location.

In the attraction, guests see some of those unique items, as well, as the damaged hull of the ship where Mary's diving-partner, Duncan the parrot (perhaps his nickname is "Salty"?) is scanning the terrain through a telescope and interacting with riders.

Nearby is Mary's diving bell with the S.E.A. motto, "Exploration Continua," and underneath is Atlantean lettering first created for the Disney animated feature film *Atlantis: The Lost Empire* (2001) that states "I come in peace."

According to the Imagineering back story, Mary's ship, the *RV Oceaneer Lab's* maiden voyage took place on July 30, 1898 (referencing the first voyage of the *Disney Magic* in 1998). It served as Mary Oceaneer's floating base for her deep-sea diving excursions and treasure hunting expeditions. Artifacts line the walls of the ship's public areas.

These include a golden sword found on a deep sea dive on December 5, 1901 (with her parrot Salty's custom diving suit accompanying it) to a more recent expedition to Castaway Cay that yielded a variety of buried treasures. Items relating to other members of the Society of Explorers and Adventurers like Henry Mystic and Harrison Hightower III are also on display.

A scroll posted by a dagger on the wall proclaims: "Welcome to the Oceaneer Lab! I sincerely hope you enjoy the assemblage of artifacts, treasures and technologies gathered from ports of call all over the world. My top-notch crew will make your visit a memorable one. Captain Mary Oceaneer." At the bottom is a raised red seal of the S.E.A.

Harrison Hightower III is represented at Tokyo DisneySea by the magnificent Hotel Hightower, Japan's version of the Twilight Zone Tower of Terror. Japanese guests were unfamiliar with the popular classic American television series so another back story had to be created.

The hotel was built by Harrison Hightower who bears an uncanny physical resemblance to Imagineer Joe Rohde. Clever Disney fans might also make the connection that the final husband of Constance Hatchaway in 1877 at the Haunted Mansion at Walt Disney World is George Hightower, Harrison's supposed brother.

Pictures in the Hotel Hightower lobby display Harrison absconding with priceless ancient treasures from around the world much to the dismay of the local populations.

On New Year's Eve in 1899 at an exclusive party to show off his ill-gotten collection, an unfortunate incident occurred with a cursed idol known as Shiriki Utundu and Harrison disappeared. Thirteen years later in 1912, the building was reopened in an attempt to preserve it, but strange things started happening to guests touring the property.

Lord Henry Mystic, the owner of Mystic Manor at Hong Kong Disneyland, also toured the world, but, unlike Harrison, did not steal the treasures he collected or conned the natives. Mystic even made friends with a mischievous monkey named Albert that he saved from a giant spider in Africa.

The curious Albert plays with a new acquisition, an ancient music box that grants life to the lifeless, and suddenly guests riding the attraction are in the middle of a chaotic collection that has mystically been brought to life.

The queue features black-and-white photographs on the wall showing the opening of Mystic Manor in 1896, and a group portrait of the founding members of S.E.A. dated 1899. There's also a Mystic Freight Depot Stage, the Archives Shop, and an Explorer's Club Restaurant, all connected within the same S.E.A. back story.

Dr. Albert Falls was the founder of the Jungle Navigation Company and the illustrious namesake of the Walt Disney World Jungle Cruise's Schweitzer Falls. Among other things he discovered a Cambodian Temple that had partially sunk into a river after an earthquake. After he died, his granddaughter Alberta Falls inherited the cargo business and transformed it into a popular tour and later added a restaurant named the Skipper's Canteen in the company's headquarters.

While most guests eat in the old Skipper's Mess Hall, behind a corridor of bookshelves is the secret meeting room of S.E.A. packed with unusual memorabilia of the members.

Barnabas T. Bullion is the president and founder of the Big Thunder Mining Company at Big Thunder Railroad at Walt Disney World. His glaring face on his portrait looks suspiciously like Imagineer Tony Baxter who designed the attraction. By the way, that middle initial of Bullion's name officially stands for "Tony."

According to the official Imagineering back story:

"Barnabas T. Bullion is the founder and president of the Big Thunder Mining Company. The longtime mining magnate comes from a powerful East Coast family and considers gold to be his very birthright by virtue of his oddly appropriate name; in fact, he considers the ultimate gold strike to be his destiny. And that is why he is having so much trouble with Big Thunder Mountain.

"According to superstitious locals, Big Thunder Mountain is very protective of the gold it holds within, and the unfortunate soul who attempts to mine its riches is destined to fail. And so far that prophecy is coming to pass. The mine has been plagued by mysterious forces and natural disasters ever since. And yet the Big Thunder Mining Co. is still in operation.

"In fact, Bullion is discovering new veins of gold and digging new shafts every day, offering a closer look at the Big Thunder mining operation than ever before. But a word to the wise for anyone attempting to visit the mountain: watch out for runaway trains."

The drilling device that disturbed the spirits of the mountain was the invention of Jason Chandler, another founding member of S.E.A. Chandler, and another character created by Tony Baxter for his unrealized Discovery Bay project for Disneyland who also appeared in early version of the Big Thunder Mountain Railroad concepts.

According to the Spring 1992 issue of *Disney News* magazine:

"A young inventor circa 1849 named Jason Chandler devised a drilling machine with the capability of boring into the very heart of Big Thunder Mountain. But a cave-in occurred on Big Thunder Mountain, burying 26 miners alive.

"They would have drawn their last breath then and there, had it not been for the inventor and his laughable drilling machine. He burrowed down into the Earth's core, rescuing the miners from certain death."

Chandler then established a scientific outpost in Northern California named Discovery Bay and funded research into strange and unusual technologies and salvaging the remains of the Nautilus and continuing Captain Nemo's scientific work.

A letter in the queue of the Big Thunder attraction from Jason Chandler to Barnabas T. Bullion has him discussing the drilling machine and warning Barnabas that with all the supernatural incidents, it might be better to move mining operations away from the mountain.

> Dear Barney,
>
> Great Caesar's Ghost, old chap, I haven't heard from you since our little misadventure in El Dorado! I am indeed sorry to hear of the second disturbance within Big Thunder Mountain, but I did warn you that you were prospecting at your own peril when I sold you the drilling machine.
>
> I took the liberty of consulting Madame Zarkov at the Museum of the Weird, and it is her considered opinion that you should abandon the entire operation at once and find a less volatile site. I wish I had better news for you, old boy, but some forces simply are not to be trifled with.

> On behalf of your compatriots of SEA, I do hope to see you around the club a bit more often!
>
> Yours in Exploration and Adventure,
>
> Jason Chandler
>
> Founding Member The Society of Explorers and Adventurers

Many S.E.A. references are scattered throughout the parks.

The Epcot United Kingdom Pavilion's Kidcot station, themed as the library of the Royal Adventurers' Society, features a "Society of Explorers and Adventurers Handbook" among its titles as well as other books referencing S.E.A. and artwork either by S.E.A. members or obtained by S.E.A. members.

The AbracadaBar at Disney's Boardwalk Resort where a group of magicians mysteriously disappeared on Friday September 13, 1940 still has a fez hat with a S.E.A. logo on it in its lounge.

Jock Lindsey's Hangar Bar at Disney Springs has a menu stating "Society FOR Explorers and Adventurers New Member Dinner welcoming pilot Jock Lindsey" with offerings referencing the adventures of Indiana Jones. According to Disney, some time before 1948 Lindsey was inducted into S.E.A. Hathaway Browne, Samantha Sterling, and Otis T. Wren of the Adventurers Club were on hand at the opening of Jock Lindsey's Hangar Bar, as seen in photos around the bar.

Merriweather Adam Pleasure, the founder of the Adventurers Club has his S.E.A. Member Fez prominently on display on the bookshelf entrance to the S.E.A. private dining room at Adventureland's Skipper Canteen.

At Disneyland, The Tropical Hideaway restaurant features canoe paddles marked with the names and expeditions of various S.E.A. members. The Bengal Barbeue restaurant has a copy of the 1899 club portrait of S.E.A. members displayed as well as other photos including one featuring Albert the Monkey.

S.E.A. was clearly inspired by the concept of The Adventurers Club, but veered from the Monty Python-like silliness of its members, rituals and traditions into a more semi-serious approach that has established a new world of adventure with new stories connections appearing unexpectedly all the time.

Indiana Jones

Rumors have persisted for years that the presence of adventurer Indiana Jones would be expanded in Walt Disney World. The most prominent proposal was transforming the Dinosaur attraction at Disney's Animal Kingdom into an Indiana Jones attraction similar to the one in Disneyland.

The ride systems are virtually identical and there was even the suggestion of keeping the dinosaurs as part of the adventure. In addition, it was proposed to expand an entire mini-Indiana Jones land like Pandora into the space occupied by Chester and Hesters. Supposedly, this would be done to promote the newest Indiana Jones film.

While all of that is still a "blue sky" concept, Indiana Jones is still prominently featured at Walt Disney World.

Dr. Henry Walton Jones Jr. more commonly known by his nickname "Indiana" is a tenured professor of archaeology at fictional Marshall College (named after film producer Frank Marshall).

In the first film, *Raiders of the Lost Ark* (1981) two top ranking agents from U.S. Government Intelligence describe Jones as a "professor of archaeology, expert on the occult and obtainer of rare antiquities." He is known throughout the world as an adventurer noted for his integrity, knowledge and ingeunity.

The character as portrayed by actor Harrison Ford has appeared in four movies directed by Steven Spielberg with a fifth film announced to start production.

Indiana Jones is featured in several Walt Disney theme park attractions including Temple of the Forbidden Eye in Disneyland (opened in 1995) and Temple of the Crystal Skull in Tokyo DisneySea (opened in 2001). Disneyland Paris features Indiana Jones and the Temple of Peril (opened 1993) that is a looping roller coaster.

Disney MGM Studios included an audio-animatronics recreation of the scene in the Well of Souls with the character of Sallah from the first film in its now closed Great Movie Ride.

The twenty-five minute long Indiana Jones Epic Stunt Spectacular! in a two thousand seat theater opened at Disney

MGM Studios in 1989 with recreations of scenes from *Raiders of the Lost Ark* and ran for several shows a day for over thirty years.

It was executive produced by George Lucas, originally directed by Jerry Rees with stunt coordination by Glenn Randall who coordinated the stunts on the actual film set.

The first scene is based on the first scene in the first movie where Jones is manuevering through an exotic South American jungle in 1936 to locate a lost Peruvian temple. Inside he seeks a small and valuable golden idol known as the Chachapoyan Fertility Idol, a fictitious artifact created for the film.

The idol used in the show is an exact replica of the one from the film. Jones must brave ancient booby traps from dangerous spikes to false floors before obtaining the treasure. Unfortunately, taking the idol triggers a huge rolling boulder that threatens to crush the intrepid hero. In the show the boulder is twelve feet in diameter and weighs 440 pounds.

To get into the seating arena for the show, Walt Disney World guests must manuever through a twisting queue that is surrounded by an overgrown jungle.

The original performer to be the stunt man portraying Indy was twenty-nine year old Kevin Brassard who was not initially told the role he was auditioning for at the time because of the secrecy surrounding the twenty-million dollar show.

Brassard, a California native, had been performing in the Hoop-Dee-Doo Musical Revue dinner show at Disney's Fort Wilderness Resort and Campground.

For nine months, Brassard and two other Indys rehearsed outside on an unassuming makeshift stage at a Disney warehouse. The training was so intense and complex that the show was not able to open until three months after the park opened.

Glenn Randall taught the performers how to crack the famous whip and throw a realistic punch.

"As an actor, I've been given one of the most wonderful entrances onto any stage in the world, and you only get to do it if you're Indiana Jones," Brassard said. "That's the rope drop."

At the debut rehearsal performance both filmmaker George Lucas and then CEO Michael Eisner rushed up onto the stage to make sure Brassard was okay after being crushed by the boulder because it looked so realistic. He was fine and the show continued.

Brassard went on to train other Indy actors and perform the part of the onstage movie director. Even in 2019, he would occasionally fill-in as needed as Indiana Jones making him the oldest performer to play that role.

The show was the longest running show at the park. Because of the Covid pandemic, the show was temporarily closed in March 2020 and in October 2020 was finally closed permanently with the cast laid off.

The Indiana Jones Epic Stunt Spectacular opened on August 25, 1989, the same year the film *Indiana Jones and The Last Crusade* was released to theaters. In 2004, Nazi swastikas were removed from costuming and props and were replaced by a stylized Greek Cross.

At the exit of the attraction is a merchandise location called the Indiana Jones Adventure Outpost. The plans for the stunt show always included some type of souvenir venue but originally it was going to be a re-creation of Indiana Jones' pre-World War II suburban Chicago house filled with artifacts from his many expeditions.

Another proposal was to have a Ford tri-motor airplane as an eating area adjoining a small merchandise shop but that was also abandoned.

"We had to come up with an idea that thematically fit the left block building which meant that one side had to look like Hollywood buildings in the 1930s but the other side had to fit the Indiana Jones story," said Imagineering concept architect Joe Kilanowski.

"So we came up with a house in Hollywood that has one side propped and dressed to look like it is being used for a movie that takes place in the Middle East. The front of the building looks like a normal house but the other side looks like an outpost."

To tie-in with the film, the outpost was meant to be a location where Indiana's crew sets out to find the Holy Grail. To aid in that illusion, Disney acquired from Lucasfilm the tank, two trucks and two cars from *Indiana Jones and the Last Crusade*.

The vehicles were meant to be part of a motor pool that were parked waiting for mechanics to work on them. To reinforce that concept, a fuel dump and machine gun nest (to protect the vehicles from being stolen or sabotaged) were added.

For the interior of the building, not just the Indiana Jones' films served as inspiration. The Imagineers studied a number of films with a Foreign Legion theme like *Beau Geste* (1939) to achieve a sense of the appropriate time with period maps of the Middle East, old rifles, scimitars and barracks-type furniture.

The interior designer, Kate Zovich, said, "Instead of doing normal merchandise fixtures, we really wanted to accentuate the theme. Usually when an attraction has an annexed shop, the function of the shop takes precedence over the theming.

"But we wanted to go the whole nine yards with the Outpost and I think we succeeded. We put together old gun cases and hung shirts off of them. We actually modified half of a wing from a biplane in order to hang clothes."

Imagineer Arden Ashley purchased many of the props that decorate the building. He noted of the exit from the attraction that "The landscaping and architecture work so well together. The exterior really draws your eye and the landscaping points you right into the shop."

Senior concept designer Tim Kirk explained when the shop first opened, "When people exit out of the stunt show, they go right past all this stuff. It's a great way to sell merchandise because their blood is boiling after seeing the show and they want to buy something. The Outpost sells hats, videos, postcards, jewelry and leather jackets—some pretty nice stuff."

Over the last two and half decades, the offerings expanded to pins, fedora hats and pith helmets, t-shirts, mugs, figures featuring Mickey Mouse as Indiana Jones and much more. A Disneyland version of the merchandise shop opened in March 1995 but was removed in 2017 to be repurposed as a new indoor seating area attached to the nearby Bengal Barbecue.

Several yards from the merchandise location and to the left of the entrance to the show, is an excavation site over an ancient well. There is a large wooden sign next to it declaring: "Warning! Do NOT Pull Rope!" The word "Not" has a line going through it.

Of course, the rope is within easy reach of the guests and the temptation is to see what might happen. Pulling on the rope sometimes elicits no response and other times an echoey voice from down in the well yelling, "Hey, what's going on up there?" or the lengthy scream of someone falling to the bottom.

According to the Imagineers, that person is the very British Dr. Dunfor Pullit, an archeologist who is supported by the rope beneath the sarcophagus stone.

Repeated pulling on the rope can generate some different responses:

"Leave off the rope old chap, be a good fellow. I have a frightfully valuable artifact down here. Oh no [crash.] I HAD a terribly valuable artifact down here."

"I say, leave off the rope old chap, be a jolly good sport. I say! Uh oh... oh no... blimey [fall, thud]"

"I say quit mucking about up there. Oh blast! Not again [fall, crash]."

"Blast it all, you don't want to pull the rope. [crash] Oh dear."

"Careful while I translate this... Let's see, um, 'twenty years of,' ah, 'sorrow to the,' ah, 'destroyer of this vessel!' " [crash.]"

There is a similar well in the interior queue for Disneyland's Indiana Jones Adventure: Temple of the Forbidden Eye.

Another reference to the movie *Raiders of the Lost Ark* is located at Disney Springs shopping and dining area.

Disney's purchase in 2012 of the entire Lucasfilm catalog for four billion dollars included the beloved Indiana Jones franchise and the first example of utilizing that acquisition is the creation of Jock Lindsey's Hangar Bar in Disney Springs.

Jock Lindsey was a minor character in the movie *Raiders of the Lost Ark* (1981) portrayed by actor Fred Sorenson who rescued Indy from the Peruvian Hovito natives with his seaplane. The character was an American freelance pilot whose background was as a stunt pilot performing in Midwest air shows.

After a flight related tragedy, he relocated to Venezuela where he was often hired to fly archeologist Indiana Jones to remote locations. According to the original screenplay, he was supposed to be British. His pet was a Burmese python snake named "Reggie".

According to the newly created Disney legend, Lindsey took Jones over Florida in 1938 to help hunt down the location of the fabled Fountain of Youth. Lindsey spotted a small town that he liked and returned in 1948 to establish an airplane hangar, air tower and runway on its waterfront and operate an air tour service.

His fellows members of the Society of Explorers and Adventurers (S.E.A.) would drop by for an occasional drink and in 1955, the area was officially established as a hangar bar and was littered with artifacts and memoribilia from their adventures.

The concrete bar top is made to look as if it was once used as a work bench. Ceiling fans are made out of plane propellers, and walls are adorned with vintage travel posters and postcards and letters between Indy, Jock and other characters.

"He only had about a minute of air time in the original movie," WDI Imagineer Theron Skees said, "and it was fun expanding on that. We were coming at it from the aspect that Jock is a pilot first and an adventurer's guide second."

In addition to references to the first three theatrical Indiana Jones movies, Jock Lindsey's Hangar Bar also alludes to elements from the Expanded Adventures such as *The Young Indiana Jones Chronicles* and *Indiana Jones and the Fate of Atlantis*, and Jock Lindsey's roles in *Indiana Jones and the Tomb of the Gods* and *The Further Adventures of Indiana Jones* story entitled *The Sea Butchers*.

The bar also contains nods to other Disney properties including *Star Wars*, *The Rocketeer* and even *Iron Man* as well as references to famous aviators such as Amelia Earhart and Charles Lindbergh.

The bar's address at 1138 Seaten Avenue, referencing a George Lucas feature film tradition to include the number from his first theatrical film *THX 1138* (1971).

From *Raiders* is the golden fertility idol at the top of the bar's bookcase. The head piece for the staff of Ra is in the lost and found bin located near the bathrooms.

From *The Temple of Doom*, voodoo dolls of Indy, Short Round and Willie Scott are on a shelf. Also from that film is a coaster from Club Obi Wan in Shanghai, China. The cool-headed Monkey drink and souvenir mug reference the monkey brain eating sequence in the film.

From *The Last Crusade*, the image of the grail cup is on sign stating "artifacts no longer taken as payment".

There are several references to Reggie, including an empty cage, a signature drink with a snake swizzle stick and an outside dry-docked steamboat named after the pet reptile.

All of the menu items have names that cleverly reference the films as well including Rolling Boulder Sliders, Tanis Tacos, Lao Che's Revenge, Dr. Elsa's She-deviled Eggs, Hovito Mojito, Poisonless Dart, Brody's Brats and many more.

Jock and Indy may be long gone but this location honors their memories and cleverly immerses guests in their legendary adventures.

The Creation of Disney's Animal Kingdom

Disney MGM Studios opened in 1989 and was an overwhelming success demanding an immediate expansion of the new park.

CEO Michael Eisner was preparing to make an announcement that the 1990s would be the "Disney Decade" that would include new themed entertainment venues and attractions.

Eisner was keenly aware of things that might compete for tourist revenue so Disney MGM Studios was meant to undercut Universal's announced plan to build a movie oriented theme park in Central Florida and Pleasure Island that also opened in 1989 would undermine the popular Church Street Station with its themed nightclubs and shopping opportunities.

Eisner also saw Busch Gardens Tampa as offering something that WDW did not. Opened in March 1959 as a beautifully land-scaped facility to promote its beer, Busch Gardens Tampa slowly kept expanding. Thanks to August A. Busch Jr. who was an advocate for wildlife the park added a twenty-nine acre Serengeti Plains in 1965 that would later expand to seventy acres.

Guests loved encountering exotic animals in the large tropical habitat as well as the many incredible thrill rides that also helped define the location.

So Eisner was enthusiastic about a WDW theme park that would emphasize live animals like Busch Gardens Tampa and include roller coasters. By January 1990, a small team of roughly seven to eight Imagineers were hard at work in a tiny, cluttered trailer with three-by-five cards and artist sketch pads to try to formulate something that was Disney-oriented.

One of the advantages to such a proposal was that Walt Disney himself was a lover of animals and a strong advocate for conservation throughout his entire life. Originally, Walt had wanted live animals on the Jungle Cruise attraction but was dissuaded because it would not provide a consistent experience for the guests and that the additional costs for the care of the animals could not be accommodated as Disneyland soared over budget.

In addition, Walt had produced a series of award-winning *True-Life Adventures* theatrical documentaries to acquaint audiences with the wonderful world of nature and animals.

I attended a two hour cast member presentation with Imagineer Joe Rohde at DAK on June 14, 1998 where he shared, "When I became involved in Disney's Animal Kingdom it was late 1989. Michael Eisner had expressed some interest in doing something to do with animals. It had come up some months earlier at a retreat in Santa Barbara. I happened to be at that retreat for design executives and this issue of 'can we do something with animals?' had come up.

"We sent a group of MBAs out across the country visiting and researching zoos around the nation and they came back with a terrifically negative report that basically said, 'Look. There's a zoo in *every* city, in *every* town in this country. They're *all* subsidized by the city, by the state, by the federal government. People pay a *third* of what they pay to get into our parks to come in...they stay for *two* hours...they buy a *drink*...they can go whenever they want...*why* would we ever do a *zoo*?' End of question, right?

"It's actually a wonderful tribute to the psychology of Michael Eisner that when he gets a report like this from his business-analysis people he goes, 'OK, you guys hate this. This has gotta be a good idea.' [laughter from audience] I mean *clearly* there are limits. We the Disney Company simply *cannot* do what is out there to be done if for *no other* reason than we're gonna charge you $50 to do it. So it *has* to be different, it *has* to be new, it *has* to be unlike anything else you can do or we simply cannot pursue it as a line of business because we can't make our per cap. We cannot do that.

"And so this was the great conundrum: What could it possibly *be* that isn't something that already *is*? And unless you can show us that it can be something that isn't, we're just not interested."

The original proposal was for the park to be a three part experience: traditional theme park attractions, a zoo-like component and a large "Epcot-style pavilion" that would provide information and education about animals.

The Imagineers knew little about what it would take to obtain, care, exhibit and manage animals so Joe Rohde brought in Dr.

Bill Conway, the respected executive director of the Bronx Zoo to educate them. It was an eye-opening education but after several visits, Conway needed to spend more time at his zoo so recommended the Imagineers contact Rick Barongi at the San Diego Zoo who had recently been promoted to curator of mammals and was a trained zoologist.

Barongi had spent time in New Jersey with Warner Brothers Jungle Habitat and with the Lion King Safari in Southern California so it was felt he would be valuable to assist with the proposed jeep safari trek.

Initially just a consultant, Barongi became more and more involved with Disney's "secret project" and pushed hard for Disney to bring on more experts. Zoologists, curators and veterinarians from around the United States, including Dr. Conway, became an advisory board that helped launch the Disney Wildlife Conservation Fund. The advisory board would become Disney's best defense when groups expressed concerns.

Their input significantly influenced the design of the park so that by late 1992, the design on paper looked very similar to the way it would on opening day. In 1993 Barongi was brought on full time at Disney after Michael and Jane Eisner visited the San Diego Zoo and Barongi gave them a personal tour. His role was not just to oversee the animal component of the developing theme park but to oversee animal operations at The Living Seas and Discovery Island.

By now the project had grown to roughly five hundred Imagineers who worked and argued with WDW park operators and a group of animal care professionals who thanks to Barongi's outstanding reputation were recruited from sixty-nine zoos across the country with many of those zoos involving multiple hires.

Earth moving equipment was set up on the property in August 1994 for the official announcement. However that announcement would be delayed by a year. The death of Frank Wells (a huge champion of the project), Eisner's heart attack, the resignation of Jeffrey Katzenberg who left to form his own company and financial challenges with the newly opened EuroDisney theme park in France and the collapse of the proposed Disney's America theme park in Virginia all worked to raise doubts about proceeding with the project as the company began to struggle.

Eisner was still convinced it was a great idea and had been intimately involved with the plans from the beginning. He was the one who came up with the names Animal Kingdom and DinoLand. He said, "We have a Magic Kingdom so why not an Animal Kingdom?"

Briefly it was called Wild Animal Kingdom until it was determined there might be confusion or legal issues with *Mutual of Omaha's Wild Kingdom*, an American television documentary series that ran from 1963 to 1988 and was still popular in reruns.

On June 20, 1995, Michael Eisner and vice-chairman Roy E. Disney formally announced Disney's Animal Kingdom to the media and that it would be "based on mankind's enduring love for animals and celebrating all animals that ever were or never existed."

The announcement was made in a ballroom at WDW's Contemporary Resort accompanied by a parade of African dancers and drummers. On the stage was a huge, painted model of the Tree of Life, inspired in part by a bonsai tree that the Imagineers had seen at the Epcot Flower and Garden Festival that would serve as the central icon for the new park.

The presentation included colorful concept paintings, a preview video and a promotional poster that featured dinosaurs, a dragon and a safari vehicle hanging off a rickety bridge.

Eisner said, "This is to the traditional zoo as the motion picture was to the stage play. It is a whole leap forward that keeps the concept of combining education and entertainment alive and well.

"Disney recognizes that the need for awareness of endangered animals and their environments never has been greater. We believe that, as storytellers and communicators, we are in a unique position to promote a deeper understanding and love for all animals."

In June and July of 1996, two young giraffes arrived. They were the first of over a thousand animals who would be showcased on opening day.

WDW's fourth theme park opened on Earth Day, April 22, 1998. Some families had been waiting overnight and so the gates opened unexpectedly early at six o'clock in the morning, a full hour before the announced opening time.

Roughly 28,000 paying guests attended that first day as well as five thousand journalists and many guests with annual passes.

The turnstiles were locked to non-resort guests by nine o'clock. The park's first guests were greeted with rose petal confetti, African bands and a keepsake grand-opening lithograph.

Dancers gyrated to the beat of two dozen African drummers. A rhythmic choir of 500 chanted in Zulu along with a backdrop of 1,500 costumed Disney cast members. There was a performance of the award-winning *Circle of Life* song led by Grammy Award winner Lebo M (*The Lion King* on Broadway).

During the song, costumed performers carried giant kinetic sculptures of animals including an elephant, a lion, a triceratops and a dragon.

It was estimated that the park had cost approximately eight hundred million dollars. Some animal rights groups had been vocal about their concerns. The Orange County Sheriff's office sent about 150 deputies but only about two dozen protesters showed up. The protest lasted approximately two hours and there were no arrests.

President of Walt Disney Attractions Judson Green addressed a group of honored guests at the park's Conservation Station. "Twenty-eight years ago, Wisconsin Senator Gaylord Nelson introduced the idea of a national celebration of nature and the environment (Earth Day)...It is our fervent hope that Disney's Animal Kingdom will be a living embodiment of that same spirit."

The first guests through the gate were Brenda Herr of St. Petersburg, Florida, her husband, Damon Chepren, and their son, Devon, who all slept in their car the night before in their quest to become the first guest family. The family received a lifetime pass to Walt Disney theme parks worldwide.

Park officials also paid tribute to their "Honorary First Family," rhino crusader Michael Werikhe and his daughters, Acacia, 9, and Kora, 7, in the ceremony at the park's Conservation Station.

Werikhe, known throughout the world as "Rhino Man," led a one-man crusade to boost public awareness of the plight of the black rhinoceros and raised millions of dollars for the conservation and survival of the endangered animal.

Roy E. Disney presented Werikhe and his family with a giant "Key of Life," in the shape of The Tree of Life, the park's massive icon. In addition, the Walt Disney Company made a monetary contribution in support of Werikhe's conservation work.

Roy said, "Just as this theme park has its roots in our films, it also represents a major departure. Once a movie is completed, it's done forever. On the other hand, Disney's Animal Kingdom — like the animal world itself — will evolve and grow. It's truly a living thing... something we are consciously and proudly calling 'Disney's'."

Eisner read from the dedication plaque for the park:

> Welcome to a kingdom of animals ... real, ancient and imagined:
>
> A kingdom ruled by lions, dinosaurs and dragons;
>
> A kingdom of balance, harmony and survival;
>
> A kingdom we enter to share in the wonder, gaze at the beauty, thrill at the drama ... and learn.

Nearly a year later, Eisner told the media, "Whatever doubts we may once have had about the Animal Kingdom's viability were answered on April 22, 1998, the day the park opened. The crowds were so large that we were forced to close our gates to further guests by 9:00 a.m.

"Over the next few months, attendance has exceeded every expectation, and the ratings from guests are the highest we've received for any park in our history. In a way, the Animal Kingdom takes us full circle.

"Thirty years ago, all you could find on our Orlando property were vast herds of grazing animals and some rather intimidating reptiles. Today, after billions of dollars in investment, we have unveiled our most original theme park concept yet: vast herds of grazing animals and some rather intimidating reptiles."

Remember that Eisner wanted Disney's Animal Kingdom to crush Busch Gardens Tampa that besides its animal attractions had thrill rides. When DAK opened there were no thrill rides because the project had soared wildly over budget to accommodate the care of the live animals so cuts had to be made.

Originally on opening day there would have been two major thrill rides. In DinoLand U.S.A. would have been The Excavator, a proposed roller coaster similar to Big Thunder Mountain Railroad. It would be in an area that was supposedly a former sand and gravel pit with an enormous piece of leftover machinery called the Excavator.

The area had been abandoned when the Dino Institute bought the property after dinosaur bones were discovered and transformed the field offices of the former business into a dormitory and cafeteria for students.

The Excavator was meant to look like a series of ore cars used to haul up the sand and gravel from the bottom of the pit to dump trucks. The paleontology students who were working in the area had reconfigured the unsafe device that had fallen into disrepair to transport the dinosaur fossils they were finding.

The marketing publicity described it as "a rollicking coaster ride through a section of the dig supposedly too dangerous to enter". At one point, the ride would have zoomed through the inside of a dinosaur skeleton.

It appeared clearly on the original concept painting of the area. It was felt that the Countdown to Extinction (now Dinosaur) attraction (since it re-used existing technology created for a Disneyland attraction) would be easier and less expensive to build, yet still attract guests wanting a thrill ride.

The other thrill ride would have been Dragon's Tower in the section called Beastly Kingdom. That entire section was "postponed" and in its place was put the inexpensive and quickly built Camp Minnie-Mickey.

Dragon's Tower was to be the land's looming major icon just like the castles in other Disney theme parks. This thrill ride roller coaster was to be housed in a tall, charred and ruined castle.

The story was that after a fearsome battle that devastated the original inhabitants, the castle had been taken over by a massive dragon as its new home. The jewel-encrusted dragon was very much inspired by the villainous Smaug in Tolkien's *The Hobbit*. Both greedy dragons guarded a vast hoard of untold treasures.

The dragon figure was to be the largest and most sophisticated audio-animatronics creature ever built up to that time. Inhabiting the nearby caves was to be a colony of bats who were also clever thieves. Hanging overhead as the guests enter, the bats' whispers would convince the guests to help them in their plans to rob some of the dragon's riches.

Guests would have been strapped into a suspended inverted roller coaster to create the sensation of flying along with the bats on this ill-advised caper in a wild chase through the dark caverns, collapsing ancient castle corridors and even the fabled gold lair. The climax would have been a confrontation with the fiery-breathing dragon, who was not pleased at the attempt to rob him.

The winged dragon would have been the major character icon of the park. DAK's logo even featured front and center the silhouette of a winged dragon marching along with the other animals. McDonald's, a corporate sponsor at the time, released a Happy Meal toy of a purple winged dragon when the park opened. Even a ticket kiosk at the entrance of the park has the head of a dragon.

As work progressed on the park, the cost of caring and maintaining the real animals caused the budget to soar past all expectations. Cuts had to be made in order to finish the park and get it open on time. Nearly 75 acres were eliminated from the Africa section.

It was decided that either Dinoland or Beastly Kingdom could be built, but not both. Since Disney was already investing heavily in its first computer animated feature *Dinosaur* (2000), Eisner made what he felt was the best decision.

By the way, Rick Barongi went on to work on Disney's Animal Kingdom Lodge but left Disney and is now a Director at the Houston Zoo. In 1998, he said, "A big company is our biggest hope of helping. Disney can affect a culture, can create the kind of caring and passion no zoo can. In the end, Disney will help zoos market the good things they do."

Judson Green, Disney Attractions president at the time, said, "Disney's Animal Kingdom is entertainment, but it would feel empty if we didn't have the passion and the breadth of knowledge. The park may go beyond even Epcot in terms of its educational value.

"That's one of the many reasons we've attracted so many talented people from both within our company and from the outside. Besides delivering a theme park experience, we'll be impacting others' lives."

The primary focus of the new park was animals and conservation. At one time, it was planned to have an Equatorial Africa pavilion at Epcot's World Showcase.

When I talked with him, Rohde explained the difference of that proposal and DAK:

"At Epcot's World Showcase, you're seeing replicas of famous buildings like the Temple of Heaven in China, the Doge's Palace in Italy, or the Eiffel Tower in France. And you're actively comparing those replicas to what you've seen in person or in media. Nobody looks up at the Eiffel Tower in Epcot and mistakes themselves for being in Paris.

"At Animal Kingdom, we didn't want to theme the Lands around specific geopolitical places. That's just asking for trouble with all the changing politics for one reason. The Africa section of the Park is not Nairobi, for example. Instead of capturing the actual architectural icons as in World Showcase and elements that relate to a very real specific place like Paris, in Animal Kingdom we are capturing the emotional feeling of these exotic lands.

"Harambe is a fictional town meant to be reminiscent of an East African port catering to tourists in modern Africa. The details are real but they are a combination from things we found in many different areas and we mashed them together. The history we created is very much based on the reality of the region.

"Harambe is themed around the sorts of things that you would expect to see if you were in Africa alongside the elephants, hippos, gorillas, and other animals that call that section their home. You really 'feel' like you've been transported to a new place where you actually could go on a two week African safari."

On their six research trips to Africa, the Imagineering team kept being struck by how many elements of a typical theme park had been incorporated into the different tourist areas.

While in Kenya at Lake Nakuru, a popular safari park, this idea was starkly apparent. When word went out over the radios carried by the Land Rover drivers that a leopard had been sighted, the news created a traffic jam.

Nearly fifty vehicles converged on the tree where the leopard was perched. Dozens of tourists leaned out of windows to photograph the animal that was roughly three hundred feet away.

"That's when we realized that the tourists' Africa is a theme park but just not a particularly well run one," recalled senior concept designer Kevin Brown. "We knew the experience we could provide in Animal Kingdom would be as good or better than that."

The research was intensive. The Imagineers took family-oriented package safari trips, from the lowest to the highest end, to get a full exposure of what a family might experience on such excursions.

They also created their own East African itinerary. They felt it was important to experience things as a group, just like theme park guests would. One discovery was that truly wild places were not accessible to the average tourist.

"The highlight of the trip was the hippos—big and strong and mean," said Rohde. "One surged out of the water with a snort and chased our boat, mouth open. We boated slowly over stretches of water where tell-tale eddies betrayed hippos lurking beneath— lots of them.

"This evening was the first time I have felt the exhilaration I expected from Africa. Fifteen-foot crocodiles and massive hostile hippos crashed through the water. As sunset drew on, the animals became more aggressive. We wanted to capture that same feeling in the park."

For DAK, Imagineers wanted guests to experience what it might be like to go on a modern safari as they had done.

According to the official back story when Disney Animal Kingdom first opened: "Kilimanjaro Safaris is just one of many companies that offers photo excursions to tourists from around the world to The Harambe Wildlife Reserve.

"After three decades of operation, it has emerged as the premier provider of safe, affordable animal-viewing safaris in their fleet of "Tembo" (Swahili for elephant) open-sided vehicles. In addition, the company hires and trains its safari drivers to offer a high level of information about the animals found on the Reserve."

One of the centerpieces for DAK is the Kilimanjaro Safaris attraction since guests would be eager to see animals differently than at a zoo. It is roughly 110 acres making it approximately the size of the entire Magic Kingdom Park.

Landscape architect Phil Schenkel along with senior project engineer Dave Dahlke had to devise a recipe for concrete for the Kilimanjaro Safari's two miles of rutted, potholed and washed out "dirt" road. They spent long hours matching the concrete color with the surrounding soil and then rolled tires through it as well as tossed stones, dirt and twigs to try to capture a seamless sense of reality not immediately recognized by the guests.

In addition, the roadway was designed to keep any water in the path separate from the water used by the animals. The potholes in the road with water actually have their own pumping and drainage system.

The Imagineers set up a test track in the parking lot at WDI in Glendale with similar potholes and ruts. However, when they took Disney Legend Marty Sklar for a practice spin, he spilled most of his coffee and his instant displeasure resulted in them going back to the drawing board to modify the design.

The ride still ended up pretty bumpy when it first opened with the park and some adjustments were made including additional padding on the backs of the seats.

Some factors in selected animals to be exhibited included if they would be active during the day, could be easily contained, got along well with the other selected animals, and how they would react to the tourists. Zoologist Rick Barongi provided input.

Originally, to emphasize the park's commitment to conservation, the attraction included a story about the dangers of illegal poachers with signage, urgent radio alerts and more. The guests were involved in a frantic chase to rescue the kidnapped Big Red mother elephant, and her baby, Little Red.

That storyline with game warden Wilson Mutua and the beloved elephants was both upsetting and confusing to guests and was redone as surveys showed guests were just primarily interested in spotting live animals.

Rohde said, "When you ride through [Killimanjaro Safaris], you do not realize the degree to which this is a manipulated landscape. The height of the little hummocks and rises in the hills just happen to be slightly higher than the sightline of a person in a vehicle, so even though there are unimaginable numbers of those trucks driving around, you are [only] aware of six."

The *Flights of Wonder* show evolved from a strictly educational presentation to a show with the comedy relief of a clueless tour guide character named "Guano Joe" who is more than a little fearful of these avian performers. Along with the audience, he learns about them and learns to love them.

Under the canvas canopy of a shady sanctuary that is what remains of the Maharajah's crumbling fortress is the makeshift Caravan Stage in the "ruins" that are now the refuge for a dazzling array of birds.

From opening until 2015, the Caravan Stage was covered with a canopy. A permanent roof was finally installed during a renovation in early 2016.

The façade of the roughly thousand person amphitheater was designed to resemble the architecture of that found in the Himalayan highlands or Rajasthan, India. The theater is situated outside the fictitious village of Anandapur, on the "trade route" towards Africa.

Approximately twenty species of exotic birds performed. While the show was entertaining, its core was a much deeper message about serious conservation themes and habitat loss. It promoted the World Wildlife Conservation Fund.

Among the species that most guests saw included Barbary falcons, macaws, Amazon parrots, Harris Hawks, ibis, vultures, crowned cranes, a Trumpeter Hornbill, Great Horned Owl, Black Vulture, an American Bald Eagle and several other interesting birds. The birds were from various continents and not just Asia. While the specific birds may occasionally be different in each show, the format of the show remained the same.

The host is an actual trainer who has spent hours with these birds. The birds are trained to react and take different actions based on audio and visual cues they have been taught. Certain noises, words or a subtle hand placement will spark an action from the birds.

While the show had been carefully rehearsed to demonstrate how birds hunt and eat, they had not been trained to do the typical tricks usually seen in such shows but merely duplicate natural behaviors with an emphasis on entertainment value like grabbing a dollar bill an audience member holds high in the air.

Groucho, the singing parrot in the show who was an audience favorite was named the World's Best Singing Parrot on the *Tonight Show with Jay Leno* after an appearance. He's also appeared on other television shows including *The Ellen DeGeneres Show*.

He was fairly unusual for most parrots because he is able to sing seven full songs including *How Much is that Doggy in the Window?*, *Camptown Races*, *Yankee Doodle Dandy*, *Alouetta* and *Jingle Bells*.

Hatched in 1986 in Kalamazoo, Michigan and raised by Theresa Barylock, Groucho was a yellow-naped Amazon parrot with an amazing ability to articulate many words and phrases such as "Look ma! No hands!".

At the end of 2017, the show closed to be replaced on DAK's 20th anniversary in April 2018 by a new 25-minute bird show, UP! A Great Bird Adventure.

The new show features Senior Wilderness Explorer Russell and his furry friend Dug from the Disney-Pixar animated film *Up*

(2009) who have journeyed to Asia and met up with Anika, a bird enthusiast, to learn more about birds from around the world like their often-mentioned friend from the film Kevin.

The new show, like its predecessor, features bird experts and close-up encounters with numerous bird species. The show now includes more than fifteen species, including toucans, parrots, macaws, an African fish eagle, and a bald eagle.

When DAK opened in 1998 it required over four million plants including everything from huge trees to even the smallest shoots of grass. There were 46,202 Vetiver grass shoots planted by Opening Day.

The number of species of grass exceeded three hundred. Just in the Africa area, more than 771,687 shrubs and nearly 70,000 trees were planted.

Suppliers were contacted all over the United States and arrangements were made for plants to be propagated in temperate zones in California, Florida, Arizona and Maryland before being shipped to the site.

A "heritage area" was created on the berm so that trees and plants there could replace plants in the park when they died.

A "browse farm" of acacia, hibiscus, and bamboo was set up to provide food for the leaf eating animals. While the different species of hoof stock may choose different plant species on which to feed, their diet is not solely dependent on African plant species. All of the animals receive supplemental nutritionally balanced diets to help maintain good health.

This "browse farm" and outside vendors produce thousands of pounds of cut browse weekly. This browse is positioned throughout the animal habitats such as the savannas for the animals to feed on which in turn reduces the impact on the planted landscape.

One of the landscape designers, Michelle Sullivan recalled, "Okapi, a rare and beautiful cousin of the giraffe eat everything so I have to spend hours scouring plant lists to see if any are toxic or there is any vegetation classified as 'noxious weeds' that means a species that might grow out of control in Florida's lush landscape."

Unlike the previous Disney theme parks, it was plants not buildings and facades that dominated the storytelling. A staff of eight landscape architects who had all been taught by Bill Evans who was responsible for landscaping Disneyland, Magic Kingdom and Epcot Center accomplished the never-before-done challenge.

"In Animal Kingdom," stated principal landscape architect Paul Comstock in August 1996, "the design challenge facing us is to help tell the story, the natural story. Landscape becomes the show in many areas. It is awesome. It is the set. It is the show."

Over a five year period, Comstock visited Madagascar, South Africa, Kenya, Tanzania, Tasmania, Namibia, China, Thailand, Indonesia and Singapore collecting seeds and shoots and establishing relationships with nurseries and botanical gardens. Material was gathered from every continent on Earth except for Antarctica.

Ancient cycads, survivors of the Creaceous Era and over sixty-seven million years old that were needed for the DinoLand area were actually found in Florida and from a collector in Eagle Rock, California.

Landscape architecture manager Carl Walsten said that one of the important things that he learned from landscape consultant Bill Evans was that "there's not one perfect answer. A red flowering tree might be one of several available, but we also need to understand whether that plant works in our micro-climate. That's where Bill's knowledge is so valuable. You don't learn this in school, but from experience.

"We even joke about our 'new species of acacia', the characteristic flat-topped trees that dot the real African savanna. The mature Animal Kingdom 'acacias' are in reality conserved thirty foot tall oak trees with 'crew cuts' that mimic the African trees."

An example of a look-alike would be the use of *Enterolobium cyclocarpa* to represent large "fever trees." Disney planted the actual fever tree, *Acacia xanthophloea,* on the savannas but they rarely reached maximum size in the central Florida climate and so were not "good show."

In 2020 Disney's Animal Kingdom celebrated its 22nd anniversary in a park empty of guests. It was planned to be a massive celebration to include honoring the 50th anniversary of Earth Day and the 25th anniversary of the Disney Conservation Fund but restrictions because of the pandemic cancelled all the plans.

Each day from April 18 to 22 would have included festivities according to Disney publicity like "a stellar lineup of expert speakers and entertainment; behind-the-scenes tours; specialty food and beverage; limited-edition merchandise signings; character greetings; photo opportunities; special Wilderness Explorers activities for kids—and MORE!"

My friend and travel journalist Seth Kubersky went to DAK on the last day it was open to the public before it was shut down and reported, "I spent the day checking in with the park's cast members, human and otherwise, and was repeatedly assured that the full-time veterinary staff would continue caring for their charges throughout the closure and had months worth of feed and supplies stockpiled, including acres of greenery and coolers of produce."

Dr. Mark Penning, Vice President of Disney's Animals, Science & Environment pointed out that even though everyone else was staying home, the animals were still there and needed to be fed, have their habitats cleaned, be observed and otherwise cared for during this time.

The park's dedicated animal care team was able to help with the birth of a baby zebra on March 21 and a baby porcupine a few days later.

DAK continues to remain a unique experience and immerses guests into many different jungles.

The Tree of Life

The first real tree planted at Disney's Animal Kingdom in December 1995 was an authentic *Acacia xanthophlosa*, grown from a seed that Disney acquired in Africa. The park has about one hundred species of real trees and shrubs foreign to North American soil.

However the tree that is most memorable at DAK is an impressive artificial one.

The Tree of Life was to capture the essence of the park with its diversity of animals and the majesty of nature.

The animals are not supposed to look as if they were carved into the surface of the tree. They are supposed to seem as if they grow out of it organically. It was designed to be reminiscent of looking up into the clouds and seeing the shapes of animals.

No one had ever before built a tree this large. It is 145 foot tall (fourteen stories tall). The branches span 165 feet across with more than 103,000 translucent, five-shades-of-green leaves that were individually placed and actually sway in the wind because each branch unit is encircled by a giant expansion joint.

Disney commissioned a wind tunnel study for the branches that determined they could withstand a blow of nearly 100 miles per hour. The leaves are four different shapes and sizes, each more than a foot long, made out of special plastic called Kynar. The bottom trunk is fifty feet wide. The Tree of Life has 45 secondary branches leading to 756 tertiary branches leading to 7,891 end branches.

The branches had to appear random but the cost of sculpting each one individually would have been cost prohibitive. Using a computer, the Imagineers were able to come up with two types of secondary branches that could be hooked to two types of tertiary branches that could be randomly assembled, turned and adjusted to create natural shapes.

The branches were assembled on the ground and then carried over and plugged into their appropriate spots by a huge crane.

The final overall look of the Tree of Life was based on a

particular bonsai tree the design team found at the International Flower and Garden Festival at Epcot.

Eventually, it was decided to utilize an oil rig as the base skeleton of the tree's trunk because it would be strong enough to hold the massive weight of the branches as well as have enough room underneath for some type of venue.

Carved into the tree's gnarled roots, mighty trunk and sturdy branches is a rich tapestry of 325 animals, many of which are endangered. Recently, with the extension of the roots into the Central Hub area, that number has gone up significantly with a deer, an elephant, Rocky Mountain big horn sheep, and a bison among others.

The Tree of Life that served as the central icon for the park like a castle was meant to be a work of art that would be a tribute to mankind's respect for nature and life on earth.

Eleven sculptors were engaged to work together to bring the artificial icon to life. That team included a sculptor from France (Fabrice Kennel), another from Ireland (Vinnie Byrne), three Native Americans (Parker Boyiddle, Craig Goseyun, Arthur Rowlodge), five Floridians (Eric Kovach, Steve Hunke, Joe Welborn, Gary Bondurant, Jacob Eaddy) and one from Indianapolis, Indiana (Roger White).

The animal sculpting was supervised by WDI senior show production designer and art director Zsolt Hormay to keep it all consistent.

"It was really important that the look of the tree flows without any interruption," Zsolt said. "The sculptors met every morning, studying a pile of wood for reference. They would discuss what each branch should be: a banyan, an emerging oak, a touch of cedar."

That same pile of wood served as inspiration for the textures of the animals like the stripes on the tiger being banyan bark and the octopus' skin modeled on oak.

The intent was to carve more than 350 animals into the base and branches and the art was to feature a mixture of styles and with some animals blending in and others standing out with high detail.

"People might look at the trunk and they might think, 'It's just brown bark' but it's more complicated than that," said production designer Ron Esposito. "We used 50 to 60 color values to reveal the animals while maintaining naturalism. The tree has a dry side and a wet side, five different moss colors, multiple lichen colors as well as brown tones, overtones, and shadow tones."

"I feel that we achieved it successfully as far as trying to create a look where the animals were grown by the tree and not just stuck on the surface," said Zsolt.

To achieve that effect, the artists had to sculpt the animals directly onto the tree, while wearing hard hats, working on scaffolding and immersed in the distracting and loud sounds of a construction site.

"In the beginning, it was a little difficult to get used to creating a sculpture every day and the fact that we just spray the cement on, you form it and by the time the sun goes down, it has to be done," recalled Zsolt.

Each artist was able to sculpt an animal or two and dedicate it to family members. Zsolt's daughter wanted him to sculpt a koala for her and so he did. He also did a baboon for his wife and a scorpion for his son.

Zsolt and the other artists found the experience emotionally moving and it helped them to better understand the importance of the tree to communicate to guests the wonder of nature and animals on earth.

"You can find a tree of life in various cultures, going back thousands of years," stated Zsolt. "To me, it's really uplifting that we can have a Tree of Life here at Disney's Animal Kingdom and have it function as an important messenger to the people."

During the early work on the tree, famous wildlife researcher Jane Goodall walked the site and asked her guide, animal care expert Rick Barongi, where the chimpanzee would be placed.

There had been no plans to include one but Zsolt found one of Goodall's photographs of David Graybeard, the first chimpanzee to accept Goodall into his society, opening the door for her groundbreaking research. Zsolt and Kennel sculpted the chimpanzee in three days and it is at the entrance to the attraction.

At one point, the base of the tree was to have had the Root Restaurant which was to have been the upscale eatery at the park. Imagineer Bryan Jowers did concept artwork for a "Wonders of Nature" show to be performed there instead. Imagineer Dave Minichiello did concept artwork for a "The Lion King" character show that later evolved and moved to a different area of the park.

It was CEO Michael Eisner who suggested during a particularly disappointing pitch meeting that bugs live in and under trees and that Pixar Animation was working on a new feature film about bugs called *A Bug's Life* (1998).

Since bugs make up nearly ninety percent of what it referred to as the "animal kingdom" it seemed natural to showcase them in some manner so it was decided to proceed with "a creepy, crawly bug-eyed adventure". Imagineering consulted directly with Pixar and while several characters from the film were used, new ones were created as well.

The decision to go with this concept was approved after construction had already begun on the Tree of Life. However, it still opened April 1998, roughly a full seven months before the release of the film that inspired it, an unusual occurrence for a Disney theme park attraction.

This 3-D experience of film and audio-animatronics educates people that insects actually help people and the environment.

The queue line into the theater was designed to create the illusion that guests were shrinking to bug size as they navigated the increasingly narrow tunnels with everything else including the roots seeming to become enormous.

Currently the nine minute show being performed in the 430 seat auditorium is entitled *"It's Tough To Be A Bug!* Starring Flik and a cast of A Million Billion Bugs" that is similar to a vaudeville revue with individual acts.

This performance is the current show produced by the Tree of Life Repertory Theater. The pre-show waiting lobby is decorated with playbill posters from past performances whose titles are parodies of popular Broadway shows. Over the years, the followings posters were displayed:

My Fair Ladybug (*My Fair Lady*), *Barefoot in the Bark* (Neil Simon's *Barefoot in the Park*), *A Grass Menagerie* (Tennessee Williams' *A Glass Menagerie*), *A Cockroach Line* (*A Chorus Line*), *Beauty and the Bees* ("Bee Our Guest!") (*Disney's Beauty and the Beast*), *Antie* (*Annie*), *Web Side Story* (*West Side Story*), *Little Shop of Hoppers* (*Little Shop of Horrors*), *A Stinkbug Named Desire* (*A Streetcar Named Desire*) and *The Dung and I* ("featuring the hit song *Hello Dung Lovers*") (*The King and I*).

Some of those poster designs were done by Imagineers Nicole Armitage Doolittle (daughter of Frank Armitage, a Disney animation background artist and later Imagineer) and Milton Noji (who worked for almost five years at Disney on both interior and exterior signage). Unlike traditional theater posters, these posters are not decorated with snippets of critics' reviews but interesting facts about the insect world.

The background music consists of a bug orchestra, sounding a lot like buzzing kazoos, playing iconic songs from these shows: *One* (Chorus Line), *Beauty and the Beast* (from Beauty and the Beast), *Tomorrow* (Annie), *I Feel Pretty* (West Side Story), *Hello Young Lovers* (The King and I), and *Tonight* (West Side Story but also includes the counterpoint *Flight of the Bumblebee*).

The theme song, *It's Tough to be a Bug*, was written by George Wilkins with lyrics by Kevin Rafferty who was the Show Writer for the project. The show's score was composed and conducted by Bruce Broughton.

"My job was to impart the facts about ten quintillion bugs in only eight minutes," stated Rafferty, who met with Ray Mendez an insect naturalist. "Ray said that, most important, they are responsible for our food, as pollinators, and they handle our waste. If it weren't for bugs, we'd all be dead in six months. That impressed me. All the acts featured in the show are based on what actual bugs do. There really, truly are acid-spraying termites."

The concept was that guests would wander through the roots of the tree into a theater space that had been hollowed-out by the bugs. Guests then don "bug-eye" spectacles in order to see in three-dimensions the world through the eyes (or multiple eyes) of their insect hosts.

Senior principal production designer Zsolt Hormay who led an international team of sculptors to carve the animals on the exterior trunk was also in charge of the bugs in the queue line for the attraction. "I get calls all the time," said Zsolt, "Any leeches? No leeches! Any cockroaches? No cockroaches!"

The Imagineers used Flik the ant and Hopper the grasshopper from the film as key figures in the attraction but also added a Acorn Weevil (The Termite-ator), Chili a quill throwing Chilean tarantula, Rolly, the dung beetle and the stinkbug Claire de Room to accompany a cast of hundreds of butterflies, beetles, ladybugs, hornets, spiders and larvae.

Some of the bugs appear on film. Some appear as elaborate audio-animatronics characters. Some only exist as puffs of air and rollers built into the theater seats. The swatter effect is created by fifty high-speed fans hidden thirty feet overhead in the rockwork folds of the theater.

When the acid-spraying termite apparently squirts guests in their face, the harmless water spray comes from the seat in front of the guest. Imagineers chose an industrial smell officially labeled "earthy" for the stinkbug's distinctive effect.

"It was a matter of getting our special effects to match the bugs," said show writer Kevin Rafferty. "All the acts we feature in the show are based on what they do in nature. There really are acid-spraying termites and quill-throwing tarantulas."

At the end of the show, an announcement over the PA system states, "Will all honorary bugs remain seated while all the lice, bed bugs, maggots and cockroaches exit first." To the left, the EXIT sign appears to be lit up by fireflies leaving the theater.

The 3-D animated portion of the show was produced by visual effect studio Rhythm and Hues. The firm that dramatically filed bankruptcy in 2013 began doing work for Disney in 1982 where they provided the computer animation for the original Universe of Energy and later created the "Big Bang" segment for Epcot's Ellen's Energy Adventure.

Walt Disney Imagineering handled the special effects including the audio-animatronics characters, wind, water, foul smells and more. At the time, Hopper the most sophisticated and advanced audio-animatronics characters that Imagineering ever created could perform a wide array of movements that make him as lifelike as possible.

Actor Dave Foley recreates the voice of Flik as he did in the original film. The voice of Hopper is not Kevin Spacey as it was in the film but Andrew Stanton who was co-director of the original film.

Cheech Marin does the voice of Chili. French Stewart the voice of the "Termite-ator", Tom Kenny the voices of the Dung Beetle Brothers and Jason Alexander as the voice of Weevil Kneevil. Corey Burton is the announcer and the voice of various bugs. P.T. Flea voiced by John Ratzenberger, Pixar's "good luck charm" who does voices in all their movies, pops in briefly for one line.

DAK: The First Year

To try to get the general public to understand that Disney's Animal Kingdom was not like the typical zoo a person might visit in a city but a new type of theme park, in 2002 WDW through its Yellow Shoes Creative Marketing division brought on Mark Simon to storyboard a thirty-second commercial spot.

The final commercial was produced by Jim Derusha of Alpha Wolf Productions and consisted of various DAK cast members declaring "Nahtazu", a fictional word that when pronounced sounded like "not a zoo".

The commercial ended with the tag line: "Disney's Animal Kingdom. It's many, many things but remember, it's Nahtazu!"

Disney stopped using the term in 2006 as it strengthened its connections with the AZA (Association of Zoos and Aquariums).

The idea of it not being a zoo came from Imagineer Joe Rohde, executive designer and senior vice president, Creative for Walt Disney Imagineering. In a presentation to DAK cast members on June 14, 1998, roughly a week before the park opened to the public, he stated:

"There's *still* people in the company who will refer to this as a 'zoo' and I mean, by no means, any disrespect or disdain to what a zoo *is*. It *is* a thing that exists in the world and is loved and valued, obviously, by their presence around the country and the world, by *gazillions* of people. The world doesn't need another big, expensive zoo with a bunch of immersion exhibits in it. That is *not* a real pressing need on the planet.

"Now, on the other hand, what we are trying to do is *profoundly* subjective, even in ways that I think many education professionals would consider to be almost dangerous. A theme park is *all* about *you* in a very specific context. *Nothing* happens to you... *nothing* is said to you...nothing is *seen* by you...that isn't governed by the overarching narrative umbrella that holds you in that place. When you move through a space, the space is *crafted* to specific narrative impact on you. That's what Disney's Animal Kingdom is. It is *not* a zoo."

The general public still did not understand the difference since DAK was unlike any other Disney theme park. Because of massive budget cuts, the park featured few attractions when it opened and some Disney fans referred to it as a "half day park" because it was felt that it took only a half a day to experience everything.

Ironically, it was physically the largest Disney theme park at 500 acres with over a thousand animals representing 250 species.

Safari Village was meant to be the thematic heart of Disney's Animal Kingdom and serve as the central hub. From that location, guests could venture out into the different sections of the park and then return.

Encircled by Discovery River, Safari Village is a lush, green island that serves as a magical departure point for each of the different realms of the park. The area was later renamed Discovery Island in 2000 after an island with that same name closed near Fort Wilderness Resort and Campground.

As the original promotional material stated, "It is a mix of tropical and equatorial styles featuring references to the Caribbean but also Polynesian influences. Strong, bright colors dominate the landscape. Animal forms decorate every possible surface of the one-storage structures smothered in many-hued tropical foliage.

"A unique vocabulary of animal images, inspired by folk art from around the world, gives the Village a playful look that celebrates the beauty and power of animals. Safari Village's shops make it the natural center of the park. It's also the ideal place to encounter a unique brand of live entertainment celebrating the special connection between humans and animals."

Safari Village has folk art inspired forms on every available surface including walls, ceilings, windowsills, gable ends and more.

The buildings are not just ornamented with animals but each facility has its own theme. Island Mercantile features animals that migrate and work—whales and wildebeests, bees and beavers. Creative Comforts features animals with stripes and spots. Beastly Bazaar has animals from fresh and salt water cavorting throughout it.

The clever theme of the Flame Tree Barbecue restaurant is predator and prey—prey are painted on the tables and predators on the chairs. Pizzafari's dinning rooms each have different themes. One room is dedicated to animals that hide in their environment. Another room is dedicated to animals that carry their houses on their backs like turtles, snails and hermit crabs. One room is based on animals that hang upside down.

For Safari Village, Imagineer Joe Rohde wanted to create a place no one had ever seen before. There are nine separate color schemes on Pizzafari alone.

"Jenna Goodman and I said, 'You want it bright? We can do bright'." said senior show designer Katie Olson. "When we did color design for Harambe we pored over books of photographs, trying to make sure we were rendering exact copies of a village in Kenya.

"Safari Village has a little bit of a tropical feelings but we just said, 'I think lime green would look really good with this color' and we tried it. At first, it was a little difficult breaking all the rules, but once we got into the rhythm of it, it became a really fun project.

"It didn't have to be recognizable as anywhere in particular and that gives you a lot of freedom. But you have to still respect the form of the architecture. We used a lot of Caribbean color and references like Mexican wedding dresses and Oaxacan carved animals. If the color design successfully supports the overall story we are telling, the environment becomes that much more magical for our guests."

Designers journeyed to Mexico to find basket weavers who could fashion wicker kangaroos to hold merchandise. In Oaxaca, Mexico, four hours down a dirt and boulder road, they found a family that carves and paints fantastically shaped animals. Imagineers ordered 300 bats, 120 bugs and 150 butterflies to hang in Pizzafari.

Principal production designer Ken Gomes actually relocated to Bali to oversee the production of more than one hundred hand-carved articles that were shipped to Florida each month. Gomes became part of village life, attending weddings and funerals and acquiring the native name of Wayan ("second-born") Sin Ken Ken ("no problem").

"The sense of community is refreshing," said Gomes. "The talent and skill in Bali are incredible resources. They don't realize how gifted they are."

Imagineer Marty Sklar said, "One of our biggest challenges in the beginning of the park was that we laid out some of the pathways in the Animal Kingdom and, the whole idea was that this was an adventurous park and people should, therefore, not have things as clear as we have made them in other parks. There were narrow, twisting, unmarked pathways. We didn't give out guide maps. Well, that only confused the public.

"They want some indication where they're going, that they understand where they're going. We had to open up a lot of the landscaping and provide clearer paths to the various attractions so that the park would work from a directional standpoint and add more signage and give out maps. People then knew where they were going and were not confused as they were when we first opened."

While much of the original DAK remains for guests to enjoy, other things that were there the first year disappeared quickly.

Discovery River Boats

Discovery River Boats closed in August 1999, making it the first DAK attraction to close.

It was intended to be a much more ambitious experience with previews of the upcoming Beastly Kingdom along the route including encounters with a unicorn, a kraken that would attack the boat and the head of a fire-breathing dragon extending out of a water front cave.

Budget cuts resulted in the ride becoming more of just a one-way transportation system between the dock from Safari Village near Dinoland U.S.A. and the Upcountry Landings dock in Asia. The trip took approximately seven to ten minutes and was similar to the Friendships at the World Showcase Lagoon.

Since there was a skipper telling bad jokes and sharing information about the park, guests expected it would be something more like the Jungle Cruise since the boats looked similar in design and were very disappointed that it wasn't especially when long boarding lines originally resulted because of the misunderstanding.

There were seven boats that were named Manatee Maiden, Leaping Lizard, Scarlet Flamingo, Otter Nonsense, Hasty Hippo, Crocodile Belle, and Darting Dragonfly.

Guests did see a few things on the voyage around the Tree of Life including a series of hot springs geysers along the shores of Africa, animal water sculptures at the Discovery Lagoon, and a large audio-animatronics Iguanodon playing in the water near DinoLand U.S.A. that foreshadowed the Countodwn to Extinction attraction where that dinosaur plays a key role in the story.

The attraction was renamed in November 1998 to the Discovery River Taxi to emphasize it was just transportation and had prerecorded narration. Animal handlers with small animals were added on the boat as part of the park's animal education initiative but did not prove to be a guest satisfier.

In March 1999, the attraction was once again renamed and was called Radio Disney River Cruise playing commentary from Radio Disney disc jockeys Just Plain Mark and Zippy with music that the guests were told was being broadcast from the top of the Tree of Life. It wasn't.

When the attraction finally closed, the boats were stored in a backstage marina and the docks used occasionally for character meet and greet opportunities or additional seating. Two of the boats were later relocated to Magic Kingdom's Contemporary Resort where they were repurposed for a Pirates & Pals fireworks voyage on Bay Lake and the Seven Seas Lagoon.

Camp Minnie-Mickey

Although Camp Minnie-Mickey was meant to be a temporary placeholder, it lasted almost sixteen years from 1998 to 2014 when it was replaced by Pandora: The World of Avatar.

Disney's Animal Kingdom faced unexpected budget overruns so cuts had to be made including an entire land called Beastly Kingdom. Realizing there would be not enough shows and attractions on opening day, CEO Michael Eisner recalled how Mickey's Birthdayland, a temporary location was built in only ninety days in 1988 at the Magic Kingdom. Eisner felt that something similar devoted to Disney characters would mimic that success.

It was hoped that once the new park was up and running that there would be an influx of revenue to build Beastly Kingdom. That didn't happen.

Camp Minnie-Mickey was themed to be a rural five acre summer fishing camp in the woodlands of the Adirondack Mountains in upstate New York where the characters were on vacation. This theme was echoed in the landscape, architecture, and street furniture that provided a homemade feeling.

At the Greeting Trails guests could usually find Mickey, Minnie, Donald and Goofy. In random places throughout the land other characters like Chip, Dale, Koda, Pocahontas, Meeko, Baloo, and King Louie among others appeared.

Along the river were three-dimensional fiberglass figures of Donald Duck fishing and catching a rubber boot; Mickey, Pluto and Goofy fishing; Huey, Dewey, and Louie backpacking with Daisy Duck.

The camp's assembly hall seating 1,375 guests was the home for the half hour *The Festival of the Lion King* musicial show that did not tell an abbreviated version of the famous animated feature's plot but was a tune-filled tribal celebration with audience participation and some unexpected surprises.

The other show was the twelve minute *Pocahontas and Her Forest Friends* in Grandma Willow's Grove. The genesis of the show came from the animal education cast at Disney's Animal Kingdom. It was meant to be similar to the animal meet-and-greet shows at zoos and other animal parks, where a trainer brings out one animal at a time and talks about its characteristics to the audience.

Pocahontas is worried that the forest is being cut down indiscriminately and runs to Grandma Willow for advice. She reminds Pocahontas of a prophecy that one creature has a special gift to protect the forest but that Pocahontas herself must discover the identity of that creature giving her the opportunity to interact with several different animals including a raccoon, a snake, rabbits, opossums, a skunk, a porcupine and in the process educate the audience about them.

The show was written to utilize the natural behaviors of the animals. The animals sometimes decided they didn't want to appear which is why so many different types of animals rotated throughout the years in the show.

A live character performer portrayed Pocahontas and there were two puppeteers who were underneath the stage for Sprig and Grandmother Willow. Grandma Willow came from the Disneyland *Spirit of Pocahontas* show that closed in September 1997.

Finally, Pocahontas realizes that the creature of the prophecy must be human beings. "Humans can destroy the forest, but we can also save it. The Earth is our home too. If we take care of it, it will take care of us!"

While there was no restaurant in the land, guests could get cookies and ice cream sandwiches at Camp Soft Serve (also known as Chip and Dale's Cookie Cabin) and funnel cakes, corn dogs and beverages at Campfire Treats (also known as Campside Funnel Cakes and Forest Trail Funnel Cakes).

The March of The ARTanimals Parade

The Disney publicity release described it as: "It's not a parade... it's not a procession...so what is it? Join us and find out as we present our fun, zany and fanciful one-of-a-kind 'moving celebration' of imagination and living art inspired by the world of animals".

It was different than other Disney theme park parades and was more of a carnival/Mardi Gras approach meant to represent a bunch of artists getting together to create their impressions of animals out of "found" items. The parade was designed to maneuver around the narrow pathways yet still stand out from the surrounding lush landscaping.

Designed by Swiss artist Rolf Knie, the parade was supposed to represent an informal and intimate celebration and featured no Disney characters or Disney music. Some of the costumes even showed the faces of the "artists" who were sculptors, weavers and painters.

Originally entitled March of the Animals, the avant-garde approach initially confused the guests so the name was changed to emphasize that is was an artistic interpretation. A band and storyteller were added to accompany the parade performers. Later, the costumes were used for entertainment and photo opportunities in the Safari Village area.

The instrumental music included songs with animal references like *Let's All Sing Like the Birdies Sing, Flight of the Bumblebee, Baby Elephant Walk, Tiger Rag, Itsy Bitsy Spider* and *Aba Daba Honeymoon.*

The six unusual floats included a lion playing a xylophone made from wooden gazelle skeletons, a frog wearing a straw hat and red-and-white striped jacket crooning to some dancing frogs, and a queen bee sitting on her honey throne while others bees tickled her with a flower and swirling ribbons.

The fifteen minute parade started near Pizzafari and wound its way through Asia and past Dinoland USA but with viewing available only on one side of the route since the pathway was so narrow. It only lasted a year.

Journey into Jungle Book

The 1,500 seat Theater in the Wild in the Dinoland USA area has featured only three stage shows: *Journey into the Jungle Book* (1998-1999), *Tarzan Rocks!* (1999-2006), and *Finding Nemo - The Musical* (2007-Present).

Journey Into the Jungle Book was a roughly twenty-five minute show that condensed the story of Mowgli and his animal encounters in the jungles of India from Disney's animated feature film *The Jungle Book* (1967) featuring the popular songs including *Bare Necessities* and *I Wanna Be Like You.*

It featured some costumed characters, human performers and innovative puppetry. During cast previews, the masks for characters had not been finished so audiences could see the performers' faces and loved it.

Later, when the show debuted and the masks had arrived, it seemed to lose its connection with the audience. Some of the costumes looked like bushes and trees that when positioned differently became animals.

Show Director was Fran Soeder who had previously directed *The Legend of the Lion King, The Hunchback of Notre Dame*, and *The Voyage of The Little Mermaid.*

After a year, the show was replaced with the high-energy half-hour concert style presentation called *Tarzan Rocks* (1999) directed by Reed Jones to tie-in with the release of the animated feature film based on the Lord of the Jungle.

Things are constantly changing at Walt Disney World theme parks and even though DAK has only been around for two decades, many things have already disappeared including things that most DAK fans never even knew existed that first year of the park including the hidden Water Buffalo Path, the Dinosaur Jubilee, and the Fossil Preparation Lab.

Joe Rohde: The DAK Philosophy

As an animation instructor at the Disney Institute, I was fortunate to be given the opportunity to attend a two-hour presentation by Imagineer Joe Rohde on June 14, 1998 for the opening team of Disney's Animal Kingdom roughly a week before the theme park opened to the public

At the time, Joe Rohde was the lead designer for DAK and he wanted the cast members to understand the thinking behind the park so they would appreciate how it was different than the other Walt Disney World parks.

He called his speech "a ritual of the transfer of stewardship" from the Imagineers to the people who would be running the park. His presentation was accompanied by slides.

Fortunately, I was able to record the lecture, and Wayne Campbell was gracious enough to transcribe it for me.

This is an excerpt from that presentation with questions removed since the answers were self-explanatory, tangential information removed, incomplete or repeated thoughts deleted, speculation about things that might develop in the future eliminated and more.

I have used some of this material in past articles that I have written but for the most part, the following material was only shared to a handful of cast members who attended the event over twenty years ago.

Joe Rohde: What I am going to try to do in two hours, is talk about *why* this park came to be, how it came to be, what the pieces of it are that make it what it is, and a little bit about the philosophy behind how we constructed it and how I hope in the future we can continue to make it grow.

I have always had a natural inclination towards natural history. Not simply zoology, but ethnology and anthropology as well. I'm an avid learner of that sort of thing.

So I sort of made it known that I was interested in this project and then I went away to Nepal for six weeks. And when I came back it was November '89 and Marty Sklar, who's the President of Imagineering, sat me down and said, "Okay, after the Christmas season is over, you're gonna start work on this animal thing that Michael Eisner wants to work on."

I had a friend—fairly highly placed in the company—who took me aside and said, "Joe, listen to me. While you were out, we had a big, big meeting of the whole company and we announced 'The Disney Decade.' And The Disney Decade is all the projects the Walt Disney Company is going to do in the next ten years and you know what? You're not one of them."

So, of course, this single person is more responsible for Animal Kingdom getting built than anything else because now I'm thinking, "Oh, yeah? Okay, now we're really gonna do this."

I went away, thought about it for a while, reconvened my little group in a really small room and we started thinking about Animal Kingdom. There were four people: Myself, Kevin Brown, Zofia Kostyrko and my support person was Patsy Tillis who has since become the Associate Producer on the park.

And we took two words: We took the idea "Animal" and we took the idea "Kingdom" and we did brainstorming...guided imagery brainstorming on these two ideas for weeks.

You come in at eight; you stay 'til lunch; you have an hour for lunch; come back in the room; you stay 'til five and work our way through the symbols, the meanings, the associations, the deviations, the permutations of what this word means.

Then we take the other word and we're gonna do the same thing until we have exhausted the kind of radiating tree of meaning and possibility generated by these two words. Then we're gonna fuse them together; we're gonna edit out everything that looks like we've seen it before; and we're gonna have a great big blob shaped like stuff we haven't seen before and that—somewhere in there—is the core of what this idea is gonna be.

Theme parks are a new thing, relatively, in the world, if you think of Disneyland as being the first theme park. There are things that pre-existed Disneyland that are in a category that might be called a theme park. They are utterly different from what we think of when we think of an amusement park.

A theme park's job is transportation. It is to mentally transport you, to remove you, to sweep you away from *here*...from everything that you think about in an everyday situation, from your worries, from your concerns, from your very perception that you are in the world that you are in.

That is why people pay so much money to go to theme parks is to be swept away. That is why the ergonomics, the human factors of theme parks, are so important. Because everything inconvenient, everything mundane that could remind you that you're still back in the world, needs to be erased.

Lines can't be too long because if the line gets too long, now you're thinking about the line and the line is full of people, and the people are just like you, and now you're back again, right?

I mean everything needs to flow and flow smoothly, just like butter, so that your mind stays in the artificially created narrative conceit that sweeps you away into another story like a great movie, like a great *book*, like a great piece of music takes you out of your life for some period of time and puts you someplace else.

Our job is to create something new and different. Something innovative. Something that is not like what is out there. There's another whole branch of the company whose job is to analyze the potential profitability of that thing. And the way you do that analysis is by comparison. Is anything wrong with this picture to you? This is almost impossible to do because if we do our job right there is nothing to compare it to.

The first experience you have of Disney's Animal Kingdom is our forecourt, before you even enter the park. It is a profoundly geometric and humanly ordered space. It is a circle surrounded by identical height palm trees, laid out in a triple arcade. It's got a linear access to a flat bunch of buildings and there is nothing else out there.

That is a summation, a reminder, a statement about where we are, where we live, what our lives are like. We live surrounded by concrete; we control the forces of nature; we order everything; we have impact on that environment and that is that statement.

As you walk through the gateway if you happen to look down, you will watch as you step off brushed concrete—which is just what any sidewalk looks like—and onto what appears to be dirt in a space of ten inches. And look in front of you and you will see nothing but jungle. You won't see a road. You won't see a path. You see nothing but jungle.

Completely natural forms...animals are in there but you might not see 'em. You'll sure see a lot of plants and water. So that's the first transition...is "that's the world we're from, this is the world we're taking you to." You've made a profound transition at that point.

We want you to have an adventure. You are supposed to be in a world of nature. Nature challenges you. We want you to have an adventure, so you walk into the park and look at the park and you don't know where the hell you are or where you're supposed to go.

There happen to be two very, very broad avenues going off this way and you cannot help but go on them because everybody goes left or right if they can't go forward and both of them, by coincidence, do end up getting you into the park. But the act of doing it is not an orienting act. It is a miniature adventure.

You're surrounded by experiences. None of these experiences are presented to you as if you need to stop and look at them. It's really not even an animal exhibit, in one sense of the word. It's a physical adventure of space that is preparing you for the mentality we want you to have when you get to the middle.

You walk under these big heavy arches and these stones lean out at you and this plant life—which as the years go by will continue to burgeon, continue to grow, continue to compress that space—you come out the other side and this is the first moment of orientation you get and it is to the tree, which is the axis of this park.

And then, finally, you see where you are. We offer you a moment of orientation, and you go down into Safari Village. Surviving adventure is an exhilarating thing. It pumps people up. It raises their level of mental activity.

One of the first things we did in the process of researching this park was to go around the country to as many zoos as we could. In the first year of Animal Kingdom, we visited 40 zoological facilities. We did not consult charts and graphs and analyses and bell curves of any form. We just observed and absorbed.

You know, officially The Walt Disney Company wasn't necessarily super, super interested and we had $250,000 to spend to get going on this and if you know anything about The Walt Disney Company you can imagine how long $250,000 will last you. It's about enough to have breakfast on.

So, what we did was buy time. We started by designing the fantasy part of the park that was to be called Beastly Kingdom because we knew how to do fantasy and fantasy creatures like dragons. And while we do that we'll travel across the country looking at zoos and we'll begin to make some connections. We'll figure out what the zoo/conservation part of this thing is and then we'll be able to work on the sort of cognitive part of the park next.

We're still sweatin' the thing of, "Well, how do we make this safari experience worthwhile? Well we need to go to Africa." So, we have our "safari sampler" experience, which literally was every form of consumable safari experience from your low-budget to relatively high-end, just to see, "Okay, what is that?" Then we were ready to come with our final proposal.

In the course of that year, none of us had ever designed a zoological exhibit before, nor did we presume that we would be able to design a zoological exhibit. What we know is stagecraft and storytelling. We don't know enough about the husbandry and management of animals to make any assumptions about what this is going to be, so we need some advice from people who *do* know.

And so I picked up the phone and I called Dr. William Conway at the Zoological Society at the Bronx Zoo and I introduced myself and told him what we were doing…what we were considering doing…and would he mind coming and spending a couple of days with us telling us what the hell we were doing.

And he was gracious enough—which is surprising when you consider this man's astounding schedule—to come and spend two full days with us at Imagineering discussing our ideas and intentions with us. And it is a credit to him that his views of what we might be capable of were more ambitious than our own. And, indeed, it was after our conversations with him that we became confident enough that we could try some of the things that we had been considering trying to go ahead with us.

We brought Dr. Conway out a couple of more times and then it really just became too much for his schedule and he recommended Rick Barongi to us. So, then it was Rick Barongi only in San Diego, right while we are nearby in Los Angeles so we're on his ass all the time.

We were haulin' him up like once a month, you know, and so that goes on for a while, right? And we're getting more and more definition, more and more definition, more and more definition and then Rick starts to go, "*Geez*…you know, I'm not the only guy in the world, here. We ought to get a whole bunch of other guys in" and so we brought people in on a one-by-one basis for a little while and then I went away to Nepal again for three months.

And when I came back, we were ready to convene a consultant group, which I think consisted of like twenty-five people. It was a *large* group of people culled from zoological institutions and conservation institutions around the country. And we would take these four-day long marathon sessions and go blow-by-blow, animal-by-animal, moat-by-moat, tree-by-tree, exhibit-by-exhibit asking questions…getting answers…taking advice…making notes…writing all this stuff down on these papers and trying to incorporate it into our designs.

Around that time, we brought Pat Janikowski in, who at the time worked for Jones and Jones and—you know, how hard is this, you sort of go sniffing around to figure out how many big zoo design firms are out there capable of handling a *gigantic* job—oh, *two*. Which one do we wanna work with? The one on the West Coast. Oh, *that's* easy, that's them. Jones and Jones. So that was easy.

So we got Pat and Jim and a few other people from Jones and Jones and, frankly, we virtually hired them away in that they moved down to California with us, lived with us, stayed with us for years now. I mean, Pat has barely seen the inside of the Jones and Jones building in the past four or five years. He's been with us. So we began to build a sense of some structure to what the animal part of this thing was, while we continued to work and define the other aspects of the park as well.

I have a profound belief in the economic value of real observation of real reference material which no experience I have ever had has lessened. So I spare no expense in sending real people to real places to see what they are really like. It inevitably is cheaper to work from an ingrained knowledge than it is to work from a book.

(Showing some slides) This is the real village of Shela on the East African coast. This, of course, is Disney's Animal Kingdom. This is a ceiling in Lamu on the East Africa coast. This is at Disney's Animal Kingdom. This is a river bank in the Selous, the Rufiji River. I shot this photograph in 1991. That's Animal Kingdom. This is a road in Africa. This is a road in Animal Kingdom. This is a rock kapi in the Serengeti. This is a rock kapi being produced at Animal Kingdom, as is this, our famous little lion kapi. This is a place we stayed in the Selous in 1991, Mbuyu Camp, which was really cool. It was so cool we had to…copy it here in Animal Kingdom. (Finishes showing slides)

Quite early on we realized that we could not proceed with this project without a very, very real conservation aspect to it. It simply would not work. It wouldn't work on a variety of levels

One was the issue of legitimacy. And, you know, one simply could not get into this business without doing something beneficial out of being in it. One was the issue of access to animals and the fact that we planned to be here for the long term, maybe fifty or sixty years.

It gets more difficult to get access to animals when legal systems are shrinking the free market of animals and you sort of have to be in a species survival program to have access to those animal populations. Probably most importantly it is good story. It makes people feel good to be in a place that is involved with all this.

Very early on we enlisted Operations people from Walt Disney World to begin to advise us about the structure of this park because, since it wasn't business as usual, we knew that we couldn't simply go with the usual assumptions. Most of the time we used Eric Eberhart, who at the time worked for Bob Lamb, and then as time went on we began using Bob himself as our advisor to craft this thing as well.

Meanwhile, of course, while we were doing all this we had no one at The Walt Disney Company say that they were actually going to build this park...which can get really tough.

At this point I am gonna talk about the ideas behind each of the lands and what makes them what they are. And I was gonna start in the center with Safari Village.

After you cross over that bridge from that jungle into the middle of the park, now you find yourself in the heart of this park. I don't know, how many of you have paid attention to this difference, but you'll notice if you do go to DinoLand...if you go to Africa... someday you go to Asia...they all look like hell. They're all sort of bio-degraded. They're all weathered. They're all aged. They're all peeling. They're all rotting. They're all succumbing to the force of nature. They are all about a kind of futility in the force of nature.

Safari Village is about the adoration of nature. And it is the only clean, pristine, beautiful, wonderful, colorful, rich, saturated area in the park. It is arranged around our tree—the axis of the park, the center of the park, the cathedral of our park rising up into the sky covered with these images like one of those Italian painted baroque church ceilings, right?

Just a complete, wholehearted, really over-the-top celebration of the beauty, the wonder, the richness, the diversity, the majesty of animal life on Earth and then arrayed around it—just like a zillion little cathedral towns in Europe—is our little Safari Village, which is also just about the love of the form and the idea of animals.

And that is why it is so joyfully exuberant and colorful and rich in detail and saturated with animal imagery and that is why we established some of the design rules for it, which were: There will be no decoration unless it is animal decoration and there will be virtually no earth tones in the entire place. It is about all that intensity of fascination, obsession, and love.

So, Safari Village is a very unique place because it is narratively neutral. Every place else you go, we go way, way, way, way, way out of our way to convince you that you are some specific other place—not here. Safari Village is kind of a no place. There's nowhere on Earth like Safari Village.

It is meant, each time you cross through it on your way from somewhere to another place, to reorient you, to sort of clean your slate and set you up again for another adventure. Safari Village is not an adventure. The adventure is across the bridge to all those different lands.

You cross over the bridge into DinoLand. DinoLand is about our American love and fascination with dinosaurs, both as real science, as part of our national heritage and as popular cult icons.

DAK is about our love of animals. DinoLand is about paleontology. Paleontology is the love of extinct animals. It's a particularly poignant form of science in that it's an unrequited love. They're dead and they're never coming back and there you are, you know, picking through their bones in the dust trying to reconstruct in your imagination the lives, the action, the vivacity of these creatures that are gone.

When you cross the bridge to DinoLand, the marquee for the land is one of those trapezoid roadside signs, you know, with the routed-out letters "DinoLand USA, friendliest fossils in America." Clearly, you are somewhere along the highway in America. You are at a place where people excavate these fossils and yet they have to make a buck, right? So, you've got these two blended ideas that come together.

There's all kinds of emotional motifs woven in to DinoLand. Probably the more dominant one is this idea of chaos and order.

The front half of DinoLand is just a mess. It looks like a construction site. A lot of the scaffolding that you see out in DinoLand is not goin' away. That's DinoLand.

Construction material, upheaval, dirt, piles of earth, piles of tools. It stands in opposition to the authority and the order and the kind of stuffiness of the Dino Institute itself, which is in the background, which represents a whole other kind of idea.

We've set up this world of students—grad students—young, refreshing, wild, exuberant; in opposition to their professors who are rather more staid and controlled. And as you look, you'll see again and again this sort of order and disarray, order and disarray, order and disarray setup.

Restaurantosaurus is an easy place to see that. You've got the sign. The sign is perfectly sane. It says "restaurant"; it is a restaurant; it says "restaurant", but one of the purported grad students has climbed up on the roof with a piece of corrugated metal and painted "osaurus" on the metal and tacked it up on the edge of the sign which is kind of an act of rebellious vandalism, against the very order of restaurant itself.

There are the live animals, which are all purported—or documented—survivors of the cretaceous era in opposition to the dead animals, which are extinct. And there is something intriguing in the opposition of these rather small, rather humble animals—I mean, even a Chinese alligator is not the biggest crocodilian in the world—and certainly the birds.

We could exhibit zillions of insects, frogs, amphibians, lizards, turtles that also would be in this category to make a point that here are these huge creatures: vast, powerful, fast, seemingly intelligent complex animals…they are just gone. And yet around us every day are all these plants and all these animals that survived some kind of event that brought about this end. That stimulates curiosity. That generates interest. That is a mystery. And that is adventure.

The reason we don't, incidentally, display a lot of amphibians and smaller animals is many of those animals that would be really, really legitimate survivors of the cretaceous era would be considered injurious species in Florida. And therefore would have to be exhibited in such a way that you, the viewer, would be aware of the containment system as a containment system and that is one of the things we have utterly avoided, if you don't notice already, everywhere we possibly can at Animal Kingdom.

You go inside the ride and once again you have this sort of rebellion against authority motif and this sort of youth/vigor/ fascination versus kind of a utilitarian use structure. The story in the Dino Institute is that the Dino Institute is not so much a museum as it is a corporation.

They're using this time machine the way we, the Disney Company, would probably use it, right? To make a lot of money. And yet there are scientists who want to use it to go save the dinosaur from extinction. They hijack the vehicle; we rocket back into the prehistoric past; we try to save these dinosaurs from extinction while all around us all hell is breaking loose as this meteor comes towards Earth.

One of the things we did with our dinosaurs, because they're almost all seen in the dark from a moving vehicle, is we hyper-accentuated certain aspects of their skin characteristics. For example, it is known that dinosaurs have these spiky nodules, you know, all over their skin but they're probably not *as* spiky as the ones that we show.

The rack of horns is a little more extreme, but there is a keratinous sheath over the horn core of these bones. And when you find the bones all you find is the bone core and anyone who's ever looked at a cow skull that still has a horn on it will know that the size of a horn can be dramatically bigger and considerably different in shape than the bone core inside of it. So, we've taken liberty with that.

Carnotaurus is a real dinosaur. No one had utilized this dinosaur at all in any form when we sort of found him in the literature. He's South American and really does have these big projecting horns over his eyes. It's really disturbing looking. So, this is our bad guy, right? We did cheat. The actual type specimen is Carnotaurus Sastrei . Ours is Carnotaurus Robustus Floridona because it's somewhat larger and bulkier than the real Carnotaurus.

These are some really very, very beautifully sculpted dinosaur figures. I want to say that both the sculpting and the interior technology of these dinosaur figures are unparalleled in our business at this time. There is simply nothing like it out there. They move almost as well as CGI figures might in a film. Very fast, very subtle movement, it's quite impressive.

We have a raptor. Exactly what raptor we won't say. They keep discovering new ones and I'm hoping they'll discover one that's exactly like this. (laughter from audience) What it's most like is a velociraptor. Now the ones that were in the movie *Jurassic Park* that were called velociraptors really didn't look much like velociraptors. A real velociraptor is about the size of a poodle. Not a real, real threatening creature. So we have a really kind of big velociraptor. So that's a lie, but it works.

Let's go to Chester and Hester's. How old is Chester? How old is Hester? Are they still alive or did they die five years ago and the shop is being carried on by their, you know, son and daughter or someone who took it on? What did they do before they opened the shop? What record of their lives does this shop hold? What can we learn and feel about the people who would make this place by walking through the spaces that they've created?

You've all walked into somebody's house that you never met before but you learn a whole bunch of things about that person. You know a lot about that person from the objects and the lighting and the arrangement of the space.

That's what we do. We want you to *feel* the presence of people and lives and histories that are, frankly, not there at all. And to do that, we ourselves have to deeply immerse ourselves in the imagined character of these people in order to bring enough reality to be convincing to each of these situations. It is clear that Chester and Hester decorated this space and lived in it.

You cross the bridge to go into Africa. In Africa is our little town of Harambe. Now, Harambe is not anywhere. It is not in Kenya. It's not in Tanzania, Zimbabwe, Botswana. We deliberately created our own principality because we want to handle conservation themes in a rather hard-hitting way and we don't wanna get a phone call from the Kenyan consulate every week. Or Tanzanian, or Zaire, or Uganda, or Zimbabwe, or Botswana, or South Africa. So we have a principality that is of our own creation: The state of Harambe.

Harambe is a Swahili word. It means, "Let's pull together." Seems like a nice idea for a town. Our town of Harambe is based on any number of coastal Swahili towns that spread down the coast, almost from the Somali border down towards Mozambique. Primarily Lamu, Shela and old Mombasa, along the Kenya coast were major influences but not entirely. There are notes from many other places in Africa woven into Harambe as well.

It is a modern place, utterly modern. It is not a long time ago. It is not the era of portly white guys with big white moustaches and pith helmets slogging through the wilds of Africa. It is not some kind of Indiana Jones-y 1930's with Nazis behind every corner. We made every attempt to de-romanticize it for a couple of reasons.

One, we are handling very timely messages. They're not romantic; they're real, and they need to be set in a real context of real values. You need to recognize these people have telephones. You know, these people have a satellite dish. They know about us and we know about them. We share this world, right?

Two, my personal belief is that in our modern world, these images say, "Adventure" more clearly. We want people to feel that it is real but just so unfamiliar. It doesn't look like home. It doesn't look like what you know. It looks unfamiliar and that is adventure.

To go on the Kilimanjario Safaris ride, you have to go through this town. This is a strange, unfamiliar place with a different language all over. You know, a different way of making doors and windows, a different way of plumbing, a different way of applying electricity, different products on the shelves and different licenses in the windows to operate a retail facility. Different everything, right? And yet, very clearly, part of our modern world of electricity, of news, of the sharing of information, of economics and values. That's where you are.

The other thing we did, quite deliberately with Harambe, is that it is profoundly geometric. It is all cubic and square. There is virtually no landscaping in it. It is a box. It is a very compressive, tight box that we put you in, because we're gonna send you out into the beauty of nature. And how will you remember to appreciate the beauty of nature unless you're reminded what it's like not to have it?

So the first thing you do is go into this urban little box and be reminded what means to feel heat reflected off a great big plaster surface and hear that sound rebounding off all those hard areas. To look at that flatness and squareness and the angles and the hardness of the lights and to see those people compressed in that space and then to go out on your adventure.

And then we do this very sort of slow seduction thing where, okay, now you get to the thatch; but it's still rather claustrophobic and close. And then you get in your vehicle and you go into the jungle, and it's still kind of contained and close. And then you get to the river and you get a long, linear view, but only on one axis, right? It's a long, linear view. You go up the hill and finally, when you come down, you finally get this release into a big area of open space.

A hundred some odd acres is not small, but it sure ain't Africa. And so we have to do everything we can to manipulate your perception of what it is, to make you believe that it's huge. It is a convincing simulacrum of a large space. It gives the impression of vast space and that is what it is supposed to do.

If you look at the map that we've created of Harambe, it's a very telling little map, right? It's got the little town of Harambe and the river, and the sisal plantation, and the cattle ranch, and the phosphorus mine, and the train line, and the other town, and the highway on the map, and more. All that is there is Harambe Game Reserve. That's where the animals are and, if the people of Harambe decide one day that phosphorus is more valuable than animals, goodbye Harambe Game Reserve!

So this is the world that we take you into. It's a world of debate, it's an active world, it's a world that is a simulacrum of the world we live in and we are going to present you with an adventure. You get in the vehicle, you go out and there are poachers in the game reserve.

They're going after elephants. We have to engage in trying to prevent them from killing the baby elephant but rather than watching this on TV or reading about it on a piece of paper, this is a physical event that is happening to you and we have done everything we can, within limits, to create the sense that it is really happening to you in that bracket of your mind that you release to the narrative.

It's just like going to a great movie. The difference is, because it is physical it is remembered and stored as a real experience and gives you the sense of conviction and drive that a real experience gives you and therein lies its conservation value. Because you end up with six to eight million people a year going around going, "Yes, we have to save these wild places. Because I have seen this and this has happened to me and I remember seeing this with my own eyes."

I can't count the number of people from Africa that we've taken out into our fake who have said, "Man, this looks just like where I'm from." People from Uganda, people from South Africa, people from Tanzania, people from Kenya, people from Zimbabwe, walking around the same place, each one of them swearing it looks like where they're from.

Conservation Station is overtly what it is. It's our nerve center to the park. It's where we deconstruct the park. You get on the train in Africa. It looks like Africa but the moment you leave, the curtain is stripped aside, and you look at our underwear for like a quarter mile as you drive up to Conservation Station and we talk about how all this is fake. How all this is here for a reason. How all this is here for a reason that is far beyond this park and involves global issues of terrific importance that we'd like you to be involved in.

We do attempt to do several things: To give you some insight into how the park operates—how the animal operations operate—to give you some insight into how it relates...you know...what conservation is to the world, and hopefully to motivate you to be involved in conservation.

I think if you were to judge Disney's Animal Kingdom by the presentational standards of a very, very fine zoo, you would find us strangely lacking in certain areas like graphics, for example. I could think of almost any exhibit that I might walk through in a big zoo that would have just lots of graphic information about the animal for me to access and to read. We really don't have a lot of information about these animals. We are not necessarily presenting these animals for that specific cognitive purpose.

Not that there are not cognitive opportunities at each viewing opportunity for an animal, but our goal is more in the arcing narrative. It's more in the experience of these animals in situations that have this hyper-accentuated reality that make you believe, that get you emotionally involved and motivate you to pursue information at your own speed, at your own discretion from a variety of choices that can be more personally sculpted.

You know the animals in Africa were frankly chosen rather opportunistically. We want animals in Africa that make you think you're out in Africa...make you believe you're in Africa... can live together in simple peace and harmony and be visible. You know that sort of boils down to charismatic mega-vertebrates.

The real thing out there is not to focus on, you know, a Thompson's gazelle, a gerenuk and an impala and why they look different from each other and, you know, how they're differently adapted to different environments. The point is to believe that you are in a living system that depends on you to stay alive.

That's what we want you to take away. You're in a living system that depends on you to stay alive. That's why it doesn't matter if you see every animal or not. It's not about seeing every animal. It's not about identifying every animal. It's about believing that every animal out there is important and important to the environment and its survival.

I do not believe that Disney's Animal Kingdom is going to negatively impact zoos. If I thought we had failed to create something that occupied its own niche, if all we had done was create an incrementally better zoo, then I think you would have a different situation. But it has been our goal to be regarded as another creature entirely. A non-competitive niche, so that we *can* co-exist; in fact, to exist symbiotically.

And I think that's terribly important because there are so many things that can be done better at a community level at a zoo that you can visit for five bucks with your family and not go broke and talk to people face to face and spend as much time as you want and come seven times a year, you know, and feel as part of your community and we can't *be* that. We are something to a planet. We're not necessarily something to an immediate community. And that just puts us in a category that's very, very different.

This is sort of a ritual of transfer of ownership, if you will. I mean, we've been on this thing for just ever, right?

And there just comes a time when you sort of, you are gone, and you hand this over to other people and they carry on. And I want to make sure that the spirit in which it was developed and sort of the ideas that underlie it are vested in somebody, somewhere so it doesn't become a mystery or a debate.

I'll be dead and some of you out here will be long gone when they have the fiftieth anniversary of the opening of Disney's Animal Kingdom

This is a delicate park because of much of what it's trying to do and I think we must all work very, very carefully to nurture it along, especially in its early years, to get its legs up and to be everything that it has the potential to be, which I happen to think is some very, very wonderful and important things.

The Forbidden Mountain

Expedition Everest—Legend of the Forbidden Mountain opened at Disney's Animal Kingdom in 2006.

The mountain-like structure is made from 1,800 tons of steel and painted with 2,000 gallons of stain and paint. It took three years and more than 38 miles of rebar, 5,000 tons of structural steel, and 10,000 tons of concrete to build the mountain. Over 200,000 square feet of rock work was done.

The structure was built by Vekoma, a Dutch amusement ride manufacturer noted for its work on roller coasters including ones for Disney theme parks like the Seven Dwarfs Mine Train in the Magic Kingdom.

The total cost for the attraction was estimated at over a hundred million dollars. It is the tallest artificial mountain in the world at 199 feet but not the tallest mountain in Florida which is Britton Hill at an elevation of 345 feet.

The Forbidden Mountain is not Everest. Everest is represented by the barren background peak on the far right that through the use of forced perspective seems even further off in the distance.

Guests are on an expedition to Everest on an old mountain railroad operated by the fictional Himalayan Escapes - Tours and Expeditions company but are taking a risky shortcut through the Forbidden Mountain to get to the Everest base camp. The attraction has nearly a mile long length of track that encompasses steep climbs, sharp plunges and a backward slide.

"The name of our story is Expedition Everest, but nothing in the shape of the 'real' Everest says, 'forbidden'," said Imagineer Joe Rohde, who was the executive designer of the attraction, in 2007. "So we created the narrative device of a foreground mountain range made of shapes that say, 'Don't go here!'

"Everest rises beyond this wall of claw-like spires, a tempting goal. The Forbidden Mountain expresses its 'forbidden-ness' in a shape that echoes the teeth and claws of the yeti itself, dominating the entire land across which the story plays out. This is one of the key principles in narrative place-making.

"The look of Expedition Everest is based on careful research into the architecture, landscape and culture of the Himalayas: research and design guided by our theme. Our goal was not to create a replica, nor to represent every aspect of Himalayan life, but to gather those specific details, which were both authentic and supported the thrust of our theme, the intrinsic value of nature.

"Expedition Everest is not meant to be a substitute for a trip to the real Himalayas; it is a fictional story told in a realistic style.

"While the environment is visually convincing and filled with accurate details, including architectural elements and props made for us by craftspeople in the Himalayas, its real purpose is to convey messages.

"The idea of the yeti as a protector is embedded in shrines depicting the yeti holding the mountains in his hands, bronzes of the yeti in the traditional 'keep out' posture of a Tibetan guardian, flyers printed from wood blocks warning visitors against offending the yeti."

The Imagineers who designed the mountain used digital imaging to create a model. They actually created 24 different ride models before settling on the one that was built. They created a virtual model after scanning with laser technology, one of their earlier models. The shell of the mountain was created digitally into six foot square pieces that fit together like puzzle pieces.

"Millions have ridden it," said Rohde. "Most of those have come for the simple fun of a great ride. But of those millions, some have come away inspired and informed by the richness of the story. And as a percentage of the huge total, that number is also large."

The queue for the attraction Expedition Everest takes guests through the Himalayan Escapes Tours and Expeditions Booking Office located in the remote village of Serka Zong in the (fictional) Kingdom of Anandapur located in the foothills of the Himalayas to obtain permits.

The company organizes a number of different tours and expeditions with "Expedition Everest" being the name of just one of their specific tours. Himalayan Escapes is operated by a native Anandapuri, Norbu, and his business partner, a British entrepreneur named Bob.

They operate out of a building that had previously been used as the headquarters of the Royal Anandapur Tea Company. They have refurbished a steam train that had been used by the tea company to bring harvested tea leaves down the mountains.

This train now takes customers to the base camp using a short-cut through the Forbidden Mountain supposedly the location of a mysterious environmental creature guardian referred to as the Yeti.

Norbu and Bob's office is filled with dozens of small details from a map of the Himalayas to a tour board depicting the status of the various expeditions.

In fact, there are so many details in the various buildings leading to the attraction vehicles that guests are unable to see it all including a yellowed newspaper clipping from *The Anandapur Reporter* "Serving the Nation for 100 Years". While some stories with headlines like "Trekkers Feared Lost" and "Herders Report Missing Yak" are missing their stories. The lead feature is complete:

Forbidden Mountain Railway ReOpens

Locals Fear Wrath of Yeti

SERKA ZONG—Despite dire warning from irate local residents, the old Anandapur Rail Services route through Forbidden Mountain was reopened today. Closed since 1934 under mysterious circumstances, the railroad, formerly operated by the Royal Anandapur Tea Co. was refurbished by Himalayan Escapes Tours and Expeditions.

The intent, say the operators, is to provide safe, efficient transport to base camp at Mount Everest and environs. Hundreds of western trekkers and climbers are expected to make the journey to Serka Zong to book passage on the new service.

In the heyday of the great tea plantations that flourished in the region, private rail lines were established to carry produce to distant markets. The Royal Anandapur Tea Company used the Forbidden Mountain route extensively in the 1920s and early 1930s.

However, beginning in 1933, the railroad was plagued with accidents. Some drew a connection between the mishaps and increasing British expeditionary attempts to reach the summit of Mount Everest, invoking the spirit of the guardian of the sacred mountain.

By 1934, continual equipment breakdowns and track breakages caused the tea company to shutter its facilities and pull up stakes. The legend of a sacred beast continued to loom large among locals, coming to a head in 1982 with the tragic disappearance of the Forbidden Mountain Expedition.

However, warnings and naysayers aside, the daring entrepreneurs behind Himalayan Escapes were determined to put on a loud, colorful show to celebrate their achievement. Local government officials in attendance trumpeted the event as a landmark enterprise, marking a new era of prosperity and opportunity for Serka Zong. It is indeed our hope that this is the case.

According to the official Imagineering back story in the queue line of Expedition Everest: Legend of the Forbidden Mountain, two business men Bob (from Australia who handles the actual booking for Himalayan Escapes) and Norbu (who has lived in Serka Zong his entire life and is best known for his knowledge of the mountain) have rebuilt the existing railroad that once transported tea in order to take travelers to the base of Mount Everest for profit.

As travelers exit Bob and Norbu's office, they begin to see shrines of the Yeti in various sizes. The majority of these shrines are showered with jewels and food, symbolizing the tremendous respect the locals have for the Yeti. Before entering the queue, guests saw more shrines and prayers flags and red paint (to ward off evil spirits).

Unexpectedly, guests sometimes take part in the story by giving their own offerings of coins to the many shrines throughout the queue. The money collected is donated to animal conservation efforts around the world.

After passing the fields of green tea leaves, travelers walk through Tashi's Trek and Tongba Shop filled with hiking supplies and equipment. The shelves holding food supplies in the queue are actually tea-drying cabinets, and there is even some "Yet-tea" among the dry goods.

Once travelers have finished their shopping, they then enter into the Yeti Museum of Professor Perma Dorje, Ph.D.

The museum which was transformed from a tea warehouse is dedicated to "the serious study of the scientific and cultural aspects of the mysterious creature known and revered throughout the Himalayas as the Yeti."

The first half of the museum focuses on the geographic region of Nepal, the people of Nepal and their interpretations of what they believe the Yeti to look like. This setting is meant to establish a sense of reality before venturing into the fantasy.

The Lost Expedition of 1982 is displayed in the museum. Legend has it that in 1982, a group of trackers went in search of the Yeti. When none returned after several weeks, a search group was sent to find these trackers only to discover they had not survived. The remains of their expedition, including their tent, hiking equipment and camera are shown throughout the exhibit.

A little more than halfway through the museum, travelers notice pictures of lowland jungle animals, midland forest animals and mountain animals. The purpose of this display is to rationalize that if these animals can survive the different areas of the mountain, then why can't a creature like the Yeti also survive?

Towards the end of the Yeti Museum, travelers notice a brown display cabinet filled with actual different discoveries that Walt Disney Imagineers made during an expedition by Disney and Conservation International to the Himalayas to once again establish a sense of reality.

Upon exiting the museum to board their train seat, travelers see one last warning sign posted by Professor Dorje: "Respect the Power of the Yeti. The weight of the evidence leads to the inescapable conclusion: The Yeti is Real. You are about to enter the scared domain of the Yeti, guardian and protector of The Forbidden Mountain. Those who proceed with respect and reverence for the sanctity of the natural environment and its creatures should have no fear. To all others, a warning you risk the wrath of the Yeti. Prof. Perma Dorje, Ph.D Curator The Yeti Museum."

Of course, Bob and Norbu can not allow the good professor to scare off potential customers and so they also post a sign that reads: "The opinions expressed by the curator of the Yeti Museum in no way reflect the views of the owners and operators of Himalayan Escapes, Tours and Expeditions."

The Yeti was the biggest, most complex audio-animatronics figure to ever be created by Disney or anyone else when it first appeared in the attraction.

It stands 25 feet tall and the movement is controlled by nineteen acuators. When operating in "A-mode" the massive Yeti animatronic figure can move five feet horizontally in a few seconds and eighteen inches vertically. Its skin and fur covering measures out to about a thousand square feet, and it's held in place by around 1,000 snaps and 250 zippers.

Most of the figure's weight would be held up by a slide and boom structure emerging from its back. It was powered by a 3000 psi hydraulic thruster that could be recharged in 20 seconds and the combined thrust of all the figure's linear actuators working together could put out a force equivalent to a jet engine. Because of this, the support base for the figure and its boom would be kept separate from the structures of the mountain and the ride track.

The final version was designed by the Imagineers after the culmination of extensive research of the Yeti's role in Nepalese and Tibetan culture and primatology to create a believable animal. These influences included the Gigantopithecus often cited as a potential identity for large ape cryptids, as well as the snub-nosed langur, a high-altitude monkey living in the mountains of Sichuan.

The figure was constructed to sit atop a 46 feet tall independent concrete base meant to hold its weight while allowing the beast to reach down on passengers in the passing train vehicles, terrifying riders and confirming that the legends of the creature were true.

By 2008, the stress caused by the Yeti's complex movement split the figure's framing which would cause a catastrophic malfunction to the ride if the figure continued running in "A-mode."

The understanding is that the fault is in the concrete base and would require an extensive refurbishment that would likely last months. The glitch is apparently not in the figure itself. In addition, with all the money the Disney parks have been losing since the closures and restrictions during the pandemic make it even more unlikely the Yeti is a priority to fix.

It has been operating in "B-mode" which meant no movement. Imagineers have installed a strobe light behind the Yeti trying to give it the appearance of movement and causing him to be referred to by Disney guests as the Disco Yeti.

The vocalizations for the Yeti were provided by voice artist Fred Tatasciore. His voice is heard in many Disney videogames and attractions as well as the giant animated troll in the movie *Enchanted* and Pacha in the first season of the animated series *The Emperor's New School.*

Creator of the creature Imagineer Joe Rohde has said over the years, "It's not an issue of maintenance access, they were part of the design team and set the standard. In fact, it was seen as a model collaborative process.

"It's an unexpected and unforeseen set of issues, very complex, with no easy or timely solutions as of yet. These guys did not ignore something or botch it. Innovation is like physical exploration of unknown spaces. There is stuff out there that you didn't know, and you only encounter it by exploration. But then....there it is.

"You have to understand, it's a giant complicated machine sitting on top of, like, a 46-foot tall tower in the middle of a finished building. So, it's really hard to fix, but we are working on it. And we continue to work on it. We have tried several 'things', none of them quite get to the key, of the 40-foot tower inside of a finished building, but we are working on it.

"I will fix the Yeti someday, I swear." Rohde officially retired from Imagineering January 4, 2021. The Yeti remains unfixed.

The only way to fix the Yeti is to close down Expedition Everest for a lengthy refurbishment where it can be accessed and worked on. Up until recently, that seemed impossible due to the attraction's huge popularity but with the opening of Pandora—The World of Avatar it now becomes more of a possibility since that area and its attractions would absorb the guest attendance.

Joe Rohde: The Yeti and Expedition Everest

Imagineer Joe Rohde led the conceptualization, design and production for Disney's Animal Kingdom since its inception in 1990. Rohde talked with Walt Disney World cast members on April 3, 2006 prior to the opening of the Expedition Everest attraction.

I was in attendance and recorded the presentation and Wayne Campbell was gracious enough to transcribe it for me.

Joe Rohde: Since we're opening Expedition Everest, I thought I would devote a lot of my comments to talking about the attraction and some of the ideas behind the attraction; how we came up with these things (and) some of the other adventures associated with getting it built.

It was a big challenge when it came time to think about Expedition Everest itself. A theme park is a little bit like a musical score. You want to write a fair amount of fluctuation and variation in what's going on in this park, so that is has a lot of diversity of emotional feelings within it.

Now, Animal Kingdom as it was opened was very pastoral, a very quiet park. Obviously a place where, you know, it's a great place to sit and look at animals. A meditative, kind of quiet, pastoral environment.

But a theme park needs to have these big, big peaks and big, big valleys, otherwise it's more like a "park" park. And so, the challenge before us was how to respond to this and do it in a way that would be consistent with the value system that was already established for Disney's Animal Kingdom.

Theme is not the surface application on things. A theme, as I said before, is the deep, underlying premise that comes before any decision about what story you're gonna tell.

The theme of Disney's Animal Kingdom, the underlying theme is adventure and personal involvement and the intrinsic value of nature. Now if we want to put in this screaming, high-thrill, zoom-slam adventure ride thing, we have a challenge trying to find a way to adapt this object that we want to put into the park to our theme.

Now we didn't start with Expedition Everest. We started with this abstract idea: Something has to go into the park, it needs to be really big so you can see it from everywhere, it needs to be physically exciting and you need to be able to see that when you look at it.

And it needs to expand the menu of this park beyond biological animals; to begin to include animals that are from the realm of the imagination, or the realm of legend, or the realm of myth. It needs to expand the menu of this park, that's what we knew.

In a sense you could consider Expedition Everest to be part of the Beastly Kingdom program. Animal Kingdom, as a premise, should be able to sustain more than known biological animals; because, when you take the word "Disney" and "Animal" and "Kingdom" and combine them with each other the logic takes you to a place that is not just live animals and science and stuff.

It took us years coming up with ideas, throwing them away, trying something else. We looked at like ten dragon ideas in the process of getting to Expedition Everest. And it's really hard to explain why they take and why they don't take. There's a million reasons.

I'm sure we will continue to add animals that are part of the imaginary world to Animal Kingdom. It is the kind of place that should have those kinds of animals. Not just dragons and griffins, but animated animal characters...animals out of fairy tales...other people's imaginary animals...it's not so narrow as like, you know, just dragons and griffins...it's meant to be a broader umbrella than that.

Finally we settled on this idea of the legend of the Yeti. Now there were several things working in our favor. We had a piece of land over there at the edge of Asia. We had an existing infrastructure—not all of it, but a lot of it, you know, that could get people to this spot. So that led us to Asia and to that upper corner of the park and that led us to the legend of the Yeti.

Now, when I say the legend of the Yeti, I'm talking about something kind of specific. There is...obviously there's the mystery of "Is there a real Yeti? Is there not a real Yeti?" And the Yeti is the Abominable Snowman. Same thing. Sorta like Big Foot but different in a couple of ways.

In the Himalayas there is this belief that the Yeti has this role as the protector and defender of these very remote and restricted areas of the Himalayas. And they tend to be absolutely pristine natural environments, so much so that when the environment is no longer pristine, if the trees are all cut down or something happens to it—the people tend to believe, "Well, okay, the Yeti doesn't live there anymore."

So the Yeti is connected to this idea of a pristine natural environment and connected to this idea that he protects and defends it and that played right into the classic value system, the underlying messages of Disney's Animal Kingdom.

All of this led us to the basic story of Expedition Everest, which is, "We the guests who show up—we are Expedition Everest. We just showed up today to this little village...little Tibetan village somewhere in the Himalayas...and the proprietors of this business have taken this train that used to go through the tea plantations, you know there's tea plantations all over the Himalayas, and they're re-routed it to go the forbidden mountains to get us to Everest, which is not the big peak sticking up there, it's that little pyramidical peak you see in the background."

That is the north face of Everest; which is, unfortunately, a really dull boring-looking mountain. It's the tallest mountain in the world, but that's really all it's got going for it. There are much, much prettier mountains. It's surrounded by gorgeous mountains that are much, much better looking and you wish they were the tall one, but they're not.

So anyway, in our story, we wanna get there, right? But our method of getting there is to take this train and to take it through these forbidden mountains and all the local people are saying, "You know, that's a really bad idea. If you go through the forbidden mountains, you're gonna awaken the wrath of the Yeti. You're not supposed to go in there, (it's) a forbidden area full of wildlife and forests and stuff that aren't meant to be touched."

And, of course, there would be no story if we didn't disobey. And, of course, the classic structure of any myth is like that, right? That's how you set the myth in motion is by going into the woods or going into the cave or going across the river. That's what sets the story in motion and then the rest of the story is resolving all the conflicts that result from making the choice to break open the seal or whatever thing you do. So that's just classic story structure analysis.

So we *do* it, right? We take the journey and we go through this whole thing and we go up into the mountains and it turns out the myth is real. The Yeti is real, blah, blah, blah.

We build this story very slowly. And what's happening is we are crafting all the different fragments of the myth of the Yeti as you walk through the environment approaching the ride. The first of 'em is, if you come from the Asian village and you look straight down towards the mountain, there's this little shrine with this little bronze Yeti sitting in it.

And the shrine is exactly in the shape of the mountain so you can kinda line it up and take this photograph of the mountain and the shrine right in front like a little statement that, you know, the Yeti is the king of the mountain. Here's the shrine, there's the mountain; the mountain's like a shrine, the Yeti's in the mountain.

Another one of these stories is, obviously, this is a story about a place that is about to change in a really big way. Quiet little Tibetan village, you know, probably has a population of 75 people. They're ranchers. They're farmers. They have some yaks. They grow some tea. You know, their life goes around in a circle every year and all of a sudden, these guys have come and built this massive tourist attraction thing in the middle of their village. So their lives are all gonna change. So everybody is like, "I hate this, I wanna go back to the way it was," or, "I'm gonna make a buck."

So here we have the Yeti Palace Hotel, which is forever "Opening next season." And there are a million buildings that look just like this all over India, all over Nepal, all over Southeast Asia. Made out of concrete...couple of floors high...brick infill... this thing is always under construction, the bricks all say "India" on 'em; just, you know, 'cause we found these bricks that say "India," in India.

So even the equipment—the construction equipment—is all like stuff that we bought overseas and stuck in there to get across the point, "This is happening right now." This thing is in the process of happening; it's changing.

And it's right next to this gorgeous old building, right? Beautifully, beautiful quaint little traditional building and then there is this God-awful cement thing with the brick and the rebar and the piles of cement and construction equipment. To me, it is just so Animal Kingdom.

And it's The Yeti Palace Hotel, so it is the most frivolous business exploitation evocation of the Yeti you could imagine within the context of this story. Every backpacker from here to California will be staying at my little Yeti Palace Hotel.

We arrive in our real village, the village of Serka Zong. Serka Zong is a Tibetan word and it's meant to be the name of this little village that's out somehow far away, even though you only walk 600 feet you're supposed to have walked like, you know…60 miles or something to get to Serka Zong, which is a Tibetan village in the foothills.

And Serka Zong refers to the fortress, and the chasm, and all of that stuff. So Serka Zong is a village in the Kingdom of Anandapur, far away from the imaginary town of Anandapur, which is also in that same kingdom. None of which exists in the real world. But it basically occupies the same space as Bangladesh and parts of India.

It's a little more traditional but it's undergoing this transformation. The big red building at one end represents what's called a "gompa" which is like a monastery or a chapel. Most of the buildings are meant to be taken to be made of rammed earth. It's a very typical Tibetan way of building. It works anywhere where the rainfall is moderate to low.

They build this big wooden thing like a bathtub. It's about the size of a hope chest or a big bathtub and it's made out of wood. It has no bottom. And they build a stone foundation about this high off the ground. Just enough so water can't get up from the ground—the water table in the ground—through the rock to the earth.

And then they set this big box down and they take earth that's about the consistency that you would make a mud ball out of that would hold together, like when you used to make little hamburger patties out of mud when you were a kids. Like that.

And they fill it up with this mud and they take these giant mallets that are like 30-gallon size mallets and they pound this earth with this mallet inside this container until it basically acquires the consistency of, like, adobe or bad sidewalk concrete.

It's amazingly tough and if they plaster it, it'll last a thousand years. I mean, there are buildings that are a thousand years old and older than that made of dirt all over the Himalayas.

We chose it because it happens to be authentic. It happens to be Tibetan. But it also happens to make the "village" part of the land, right? So the village feels like it is consistent with the land, with the mountain, with the environment 'cause this village is part of the natural system that's being intruded on by this other thing.

So we deliberately chose this style of architecture not just because it's visually authentic, but because it pushes our story forward another step by being earthy, basically. And then you might have read, somewhere in all the various conversations about the park, about the sort of ritual uses of color on the buildings. If you go look at the village, there's all these different colors painted on the building and all that color is symbolic.

Now, once again, we went to the Himalayas. We went all over the Himalayas. Did research all over the place, but we chose a very specific style of architecture to evoke because of the use of color symbolically like this.

'Cause when you look at these buildings, it's obvious that something is going on that is more than just the functional use of the building and that it's something you don't necessarily understand. And all of that is part of building a mood and building a story in the village that is consistent with what we're trying to move forward in the story of Expedition Everest.

So we've got this red color, which is often used as a kind of a defense against you know, scary things. You'll see it around doorways. You'll see it around windows.

There's these stripes that you'll see painted on some of the buildings. These black, white and red or black, white and yellow that represent—the black represents kind of the underworld spirits, and the white represents kind of heavenly spirits, and the red represents things that are with flesh and blood; things of this Earth.

It's not blood, but it represents the idea of living things. The Yeti is considered to be a living thing, so you see a lot of red. We put our little totems out. All kinds of clues as to how these people think.

And then, of course, there's the Yeti mandir (Hindu temple), which doesn't look like anything else—hopefully that makes people look at it—and then the whole mandir, and I don't know if you guys know, if you've read any about this, but this is really kind of cool.

We have done work before at Animal Kingdom with various partners that we have in Nepal who do architecture, wood carving, stonework, bronze work. But this time we gave them a huge assignment. They basically did the design of most of the wooden elements you see at Expedition Everest.

In particular this structure, this mandir structure, which is about 35-feet tall and almost the entire exterior—the bronze work, the carved woodwork, everything you see—came from Nepal; was designed and built in Nepal for us by these traditional woodcraft guys.

I'm sure their hearts would be broken to see how we distressed and aged it with, like, jackhammers and, you know, sandblasters to make look old but it was designed and it was deliberately designed to incorporate all these images of the legend of the Yeti.

So, the Yeti as a fierce protector of the mountain. The Yeti as the destroyer of yaks. If you look at the thing, it's Yeti, Yeti, Yeti, Yeti, Yeti. Everywhere you look there's carvings of Yeti, so it is the Yeti mandir.

And then, within it, is the little inset kind of shrine area and that has a bronze of the Yeti. Once again, this belief in the Yeti, this idea that the Yeti is the defender and protector of the mountain definitely exists. There's not a lot of actual visual design to go along with that concept and that has to do with really complicated kind of Tibetan...the way they think of things, in the sense that they believe in the Yeti as a real creature—he lives out there in the forest, he comes down, he eats my yak, he's a real animal— but sometimes he's also the divine protector of the mountain.

But we said, "No one will understand that." So we need to create images of the Yeti as the protector of the mountain, but use the real Yeti—use the "Yeti" Yeti. And once that they got that this was like a translation—that they needed to do this translation in visuals for us—then everybody was, "We'll do that."

So they created this bronze for us of the physical Yeti, and he's in the traditional pose of any protector spirit with his one hand up holding this mountain in his hand and the other hand is out saying, "Stay out!" And he's got his little bent leg posture and he's got his little skeleton helper guys who—the whole meaning of a skeleton in Tibetan art is different than in our art form. It sort of represents the human spirit liberated from the limitations of the human body.

But these are the guardian protectors of the Yeti and he's on his mountain, and he's protecting the mountain and he's got his hand out. And then, of course, it's filled with all these little offerings to the Yeti, 'cause "We've gotta put out little things in there or the Yeti's gonna go wild and tear apart the village."

And then we did all this work to age down the wood around the opening to make it look like people have been doing this for, I don't know, a hundred years... maybe five hundred years.

So, anyway, all of this building up a mood and a tone—a certain tone—and that's the mythic, mystical tone of the legend of the Yeti. The other place is The Yeti Museum. The Yeti Museum, basically, is another way of telling the story.

This is like a very logical way of telling the story where you go through the museum and if you didn't pick up on any of that, now we have this very logical presentation. "This is the Himalayas...these different kinds of people live in the Himalayas...some of 'em live like this...some of 'em live like that...they live all over the place...they all have this legend of the Yeti...here's what all that stuff looks like.

"And then all these Western people came to the Himalayas and they looked, too, and they saw stuff that they thought looked like the Yeti and it looks like this. And incidentally..." And then there's the made-up stuff like the lost expedition. "The Yeti's big. He must be big. Look, here's some photographs of the Yeti. You might see this if you keep going."

Then there's a whole thing about, incidentally, the Himalayas really are a place with real bio-diversity—tremendous bio-diversity—where new animals are discovered every year. We just discovered some, for real. So it's a place where plausibly there could be a Yeti and just because there's really an animal doesn't always mean you see it.

Here's how we find animals we don't always see, including things like footprints. Here's a giant footprint. You know, on and on and on and on and on until you get to, you know, "The Yeti is real. You should beware. Blah, blah, blah."

And, of course, then there's the room where the proprietors of Himalayan Escapes—which I find to be a humorous name for a travel company where you end up escaping from the Yeti— basically disavow all that. And then you go into their prep room which is all about the Sherpas and how the Sherpas are gonna help you with everything you do.

Just to be clear, one of the things we do try to do—just one little slight public service for these Sherpa people of the world—is to make sure that we make it clear to people who ride Expedition Everest that Sherpa is an ethnic type, not a job.

You cannot hire yourself out to be a Sherpa; you are a Sherpa. Then you hire yourself out to do a job. And a lot of people use the word Sherpa as if it meant, "Guy who carries heavy stuff."

If you are one of those who use Fastpass and miss all that story-telling and just get on the train, totally oblivious to all that other storytelling, you start your journey and you're riding through, you know, the foothills of the Himalayas and you come along and there's this big fortress—this ruined Tibetan fortress—guarding the approach to the mountain. And inside the fortress, yet again—reiterated for the last time—is the image of the Yeti, protector of the mountain and the eerie ceremonial music.

So there you go up under the mural of the Yeti, defender of the mountain. You go on a bridge—kind of classic mythic thing—you cross a gap that separates two worlds: A man-made world, right? Wood fortress, architecture, paintings and places where—so far—everything we've encountered about the Yeti has been human-made.

Statues...paintings...photographs...rumors...human-controlled evidence of the Yeti. Now we're gonna cross this magical boundary into another world: A world of nature...a world of the mountain...we're going to the Forbidden Mountain, it couldn't be more obvious...and now everything changes 'cause, from here out, all we see is evidence that the Yeti is real and that has been made by the Yeti.

From the first moment that we see that evidence, there's also a change in the flow of the ride, right? So you're riding along and you're riding at a certain kind of speed that's not very fast. And when you come to the broken track scene, where you see the footprints, where you see the damaged track, where you see that the Yeti is real...the little line snaps, right?

The snapped connection between the controlled human world where everything happens where it's supposed to and the crazed world of mythology starts there.

That's why from *there* it turns into the scary-fast-thrilling ride. Finally you see the Yeti, guardian of the mountain, as real as we could make him be, and it is sort of both a revelation that the

Yeti is real—that's kind of a reward and it is kind of the end of your whatever you want to call it, your mythic adventure that's returning you back to the world of humanity—and you're back to humanity almost like it was a dream right? Like it almost didn't happen, just like a fairy tale.

You know, we made twenty-four clay models of the mountain by hand before we got to the one that we did digitally.

The other challenge that we set before us was making the Yeti real; making a Yeti that could both seem real and be this other Yeti—the guardian of the mountain Yeti. So we did, in fact, blend both of those ideas into making our Yeti.

Most people in the Himalayas believe the Yeti is real. It is not like Big Foot. It is not something that like six rednecks in a bar think is real and everybody else thinks they're crazy. That is not the Yeti. When you go to the Himalayas, it's really hard to find people who don't think the Yeti is either real right now or was real a few years ago. The Yeti is real to these people.

We wanted try to make our Yeti as real as possible and one of the things we did was talk to real Sherpas about the Yeti. "What do you think it looks like? How does it move? How big is it? What do we know? What do we know that people have ever said about the Yeti?"

So we got all these interviews from people; we got all these stories; we had that aspect of the Yeti. And then we also did a bunch of scientific research, going, "Alright, alright. If there really was a Yeti, what might this Yeti really look like and how could we make a Yeti that would incorporate the descriptions but also incorporate the logic of a real animal that could really live there?"

And one of the animals that we looked at is this, 'cause it's obviously one of the creepiest animals in the world is a Szechuan golden snub-nosed monkey. They're very, very rare. They used to not be rare at all, they used to be all over the place; but now, of course thanks to us, they're rare.

And they, obviously, they live in a very cold area; an area where it snows in the winter. And unlike many animals, they don't migrate down the mountain to a warm place. They stay in the snow all winter and they've adapted to this cold weather environment.

So we basically took this monkey—the idea of this monkey— and we make it bigger and bigger and bigger and bigger and we took some ape-like characteristics and we blended them together to get our Yeti. So if you look at our Yeti and think of this monkey you'll see all kinds of interesting parallels between our Yeti and this monkey, which we just sort of blended together to get something that you could believe would be real.

The Yeti doesn't live on the mountain. He lives in the jungle. He goes up into the mountain. We made our Yeti's fur exactly the same color and texture as these incredibly dense festoons of Spanish moss that hang in all these Himalayan forests. So if our Yeti was in that forest, standing still, he would be invisible.

There are areas in the Himalayas that are protected realms that are protected in part because of their belief that this is an area where the Yeti lives, and he is the protector and defender of it so we don't go there and we don't mess with it. We don't cut down trees. We don't hunt animals. We don't grow crops. We don't build buildings. The only thing in this environment is a little monastery somewhere. And they think of these environments like a big mandala—like a big sacred shape.

And so we put together this big expedition with Discovery Channel, with Conservation International to go precisely to these areas in Nepal and in Szechuan, the western half of Szechuan. The big half of it is almost all Tibetan cultural area.

It looks like you're in the movie *King Kong* when you're in these forests. It's so thick you can't move. It's utterly uninhabited except for that little monastery and this little cluster of farms that support the food for the monks.

I went to Tengboche Monastery, which is right next to Mount Everest. Beautiful little setting, you know, all alone in the middle of the mountains. Spoke to the Lama about the whole legend behind the skull cap and all that stuff. And then I also went to this other monastery, and this was the place where the whole story kinda came together for us.

In this Tibetan area of Szechuan, China is this teeny monastery. It is like a hundred-and-fifty feet on a side, not even an acre footprint to this monastery. It's been there for a thousand years. The site has been a sacred site for two-thousand, five-hundred years.

The monks of this monastery totally believe that it sits in the realm of the Yeti. They claim that from this point they look out across this meadow, they see the Yeti every monsoon season at the other edge of the meadow...the Yeti lives in this forest...he protects this entire forest and therefore protects this monastery. Therefore, the monastery has a reciprocal duty to protect the forest in which the Yeti lives, which they indeed do. The Yeti is the defender of this environment and that they, therefore, are defenders of the Yeti.

Here's exactly what I think: There's too much evidence for some kind of real creature for there to be no real creature behind the legend of the Yeti. I think it is something real, somewhere in the background, that has migrated and mutated into a series of legends, some of which are very obviously fairy tale legends. I wanna stress that what we have done is a story. And it is constructed like a story.

As Imagineers, we were very privileged to have that experience ourselves and we did try our best to incorporate some sense of the feeling of all that into what we built at Expedition Everest.

The Pandora Jungle

Based on Oscar-winning filmmaker James Cameron's record-breaking box-office hit movie, *Avatar* (2009), Pandora opened in May 2017 at Disney's Animal Kingdom in the area formerly occupied by Camp Minnie-Mickey. It is a much different jungle than one on Earth although there are some similarities.

For the movie, filmmaker James Cameron envisioned a moon called Pandora about 4.37 light years from Earth in the Alpha Centauri system orbiting the gas giant Polyphemus, with an atmosphere on the moon un-breathable for humans without assistance from Exo-packs.

Earth personnel in the presence of the Resources Development Administration (RDA), a quasi-governmental company, travel to this distant place in the 22nd century primarily to mine a rare mineral whose superconductive properties allow it to float in magnetic fields.

In addition, scientists studying the indigenous humanoid species called the Na'vi and the unusual fauna and flora also accompany the private security contractors employed by RDA.

Cameron meant to draw parallels between the lush, tropical forests of this science-fiction inspired moon and the supposed devastation of the ecology on the current Earth where humans have turned their planet into a global urban slum where little remains of a functioning natural ecosystem.

He also wanted to make connections between the Na'vi's spiritual relationship and responsibility to their world which have allowed it to flourish.

The new land at DAK welcomes guests to this lush world of the habitable moon in the Alpha Centauri system, set generations after the human conflict with the native Na'vi inhabitants of the movie has ended, and peace prevails. According to Imagineer Joe Rohde, the premise for the new land is that *Avatar* was not a movie, but rather a documentary.

Alpha Centauri Expeditions (ACE) now allows eco-tourists to enjoy some of the legendary delights of the planet, including enormous floating mountains where waterfalls cascade down the mountainsides into meandering streams and pools, a bioluminescent forest with exotic plants that illuminate with a dreamlike quality in the evening, winged mountain banshees and more.

In partnership with ACE, visitors have the opportunity to explore the values and culture of this exotic place, and celebrate the striking beauty and overwhelming power of the natural world.

A Na'vi-built drum circle, Na'vi totems, and other cultural items are scattered through the area. Tour guides from Alpha Centauri Expeditions, scientists from the Pandora Conservation Initiative (PCI), and even an occasional eclectic expatriate interact with visitors and help them understand what they are encountering.

Pongu Pongu (meaning "Party Party" in the language of the Na'vi) is the center of the expat community, and offers various liquid libations and some snacks. It is located near the shop Windtraders where visitors can purchase Na'vi cultural items, toys, science kits and more.

The quick service dining venue Satu'li Canteen (pronounced "Sa-too-lee"), a Quonset-hut-style building, was once the main mess hall of the Resources Development Administration base (the main antagonist in the film).

Now the canteen is owned and operated by the Alpha Centauri Expeditions tour company and has been redesigned into a beautiful museum-like dining room for visitors. The interior has been transformed with colorful Na'vi items filling the walls and hanging from the ceiling — hand-woven tapestries, natural Pandoran elements and even cooking tools decorate the restaurant.

Producer and director Cameron stated, "I think I knew (the theme park version) was going to be a pretty amazing world but I was still thinking 'movie'. You can walk around and smell the world, touch the world. I wander around with a sense of wonder myself. I had an amazing time working with the Imagineering artists as they conjured all of this.

"This has been a transformative adventure for me. It's certainly transformed my perception of what is possible in the real world. If you had asked me ahead of time, I would have said this is not possible. What they have created here is not possible."

Imagineer Joe Rohde told the media, "We are taking our guests on a journey to this world in an experience that's as realistic and immersive as possible. In the movie, the world of Pandora is a setting for the action and characters whose story we follow. Here, guests are the primary characters immersed in an extremely vivid, authentic experience.

"We've been welcomed into the culture because of our motives. We're here to learn. We're here to educate ourselves. We're here to become better stewards of our planet. The world in which the Na'vi live is in order because they care about it. They care for it. It is not enough to care about the world. You have to care for it. You have to do things. Take action."

Avatar Flight of Passage is a simulator attraction that allows guests to climb atop a mountain banshee for a breathtaking, multi-sensory flight over the moon's incredible landscape. The experience mimics the memorable rite of passage bonding scene in the original film. The journey includes a face-off with the most feared predator of Pandora, the Great Leonopteryx.

Na'vi River Journey allows guests to sail serenely down the Kaspavan River in a reed boat gently winding through a bioluminescent rainforest in the Valley of Mo'ara on the planet of Pandora.

The Na'vi, the indigenous people of the planet, are seen throughout the ride in scenes where they are hunting and gathering. Native wildlife can be seen on the nearby banks including the dangerous viper wolves and gentle woodsprites as well as mysterious glowing fauna.

All of the activity seems to be heading in the same direction and the lazy river journey culminates in the appearance of the Na'vi Shaman of Songs, who is radiating positive energy into the forest. The rough translation of her song basically thanks the Great Mother for the many gifts that allow the Na'vi to live well in the forest.

All of the other creatures have actually been presented as realistic projections on layers of screens that are positioned inside the magnificent scenery. The Na'vi Shaman of Songs is the most complicated audio-animatronics figure ever created by Walt Disney Imagineering.

"The shaman is even more extraordinary than we expected," said Rohde. "Her facial expressions, little movements in the cheek, tiny movements in the eyelid—each one of these carries an emotion she's capable of conveying."

According to Executive Creative Director Stefan Hellwig, "the queue begins on a path that winds its way around various textiles created by the Na'vi as well as their totems of the magical Shaman of Songs. The pieces are intricate works of art and give you a taste of the fascinating people you are about to see.

"Above the queue is another intricate hand-woven piece that actually serves as a map of the river that winds through Pandora. The blue ropes represent the river, and the other areas represent the rest of the bioluminescent forest. At night, this piece takes on new life as it is illuminated with light that moves, showing where various life forms are as they journey down the river."

Rohde added, "Na'vi River Journey is a very sweet, lyrical adventure through a spectacular visual environment that just becomes more and more spectacular as you go on. The bioluminescent activity of the plants around you unfolds in richer and richer scenes in really just a very uplifting, wonderful kind of journey.

"It is a ceremonial forest. We're bringing to life everything from the largest creature you might encounter to the most microscopic. Animals will appear out of the underbrush—big Pandoran animals will appear at the edge of the forest and you'll hear the very complicated calls they issue back and forth."

In the Animal Kingdom's version of Pandora, the Na'vi people make appearances only in the two attractions and in artwork throughout the area. Disney claims this is to have guests see the area from the Na'vi point of view as well as the more probable reason of the difficulty in creating realistic costumes for the unique creatures.

The Na'vi people, according to Disney, "possess humanlike consciousness and intelligence. The average Na'vi is three meters tall with cyan-colored skin and bioluminescent markings. They have large almond-shaped eyes, long torsos and a prehensile tail."

Cameron utilized a team of expert advisors in order to make the various examples of fauna and flora in the Pandoran jungle as scientifically feasible as possible. The Pandoran ecology is inter-connected from the floating mountain ranges to winged banshee predators.

For a 2010 interview in the *Los Angeles Times*, Jodie Holt, chairwoman of the department of botany and plant sciences at UC Riverside talked about her contributions to the plant life on Pandora.

All of her degrees were in botany and she taught general botany for twelve years, challenging her students to analyze plant morphology and anatomy to how plants adapt to the environment.

Holt said, "After being briefed on the plot and being shown early images of the plants on Pandora by (film producer) Jon Landau, I met with Sigourney Weaver [who plays botanist Grace Augustine in the film] and set designers to talk about how a field botanist would study and sample plants to learn about their physiology and biochemistry.

"We also talked about the idea of communication among plants, and between plants and the Na'vi, and how that might be explained. Subsequently, I worked with a set designer to ensure that his designs for the field and lab equipment were credible.

"Since life on Pandora was intended to adhere to our known laws of physics and biology, it was not credible to me to suggest that the plants had any kind of nervous system. Instead, I suggested that communication among the plants could credibly be explained by signal transduction, an area of research that deals with how plants perceive a signal and respond to it.

"Jon Landau called to ask if I would be interested in writing descriptions of the plants, including fabricating Latin names, to be included in the games and book that were planned

"For plants that resembled Earth plants, I gave them similar names, such as *Pseudocycas altissima* for a plant that looks like a tall Earth cycad. Others I named for their appearance, such as *Obesus rotundus* for the puffball tree.

"The movie is only about 150 years into the future, which is not a lot of time for major evolutionary advances. The real question I dealt with was how the environment on Pandora (eg. atmosphere, gravity, soil) would have selected the many unusual, bizarre plants found there, as well as some that look very much like plants currently found on Earth.

"For example, the atmosphere is thicker than on Earth, with higher concentrations of carbon dioxide, as well as xenon and hydrogen sulfide. Gravity is weaker. And there is a strong magnetic field.

"Given the role of the environment in plant evolution, one would therefore expect to see gigantism, less of a gravity response (which makes stems grow up and roots grow down), and possibly a response to magnetic fields, which I named 'magnetotropism'."

Throughout the DAK area are examples of some of Pandoran plants from that research.

Disney published a flyer explaining what they were for guests to identify when the area first opened: "The diversity of Pandoran plant life and its range of size and complexity suggest that the environment of Pandora acts as a strong force for natural selection. The environmental factors that plants experience on Earth—radiation, water, atmospheric gases and gravity—are present on Pandora, although their characteristics differ profoundly."

The plants that Disney identified were:

- Spiny Whip: The cup-shaped top of this plant collects raindrops and many species of birds use the plant as a source of water.

- Panopyra: This plant captures water and minerals from dew and fog. The Na'vi collect the liquid and use it as a healing drink.

- Vein Pod: The pods produced by these trees help to detoxify the atmosphere on Pandora, maintaining stability in the environment.

- Flaska Reclinata: This plant absorbs, condenses and purifies atmospheric toxins on Pandora.

- Dapophet: The leaves at the top of this plant have healing properties used by the Na'vi, while the leaves along the stem store water and are used as portable hydration.

- Puffball Tree: This tree is an important plant on Pandora for purifying the atmosphere. The Na'vi also harvest its leaves for salt.

- Grinch Tree: This tree grows in a hunched shape with a twisted trunk and bluish bioluminescent leaves.

To maneuver through the thick jungle and toxic atmosphere, Disney added a demonstration of the Pandora Utility Suit. This human powered suit helps demonstrate how technology is being used to restore the ecosystem on Pandora. The Pandora Utility Suit is inspired by the iconic Amplified Mobility Platform (AMP) suits of power armor from the original film.

The first military exoskeletons in the mid-21st century evolved into the Mitsubishi MK-6 Amplified Mobility Platform (or "AMP" suit) that could be used in different environments from arctic to jungle to desert. The human-operated multi-purpose mechanism amplifies strength and mobility while providing protection in toxic environments. It was designed to mimic the form of a human with two legs, two arms and dexterous hands.

In the original film, the suits were used primarily to defend the base and for patrol duties, but also appeared in the battle at the Tree of Souls scene and Colonel Quaritch's final attack on Jake Sully.

The Pandora Utility Suit is the next evolution of the AMP suit, and was created to assist in the restoration of the environment. It has a streamlined design with no protective cockpit, unlike the AMP suit.

Its sleek structure and technical upgrades make it the perfect tool to collect plant samples, study flora and survive Pandora's wild terrain. It protects its operator from Pandoran hazards while doing ecological research for the Resources Development Administration and its Pandora Conservation Initiative.

Perched ten feet high, a human pilot straps into the cockpit of this exo-carrier and controls its powerful, yet agile movements. The giant walking suit was designed with articulated hands and a shoulder span of more than five feet. It also bears claw marks and battle scars from a Thanator—an alpha predator on Pandora that apparently attacked it.

As the suit traverses the land daily, its pilot interacts with guests, sharing details about the land's otherworldly landscape, and highlighting the importance of preserving nature.

The Pandora Utility Suit is a collaboration between Disney Parks Live Entertainment, Michael Curry Design Inc. (that previously supplied the 120 towering puppets for Epcot's Tapestry of Nations parade, and the puppets for DAK's *Finding Nemo—The Musical*), WDI and Lightstorm Entertainment (*Avatar* director James Cameron's film production company).

The suit made its official debut on April 22, 2018, the anniversary of the opening Disney's Animal Kingdom, and appears twice daily, usually in the area outside Satu'li Canteen.

Show Producer for Disney Parks Entertainment Tony Giordano stated: "We knew when the land would be opening there would be some great opportunities for entertainment. Lightstorm suggested a suit that would fix the environment rather than the one in the film that destroyed the environment.

"They drew this amazing drawing of a scientist picking a piece of fruit out of the tree. Our partners at WDI looked at that drawing and made it into a reality. And then the Michael Curry Designs actually built the suit. The final product is a great partnership between those three groups."

One of the things that makes a Disney theme park experience so memorable and so different from other entertainment venues is the elaborate, detailed back stories that helps immerse guests into a new world. It is these back stories that are used as a reference to keep everything consistent and with a sense of realistic fantasy.

Pandora is yet another example of how Imagineers can transform a small section of the familiar topography of central Florida into a jungle that is quite literally out of this world.

The Walt Disney Company sometimes in official publications have spelled Adventurers Club with an apostrophe between the "r" and "s" and other times with an apostrophe after the "s". I feel that this inconsistency is perhaps in keeping with the maverick spirit of the club.

The Adventurers Club was truly a once-in-a-lifetime experience with a dysfunctional family of charming and clever personalities who welcomed you as part of the family in an atmosphere that only ever existed in the imagination.

That is why so many of us want to continue singing songs like "Adventure Keeps Calling My Name":

> Home, I'm home; it's great to be here
> But adventure keeps calling my name
> I'd like to stay for about a year
> But adventure keeps calling my name
> It just keeps calling my name

PART TWO: The Complete Adventurers Club Guidebook

The Mythology and Reality of the Adventurers Club

"Do not cry the Club is gone. Smile that it ever existed."

The sign posted outside the Adventurer's Club:

> *Welcome to Adventurers Club*
> *You who crave danger and snicker at fear*
> *Will find most agreeable company here*
> *Thrill seekers, nomads, high-flyers and low*
> *Rovers, explorers and getters of go*
> *From every far corner, you'll meet at this hub*
> *The world is your oyster, the pearl is our club!*
> *Tonight!*

The Adventurers Club officially opened in Pleasure Island on May 1, 1989 along with the rest of the entertainment complex. The Adventurers Club officially closed September 27, 2008.

Some of the following information appeared in two different self-published, limited edition pamphlets of less than fifty copies each that I produced in 2008 and 2010 for fans of the Adventurers Club. Some of that material and the format of the presentation of the information from those pamphlets has been "borrowed" by others without citation during the last decade. Some of my rough draft articles under my pseudonym of Wade Sampson were published by MousePlanet.

Information was obtained from exclusive interviews with performers, staff, and Imagineers. In addition, material was personally reviewed by me at the Walt Disney World Entertainment Library several times at the Main Gate complex. That library was closed in 2009 and was later dismantled. Some material was dispersed to other Disney libraries but in general, sketches, notes, photos, scripts, videos, file folders and more of no longer active shows were purged to save money on storage and insurance.

NO APOSTROPHE. While I did discover some early Disney documentation with the apostrophe in the name Adventurers Club, the official nomenclature for Adventurers Club verified by the Walt Disney Company has no apostrophe. However, Disney is notorious for being inconsistent.

The Pleasure Island Story (1986-2010)

At a press conference July 21,1986 on the Empress Lilly, CEO Michael Eisner announced to the world that a new concept in Disney nighttime entertainment would be opening on the parcel of land at the west end of the Disney Village Marketplace. It would be an entire island of themed nightclubs and stores called Pleasure Island.

Eisner told the media that he had decided that it was pretty quiet on Disney property after dark except for the fireworks at the Magic Kingdom and Epcot. So he had decided there was needed an after-dark entertainment location for guests, Orlando residents and conventions.

Disney's Pleasure Island was the solution with construction to begin in August. It would be a six-acre island opening Spring 1988 and would be "a place to go when the sun goes down… in a nice Disney way" according to Eisner.

Attending the press conference with a miniature model of the Pleasure Island layout was Madame Zenobia (portrayed by actress Anita Goodwin), who Eisner said would be the hostess of the Adventurers Club and "who will read your palm and tell your future and consult with our studio execs about what pictures we will make."

Also there in full beard, pipe and a brimmed sailor cap looking a bit like Popeye's scruffy father was Captain Spike (portrayed by Craig McNair Wilson who had directed improvisational shows for Epcot's World Showcase) who would run the waterfront club, Madison's Dive, and tell salty stories about his love of a mermaid inspired by Madison the mermaid from the Disney hit film *Splash* (1984), a particular favorite movie of Eisner's.

The Disney "nightclub district" got its own team: Rick Rothschild (show producer), Chris Carradine (architect), Joe Rohde (art director), John Kavelin (designer), Craig McNair Wilson (writer and director of improvisation) and then later many others joined the team including Tony Anselmo (designed and directed the interior effort for Mannequins), Tom Sherohman (the original director at the Comedy Warehouse) and Roger Cox, (director and writer for Adventurers Club).

However, this was not to be the infamous Pleasure Island of the Disney animated classic, *Pinocchio* (1940), where naughty little boys drank beer, smoked cigars, shot pool and turned into jackasses. Walt Disney Imagineering created an extensive and convoluted storyline to explain the history of the shopping and dining district.

Chris Carradine whose official title was Vice President of Design Development for Concept and Design at Walt Disney Imagineering stated, "Disneyland and the Magic Kingdom at Walt Disney World have classic stories of the frontier and pirates and the storybook legends, which are retold in a new way—but these stories are familiar to everyone. Pleasure Island also has stories to tell but they're stories that haven't been told before.

"When you go to Pleasure Island, you have to find out the stories while you're there, and that's the adventure. It's a night-time adventure, a sort of urban *Stand by Me* (1986), where a group of kids can get together and explore the place.

"Sometimes people may go to Pleasure Island and won't be able to solve all the mysteries about it. The buildings have clues to tell you about the mysteries, but some of them will be obvious and some won't. It's almost like a scavenger hunt, but instead of treasure you'll be collecting bits and pieces of a mystery story, like someone in a detective novel.

"When you visit Pleasure Island, you won't know if you're one of the characters yourself — because you might become part of the story. You become part of the mystery."

According to the Walt Disney Imagineering back story, in 1911, a Mississippi side-wheeler steamed into Lake Buena Vista and dropped anchor. The captain of the vessel, an adventurous Pittsburgh entrepreneur, Merriweather Adam Pleasure, saw that on this island he could create a one-man dominion like Thomas Edison's Menlo Park or William Randolph Hearst's San Simeon.

Pleasure was an inventor, industrialist and bon vivant. He envisioned a manufacturing center, research lab and development facility, as well as a social gathering spot for the famous and well-to-do.

His motto was "Fun for all, and all for fun!" Pleasure was known to all as "The Grand Funmeister" after being called that name by the U.S. Secretary of Agriculture in 1927. (A "Grand Funmeister" icon of a yellow half moon face with an open smiling mouth decorated Pleasure Island in its earliest days.)

The boat was to serve as home, guest house and entertainment center while construction began on the island. Living on the boat with his Italian wife, Isabella; his sons, Stewart and Henry; and his daughter, Merriam, Pleasure built his island empire and founded a canvas manufacturing and sail fabricating industry.

The Florida climate favored his business, and though the merchant sailing industry was in its twilight, pleasure yachting and the need for canvas for tents during World War I assured his immediate success. The business was known as Pleasure Canvas and Sailmaking LTD. The first buildings went up in 1912.

The Pleasure family soon outgrew their showboat home. In 1918, they moved to a Bermuda-style mansion overlooking Lake Buena Vista. The Pleasure Family Home (which in 1989 became Portobello Yacht Club, serving Italian food because Isabella was Italian) was designed so that Isabella Pleasure could host hundreds of tea socials, garden parties and croquet tournaments, featuring fine food and uninhibited conversation. As Mrs. Pleasure often said, "If you don't have something nice to say about someone come sit next to me!"

"Lilly Plaza," the area directly in front of the docked paddle wheeler, was officially christened in 1922. Originally a turn-around for the limousines of guests visiting the Pleasure family houseboat, the plaza was remodeled for the July 4, 1937 debut of the 118 member Pleasure Island Philharmonic Concert Band (PIPCB) conducted by Maestro Don G. O'Vanni. The PIPCB concerts on this site always ended with a piece Mrs. Pleasure commissioned, the haunting "Fugue for Triangle, Piccolo and Steam-powered Riverboat Whistle."

Aware of the Westering circumnavigations of Irving Johnson and the youthful crews of his Yankee Clipper, Merriweather Pleasure commissioned the yacht *Dominoe* (named for his then-favorite pastime and yes, this was the official spelling with the additional "e" on the early Imagineering documents) in 1929, which brilliantly foresaw the awesome J-boat formula.

With his eighteen year old daughter, Merriam, Pleasure embarked on a series of eastward 'round-the-world voyages. He turned the business over to his two sons: "Awkward Stewart" Pleasure who pursued the sporting life and Henry who was known as "The Mad Genius of Lake Buena Vista" and who succeeded in creating a Cellular Automaton (sort of an early version of an artificial intelligence robot that was later discovered still functioning by the Imagineers).

Merriweather and his daughter returned from their many expeditions with a vast treasure from their journeys filled with adventure and discovery. The souvenirs eventually overwhelmed Pleasure's comfortable Bermuda-style house and Mrs. Pleasure threatened to eject her husband from the house unless he found a place for the books and artifacts collected on these trips.

An imposing building on the opposite side of the island was designed to house Pleasure's huge personal library and archeological trophy collection. Pleasure reportedly won the plans for the building in a game of dominoes. A domino design was still evident on the outside of the building.

The building became the headquarters for the Adventurers Club five years later in 1932. The Adventurers were Pleasure's zany band of globe-trotting friends, yachting cronies and hangers-on who all swapped tall tales. Exotic trophies of the members' outlandish expeditions and riotous adventures were displayed on the walls.

It was also in 1932 that Merriweather Pleasure created the "Adventurer's Creed" which was framed in the Zebra Mezzanine: "We climb the highest mountains, just to get a better view. We plumb the deepest oceans 'cuz we're daring, through and through. We cross the scorching desert, martinis in our hand. We ski the polar ice cap in tuxedo, looking grand. We're reckless, brave and loyal and valiant to the end. If you come in here a stranger, you'll exit as a friend."

The Pleasure Perfect Upholstery shop (which became in 1989, the shop Changing Attitudes selling apparel and accessories) had six full-time seamstresses working to refurbish the interiors of the custom yachts in the Pleasure Island dry dock.

In 1934 the shop was responsible for stuffing the head of a rare Mongolian Yakoose for the Adventurers Club. This profitable sideline ended in 1943 when a war-time shortage of kapok put taxidermy on the endangered species list.

Between journeys, Pleasure returned to his beloved island and devoted himself to a quest for reusable energy and the conversion of some of his factories to mysterious laboratories that included the construction of an experimental flying vehicle as well as broadcasting messages to outer space (in 1989, the home of the club XZFR Rockin' Rollerdome).

Unfortunately, the Funmeister's good fortune ran out in 1941. The *Dominoe* was presumably lost with Merriweather, Merriam, and all hands, having been reported pitch-poled in a howling summer storm while attempting a circumnavigation of Antarctica in December 1941. After Pleasure vanished at sea, the Adventurers Club was closed and sealed.

Mrs. Pleasure died in 1949 resulting in the disbanding of the Pleasure Thespian Players and the closing of the Power Station (in 1989, it became the Comedy Warehouse) where they performed elaborate Central Florida historical pageants including the seminal *Song of the Seminole*.

The canvas business continued to be successful for more than a decade until Henry's poor business decisions and Stewart's lavish lifestyle forced Pleasure Canvas and Sailmaking into bankruptcy in 1955. As a note of finality, Hurricane Connie inflicted near-total destruction two weeks before the creditors' sale leaving the island an un-saleable shambles.

This was the same hurricane that transformed Placid Palms Resort into Typhoon Lagoon. Many of the contents of the various Pleasure Island buildings were strewn across Lake Buena Vista by the winds of change and some debris ended up at Typhoon Lagoon.

The once bustling harbor community became a ghost town. But in 1987, Disney Imagineers re-discovered the island. Some buildings were renovated and some, like the Adventurers Club that had survived disaster, were reopened.

The legacy of "America's First Family of Fun" was revived and according to the fictional "Jasper W. Linedozer", the self-proclaimed semi-official Pleasure Island historian who wrote the pseudo-historical plaques on the island, "along the streets of this reawakened Island you can sometimes catch a glimpse of a portly, but strangely ethereal man, dressed in a yachting cap and natty plus-fours. Or perhaps you'll be sitting in a restaurant booth or a cozy corner of a nightclub when you hear a voice murmur quietly, 'Fun for all—and all for fun!'"

This colorful history devised by the Imagineers continues for many, many more highly detailed pages connecting every building on Pleasure Island to the legacy of Merriweather Pleasure including the AMC Theaters at the far west side.

There were two real life inspirations for Disney's Pleasure Island. Imagineer Chris Caradine was impressed with Granville Island in Vancouver, British Columbia, Canada. There, a manufacturing village that had fallen on hard times had its buildings transformed into restaurants, theaters and shops in the 1970s and became a popular destination for both the residents and tourists. Some of the colorful artistic signage there was also adapted for the Disney version.

The second inspiration was the Church Street Station area in downtown Orlando, Florida. By 1985, it had become the fourth most popular tourist attraction in the state of Florida, right behind Walt Disney World, Sea World and Busch Gardens.

Its colorfully themed clubs like Rosie O'Grady's Good Time Emporium, the Cheyenne Saloon and Opera House, Phineas Phogg's Dance Club and Lili Marlene's Aviator's Pub and Restaurant along with the Church Street Station Exchange, a three story shopping emporium featuring dozens of shops and restaurants, were a favorite nighttime spot for both locals and tourists.

"At some point, we dug out an aerial photo of WDW Shopping Village and noticed a little peninsula at the far end adjacent to the Lilly Belle restaurant and how easy it would be to make it an island," remembered Craig McNair Wilson, an Imagineering consultant who worked on the project.

Originally a peninsula, Disney dug a trench separating it from the Disney Marketplace. The trench that makes Pleasure Island an island is technically a water quality drainage feature. In most locations, Disney digs aesthetically pleasing ponds to hold water and allow sediment and heavy metals to settle out before discharging to canals and rivers.

At Pleasure Island, the theme of an island makes that pond more like a small waterway isolating the island from the mainland with three footbridges at different locations providing access for guests to the area.

"We began to riff and created the mythology and back story of Merriweather Adam Pleasure," continued Wilson. "We all improvised it and it grew and grew…at one point, the full mythology was way too long and Marty Sklar called me into his office and asked me to rewrite it in one voice and make it pithy, brief, and fun. The now famous Pleasure Island plaques were excerpted from that document: *The Final, Ultimate, Semi-Official History of Pleasure Island.*"

When the Island opened, there were twenty-six plaques placed at the entrances of the island and on the individual buildings by the Pleasure Island "Histerical" (sic) Society to explain the mythology of the island in elaborate detail.

Unfortunately, these dark black out-of-the-way plaques were difficult to find and read at night, especially after guests had too liberally enjoyed the alcoholic offerings in the clubs. As a result, neither guests nor cast members discovered the complete history of the island or fully understood the complicated connections.

The clubs that eventually opened were considerably different than the original plans. Madison's Dive was soon cancelled with some of its special effects like a sinking ship in a bottle moving to the Adventurers Club. A planned Jazz Club transformed into a Country and Western location when Eisner saw the popularity of a similar venue at Church Street Station in Downtown Orlando.

A proposed magic club very reminiscent of the famous Magic Castle club in Los Angeles was never built and again, some of its elements were incorporated into the Adventurers Club.

"We wanted a T.G.I. Fridays open twenty-four hours where the Portobello Yacht Club is today," recalled Wilson. "We presented Marty (Sklar) with a menu of fifty food, entertainment, and retail ideas for Downtown Disney and West End. There were a few Disney attractions in the mix that various teams had been playing with, including 'Do It Yourself Disney' that eventually evolved into DisneyQuest.

"The list included House of Blues, T.G.I. Fridays, a 1940s era Hollywood Canteen (dance and supper club), All That Java (coffee and jazz club), Villains (a/k/a Villains Volt, an 'underground' haunted night club themed on classic Disney Villains), and 100 Acres (from the stories of Winnie the Pooh) which would have been a nighttime day care for kids while adults shopped and dined.

"I was very excited about a twenty-four hour diner inspired by Orlando's Bubble Room, but completely decorated and stuffed with antique Disney memorabilia. From the outside it would be a classic, stainless steel American diner with flashing neon signs. Inside, you would find hearty dishes with the best Disneyana we could find, buy and borrow including authentic Disney movie props. The name would have been 'W. Elias's' as a tribute to Walter Elias Disney. It would have been located where Planet Hollywood is today."

For a variety of reasons including cost and time since the project was running over deadline and over budget, all of these proposals narrowed down to the clubs and restaurants that actually opened in 1989:

Mannequins Dance Palace (with a large rotating floor and overhead mannequins attired in a variety of theatrical costumes); Neon Armadillo Saloon (a country and western location inspired by the extremely popular Cheyenne Saloon and Opera House at Church Street Station that Eisner visited.

XZFR Rockin' Rollerdrome (a dance club with a skating rink on the upper floors); Videopolis East (a non-alcoholic club catering specifically to people younger than 21); the Fireworks Factory (a restaurant specializing in barbecue to match the "burnt" theme of a stray spark from Pleasure's cigar that had set off fireworks and blackened the interior of the building)

The Portobello Yacht Club (an authentic Northern Italian cuisine restaurant); Merriweather's Market (a food court with four distinct sections where everything was cooked to order); the Comedy Warehouse and the Adventurers Club.

In addition, there were many shops unique to the location including Avigators Supply (featuring aviation and clothing merchandise with a winged alligator who was supposed to be another mascot of the Island just as Lagoona Gator was to later become the mascot of Typhoon Lagoon)

YesterEars (selling Disneyana items); Suspended Animation (selling Disney artwork) and Jessica's of Hollywood which opened in 1990 and showcased a giant two-sided neon sign of Jessica Rabbit with sequined dress and swinging leg who sat atop the light purple colored building to entice customers inside to purchase jewelry or nightgowns that featured her logo.

When the Jessica's of Hollywood shop closed, the sign was re-positioned on a building near the West Side footbridge and became a symbol of Pleasure Island.

When Pleasure Island officially opened May 1989, it went through some changes almost immediately as the Disney Company adjusted to running a night club district for the first time.

Almost a year later, April 1990, an admission gate was placed at the front of Pleasure Island (using redesigned train cars from the closed Fort Wilderness Resort and Campground railroad as ticket booths) so that guests who wanted to visit the area after 7:00pm now had to pay roughly ten dollars for the pleasure.

To encourage guests to visit at night after their day at the Disney theme parks, from 1990 through New Year's Eve 2005, Pleasure Island celebrated New Year's Eve every night with a street party at the West End Stage at midnight with lots and lots of confetti, professional dancers and musicians, loud blaring music and all of the festivities finishing with a countdown climaxing in a fireworks show.

Over the years most of the restaurant and store venues changed radically. Pleasure Island Jazz Club took over the space of Merriweather's Market in 1993. XZFR became the Rock'N'Roll Beach Club in 1990 because of possible safety issues with the skating rink that was replaced with billiard tables and other games.

BET (Black Entertainment Television) Soundstage Club took over the Neon Armadillo location in 1998. 8TRAX (a 70s/80s music club) replaced Videopolis East in 1994. The Fireworks Factory changed to the Wildhorse Saloon (Country and Western club) in 1998 and finally Motion (dancing to Top 40 tunes) in 2001. Stores changed as well.

These severe changes from the original concept were indicative of the challenges of operating such a unique venue. In the process, the storyline of Merriweather Pleasure was slowly lost as it did not adapt easily to these new businesses and guests showed no interest or understanding of the existing Merriweather Pleasure mythology.

Major renovations to Pleasure Island were made in March 2006 in an attempt to reverse declining attendance. By this time, there was no longer an evening entry fee to Pleasure Island and as a result, the area was attracting large groups of rowdy local teens who came to just hang out and cause trouble which was considered undesirable for a Disney family location.

In late June 2008, Disney announced that the six remaining nightclubs at Pleasure Island would close by September 28, 2008, to make room for additional family-oriented entertainment.

Only two of the original clubs had remained in continuous operation for nearly nineteen years, the Comedy Warehouse and the Adventurers Club. The Comedy Warehouse (with its tiered interior decorated with authentic Disneyana memorbilia on the walls) opened with a scripted show entitled *Forbidden Disney* that poked good natured fun at Disney and the tourist experience.

However, within a year, the club transformed into a typical improvisational comedy club where the talented performers solicited suggestions from the patrons to create short humorous sketch comedy.

For the most part, the Adventurers Club continued to provide the same type of entertainment for almost two decades. It was meant to resemble a 1930s World Explorers' club decorated with many "treasures and artifacts" brought back from far off expeditions. Many of those artifacts were not as inanimate as they first appeared and often came to life throughout the evening to entertain the guests. Official club officers and members interacted with the guests the entire evening by telling stories and introducing them to the club's customs and activities.

The announced reason for having an "Open House" for new members to the exclusive club every evening was to help pay off the lease on the building "one drink at a time" at one of the three bars in the building.

A large sign outside the entrance proclaimed: "Welcome to the Adventurers Club! You who crave danger and snicker at fear will find most agreeable company here. Thrill seekers, nomads, high-flyers and low, rovers, explorers and getters of go, from every far corner, you'll meet at this hub. The world is your oyster. The pearl is our club! Tonight!"

Situated toward the top of the winding Hill Street, the odd looking building exterior was decorated with a variety of strange surprises from a crashed plane in the front lawn to monkey skulls on spears and ancient pottery cluttering the entrance.

The logo for the Adventurers Club, a globe and compass with overlapping banners, was created by Imagineer Joe Rohde as an homage to the logo of the *True Life Adventures* documentary film series made by the Walt Disney Company in the 1950s.

The active members included Hathaway Browne (daredevil aviator and ladies' man), Otis T. Wren (club treasurer and ichthyologist), Fletcher Hodges (club curator), Pamelia Perkins (club president), Samatha Sterling (explorer), Emil Blehall (from Sandusky, Ohio and contender for the Balderdash Cup), Graves (club butler) and the maid. Over the years, there were a variety of maids including Sugar Snap, Kiki McGee, Gabby Normal and Dusty Cabinets.

The club was also home to some not quite human members as well including Fingers Zambezi (the invisible spirit who played the organ in the library), Colonel Critchlow Suchbench (club glee master and chief of club security who in actuality was a large scale puppet torso nailed to a chair in a balcony on the wall), Babylonia (the great stone goddess whose talking head was nailed on the wall over the restroom entrance), the Yakoose (half moose and half yak who instead of being sent to the taxidermist was mistakenly sent to the upholstery shop), Beezle (the head of a genie who floated mysteriously in a cabinet in the Treasure Room) and Arnie and Claude (two talkative masks in the Mask Room).

The festivities each night included shows devoted to honorary member inductions, the Balderdash Cup competition, an episode of the radio cliffhanger show *Tales of the Adventurers*, and some odd activities in the Treasure Room and Mask Room. These were the primary shows that delighted guests over the years but other shows, especially for holidays or special events, also came and went.

Jim Steinmeyer, legendary designer of magical illusions and theatrical special effects who was working with Imagineering at the time, stated, "I really think that the Adventurers Club is a perfect blend of two personalities: Joe Rohde and Roger Cox.

"You see Joe's sense of visual fun and old fashioned adventure, and you experience Roger's offbeat humor and loving evocation of these old-fashioned, bigger-than-life personalities. It was a project that fell outside of the usual Disney formula, and worried everyone before it opened. Roger was very un-Disney in his thinking and Joe was always deliberately pushing the envelope."

Larry Hitchcock, who worked on the Pleasure Island project and was responsible for bringing in Roger Cox as the writer concurred, "I agree Roger delivered the text, and Joe the visuals but they pushed and fulfilled each other. Roger's prose painted a picture. Joe's art suggested a story."

Production designer Susan Cowan who was referred to as Rohde's right hand on the project said, "The Adventurers Club remains a favorite project of mine after all these years. As art director, I production designed all the show elements, including the illusions provided by the talented Rock Hall and Monty Lunde of Technifex.

"I also bought about ninety-five percent of the fifteen hundred plus props. I am sure the finance department at Imagineering will never forget me. Lots of receipts scribbled on brown paper bags because many of the props were bought at my favorite haunt, the Rose Bowl Swap Meet in Pasadena.

"By the way, Joe who was the primary art director on the project painted the artwork (for the two paintings) that hung in the library. He and I are rendered in both of the paintings along with Roger Cox, the show director, and Rick Rothschild, Pleasure Island's show producer (and Chris Carradine)."

In January 1990, Walt Disney World Entertainment Chris Oyen was brought in as a show writer and director of both the Adventurers Club and the Comedy Warehouse to maintain, and where necessary, modify the experience so that it was consistent.

Oyen was responsible for creating the character of Samantha Sterling, readjusting the performing matrix so that there was a beginning, middle and end to the evening, created and edited the *Adventures Almanac* newsletter and wrote several new show segments. Over the last decade of its operation when Oyen went on to other entertainment assignments, several other directors rotated into the venue supervising the established shows.

When guests entered the club the top floor was known as the Zebra Mezzanine because of a zebra designed bar styled by Rohde that was prominetly placed there. The walls were covered in ancient artifacts and yellowing photos all connected with the exploits of the members with captions explaining their significance.

A winding staircase (or a slightly hidden elevator) led down to the circular Main Salon. This central room of the club was filled with more artifacts and photos as well as the head of a Yakoose (Voiced by Tom Sherohman, it would spring to life unexpectedly to talk to the guests), the Colonel who would help induct new members with the creed and lead them in songs, Babylonia who would flirt with the patrons, and a replica of the Artemision

Bronze statue, commonly known as the "javelin thrower statue" or at the club itself as "Zeus with a Fishing Rod" (with the fishing line entangled in exhibits overhead).

Along the sides of this Main Salon were entrances to four additional rooms: The Mask Room (where the masks on the wall would spring to life like in *The Enchanted Tiki Room*), The Treasure Room (holding the cabinet with the floating head of Beezle the genie along with other assorted treasures), The Rest Room and The Library (where the primary shows were performed on a raised stage).

Steinmeyer summed up the continuing appeal of the experience, "To me, the charm of the Adventurers Club was that it was eccentric and unexpected. The humor was unpredicatable and off beat. But it all seemed to make perfect sense, unto itself. That's the comfort of the Adventurers Club, really.

"You've gone to someone else's party. They've been throwing that party for a long time. They're experts at it. But over the years, it's taken on all of their personalities and quirks. Audiences felt they'd fallen into a rabbit hole and experienced another world."

The final public performance at the Adventurers Club was the night of September 27, 2008 to a crowd that overflowed into the street. The premise of the final show was that the Adventurers had failed to raise enough money in their nightly RadioThon to pay their lease, and the members were being immediately evicted.

Fortunately, Marcel (a Missing Link character who disappeared during the early years of the club) had become filthy rich due to lucrative investments and had returned to whisk the club members away for a year long safari. They marched out of the club, followed by their fans, and the club was officially closed except for a few special private events held during the following year.

About an hour before the doors opened, many of the actors came out in their street clothes to loud cheers. They posed for photos, answered questions, received gifts, and thanked as many fans as they could for their support over the years. A huge video screen was placed outside so that fans outside in the street could see the final library show.

The very next week, the National Fantasy Fan Club (now known as the Disneyana Fan Club) attended the location as part of their annual convention for a performance and meeting at the club.

Disney had several groups pre-booked for private parties at the Club and offered to honor those bookings through the end of the year or to refund the money or offer another venue. It is not surprising that all of those groups preferred attending the Club.

What was surprising is that location still continued to function in that capacity for another year. On Thursday, September 24, 2009 Lou Mongello had a group party there with performances. On Friday September 25, it was the Congaloosh convention that attended performances there.

Finally, on Saturday, September 26, 2009 there was an exclusive final farewell with Disney executives before the location was closed and the interior stripped with some of the props being sent to the Mystic Manor attraction in Hong Kong Disneyland.

Some props including Merriam's pet peacock Scooter and the Zebra bar were placed in a Downtown Disney West Side merchandise shop D—Street. Scooter was given his name by the Viceroy of Ceylon, Sir Manning Hubley Sommerset, in 1931.

Disney archivist Dave Smith walked the location to select a few items for the Disney Archives. Imagineer Joe Rohde took a few props that had sentimental value since it was one of his first major projects as art director.

The last performance of the cast took place at Disney's Contemporary Resort on November 23, 2014 as part of the Disney D23 Destination D event where some original cast members reunited for a revised performance and a "membership renewal" ceremony.

With the closing of the Adventurers Club, the last bit of the Merriwether Adam Pleasure story finally disappeared from Pleasure Island, leaving gutted buildings, boarded up entrances, blocked pathways and a ghost town feeling that ironically resembled how the Imagineers supposedly first found the location over twenty years earlier.

"Our decision is largely based on guest feedback," said the official Walt Disney World statement in July 2008 explaining why the clubs were closing, "We are seeing more demand for shopping and dining experiences and less demand for clubs."

In actuality, the primary reason for the closing was a failed business pro forma that presumed that Pleasure Island guests would club hop and so might spend only fifteen to twenty minutes in the Adventurers Club instead of all evening.

In addition, the pro forma assumed that during that time guests would purchase several drinks that would offset the overhead cost for performers and maintenance of the delicate special effects.

It never occurred to anyone that a guest might not buy a drink at all but remain for the entire evening enjoying the entertainment. The performers were all Equity (the theater union) members and their salaries were significantly higher than the usual cast member salary and in addition had other stipulations in their contracts included mandated breaks and higher overtime.

So the on line petition by fans to try to save the location or have the Walt Disney Company re-locate it elsewhere like Adventureland at the Magic Kingdom or the Polynesian Village Resort had no impact at all despite the thousands of signatures that were gathered.

At one point, the Disney Vacation Club considered taking over the venue as an exclusive location for its members. That was just one of several proposals that unfortunately failed to materialize.

Only one new venue opened on Pleasure Island. The Paradiso 37 restaurant opened in 2009 in the location of the old Avigators Supply building next to the old Adventurers Club.

On November 18, 2010, Disney announced the section of Downtown Disney known as Pleasure Island would receive a massive three-year renovation to include "stylish boutiques, innovative restaurants," and a "lakeside park" and would be called Hyperion Wharf in an attempt to revitalize the area and attract new businesses.

Almost a year into the project, Disney put the plans on hiatus as they discovered that they faced challenges getting prospective new tenants into the area, especially because of the lingering negative reputation of the location in its later years.

Disney decided that instead of just spending money to create a "bandage" for the bruised Pleasure Island section that it should expand the proposal to re-design the entire Downtown Disney area into a cohesive story line.

However, rather than create another overly complicated Merriweather Adam Pleasure back story as was done for Pleasure Island that provided problems when buildings changed use or new areas had to be built, the Imagineers developed a simpler, more organically Florida story that would easily change for any future adjustments.

"We looked at a lot of different types of plans over the years and took our time to really decide on what was the best approach for this area and we landed on Disney Springs," Walt Disney World Imagineer Theron Skees, executive creative director of the project said in 2013. "It's kind of a unifying storyline that we felt would really reinvigorate the property and really give it an identity all of its own."

Inspired by the small Florida towns that developed in the early 1900s around bodies of water, the storyline is that Disney Springs also attracted its first settlers "more than a century ago" and, over the decades, the town continued to expand around the natural spring into four distinct districts: Town Center, The Landing, Marketplace and West Side.

The Landing would occupy the land previously designated as Pleasure Island. The Adventurers Club building would be reformatted as The Edison, referring to inventor Thomas Edison. The Edison was once the power plant for the town. Its design was meant to evoke the steam powered age of innovation.

The restaurant is promoted as a "lavish industrial Gothic-style destination for fine food, handcrafted cocktails and exciting nightlife." The impressive, detailed decor includes actual antique pieces and a large industrial-style mechanical clock at the main entrance.

Different dining areas have their own themes including: The Boiler Bar, The Ember Parlor, Telegraph Lounge, The Patent Office, The Tesla Lounge, The Radio Room, Waterfront Patio, and The Lab. Antique boilers are a focal point for guests who enter The Edison from the Enzo's Hideaway tunnels or any guests that make their way downstairs.

It was hoped that Disney Springs would be seen as more upscale and family friendly with these changes.

However, for those Disney fans who experienced Pleasure Island and especially the Adventurers Club, the ghosts of Merriweather Pleasure and his raucous friends still haunt the area.

Rick Rothschild, the Executive Producer, Entertainment Center Projects, Walt Disney Imagineering stated in 1989: "We've done a lot of homework by traveling all over the world to look at different night clubs and complexes. What we've done here is beyond what anyone has ever attempted before. If Disneyland is fantasy made real, then this place is reality made fantastic!"

New Member Induction Ceremony

The Adventurers Club Entertainment Mission Statement (1989): "Our goal is to create the highest quality entertainment experience possible, in accordance with both Pleasure Island and Disney standards, values and principles, in order to captivate our guests imagination and capitalize on their senses of humor, so we can create an environment that makes each guest feel that they have not only experienced the Adventurers Club, but they are welcome and valued *members* of the Club."

"Come in a stranger...leave a little stranger." New member induction ceremonies were held in the Main Salon each evening at 8:40, 9:50 and 11:20. Chris Oyen formalized the ceremony into three parts.

1. THE SALUTE

Raise your right hand. Open the fingers wide.

Place the right hand, not touching your body, just above your navel.

If you place it below your navel, that is an entirely different club.

Make a few "fishy waves" wiggle movements back and forth with your hand.

Lift up your hand to you mouth as if you were going to take a shot of alcohol.

Continue the movement higher so your right hand is raised high in the air.

Shout "Kungaloosh!"

("Kungaloosh" is an "all purpose" word like "Aloha". It means "Hello", "Goodbye" or "Kiss me quick before the lava flow engulfs us".)

2. THE CREED

Raise your right hand and repeat the *Adventurers Club Creed* written by M.A. Pleasure in 1932 according to the copy posted in the Zebra Mezzanine.

> We climb the highest mountains
> Just to get a better view.

We plumb the deepest oceans
'Cuz we're daring, through and through.
We cross the scorching desert,
Martinis in our hand.
We ski the polar ice cap
In tuxedo, looking grand...
We're reckless, brave and loyal
And valiant to the end.
If you come in here a stranger,
You'll exit as a friend.

3. THE ALL PURPOSE THEME SONG (MUSIC AND LYRICS BY LYNN HART)

Chorus

Marching along, we're Adventurers
Singing the Song of Adventurers
Up or down, North, South, East or West
An Adventurers life is best

Verse (each paragraph sung by a different character)

We've been chased by angry dingoes
Took a bath with Pink Flamingoes

Eaten Passion Fruit in East Beirut
We shot down with our guns.

In the Grenadines, we rested
In the Philippines were bested

By a flummox in out stomachs
That soon had us on the runs.

I went hunting in Tijuana
Where I bagged a wild iguana

We hopped a train in old Bahrain
Purely for the fun.

Then I got into hot water
Had to wed the Chieftain's daughter

But we traded her for beaver fur
And a poison blow dart gun.

We've hunted tigers in Tunisia
Counted geigers in Magnesia

Been shot in spots by Hottentots
Drank Dandelion Gin.

Got nibbled in Bothswana
Turned to kibble by piranha

Caught Malaria in Bulgaria
By Jove, what a week it's been!

Chorus

Marching along, we're Adventurers
Singing the song of Adventurers,
Up or down, North, South, East or West
An Adventurers Life is Best,
An Adventurers Life is Best!
Kungaloosh!

The Membership Plaque

FOUNDER
Merriweather Adam Pleasure

FOUNDER'S CIRCLE
Otis Wren
Pamelia Perkins
Hathaway Browne
Merriam Pleasure
Col. Critchlow Suchbench (misspelled on plaque as "Sunchbench")

MEMBERS EMERITUS
Dr. Fielding Ratzkwatzky
Maj. General C.K. "Bob" Waggleberry
Richmond Linedozer
Pygmalion "Piggy" Venables
B.W. "Icicle Ike" Jakookie
Kennigton Schnabel
Sir Langton Dithers
Lowell Battbarton
Emil Bleehall

MEMBERS
McDabbler Twelvetrees
Alvin W. Chowderflute
Sir Reginald Phyfee-Hardwicke
Linus Van Aukerman
Mumford L. Gertz (a reference to Imagineer David Mumford)
Clyde McBeebee
Dr. Geofrrey T. Spaulding
Noah X. Malmborg
Embrey Z. Harumphinger
Julie Harbert-Harman

Bascombe H. Potter III
Hardwick "Bugsy" Van Loon
Cowley W. Frink
Burlwood Carrutters Jr.
Chester Babbit Rawlinson
Florence Arrot
Tarleton Feldspar
Coombs "Lucky" Lupree
Erwin "Pops" Einbinder
Davila Willoughby
Pieter Hoots

MEMBERS OWING DUES

S.R. "Bob" Bobenmeyer
Knute "Big Swede" Belasco
Rev. Charles A. "Tick" Bitterford
Eben Cockley

PERMANENT MEMBERS

- **Hathaway Browne:** Club aviator and Casanova.
- **Otis T. Wren:** Club Treasurer and Ichthyologist.
- **Fletcher Hodges:** Eccentric Club Curator.
- **Pamelia Perkins:** Club President.
- **Samantha Sterling:** Explorer and cabaret singer.
- **Emil Bleehall:** Junior Adventurer and pigeon trainer from Sandusky, Ohio who is a contender for the Balderdash Cup.
- **Graves:** Club Butler.
- **The Maid:** There are many maids although only one on duty each night including Sugar Snapp, Beullah Belle, Kiki McGee, Gabby Normal and Dusty Cabinets who have worked in the Adventurers Club over the years.
- **Colonel Critchlow Suchbench:** Club Gleemeister and Sergeant-at-Arms on duty. He has a peculiar talent of sleeping with both eyes open. Usually, he can be cajoled into leading his fellow adventurers in song when the audience yells: "Free drink, Colonel?" He will respond, "Gin and

tonic!" and often some other additional comment like "And a banana daiquiri for the monkey I am sitting on!"

- **Babylonia:** A giant stone face of an ancient goddess on the wall

- **The Mongolian Yakoose:** Half yak and half moose. It was mistakenly upholstered rather than stuffed in 1934 by The Pleasure Perfect Upholstery shop. Voice by Tom Sherohman the first director of the Comedy Warehouse.

- **Arnie** (Mask of Comedy) and **Claude** (Mask of Tragedy): lifetime partners

- **Beezle:** the head of a genie imprisoned in a lamp in a cabinet in the Treasure Room. He wants a body and a date with the lovely maid who dusts his cabinet.

- **Fingers Zambezi:** paranormal piano protégé who inhabits the Library organ. Apparently, the massive organ plunged through the rotted floor of the loft, killing the organist in the process. Not one to let a little misfortune stand in the way of his passion to play, the now-ghostly organist appears nightly to take request while magically manipulating the keys and pedals.

  Jim Roberts was the primary pianist doing the role of Fingers Zambezi for the last 13 years of the club, although others like Steve Watson also filled in doing that role. By the way, one of the sheet music sheets on the organ in the library was the song *Laughing Fingers*.

MISSING MEMBERS

- **Sutter Bestwick:** Contender for the Balderdash Cup

- **Chilton Thompson:** Sound effects man for *Tales of the Adventurers Club* radio show and another contender for the Balderdash Cup.

- **Sheila Griffin:** Performs the role of Greta in *Tales of the Adventurers Club* radio show.

- **Madame Zenobia:** the mysterious former proprietress of the Club and alleged granddaughter of M.A. Pleasure who reads palms and tells fortunes. The character was later identified as Madame Zarkov although most fans agree that this was an entirely different character just with similarities to Zenobia.

- **Mandora:** Adventuress and cabaret singer currently on "urgent business somewhere in the Andes."

- **Abdul:** doorman and security guard.

- **Marcel:** Officially, Marcel is "the Missing Link" and according to the official WDW Entertainment description, he is "wearing the livery of an apprentice bar man. He moves about the Club silently doing his thousand and one chores. Marcel's looks are much closer to Australopithecus man than to an ape." His purpose was to help the male performers (and the early show was primarily male) to get from one side of the club to another in the days when they played more than one character a night so that all they had to do was put on the monkey mask.

  When the performing matrix changed and that was no longer necessary, Show Director Chris Oyen sent Marcel away and replaced him with his own creation, Samantha Sterling, an Amelia Earhart type adventuress who came from a good family but was "rough and tumble."

- **F. Godfrey Wells:** On the wall to the left of Colonel Suchbench, and about halfway down, was the following plaque: "F. Godfrey Wells. A Tribute. Best Friend of Merriweather Adam Pleasure. World Class Mountaineer, Alpinist and Cragsman. Borrowed an ice pick from the Zebra Bartender and used it to scale Everest, 1932. (Didn't get the credit he deserved, despite being the *only* man to scale the world's highest peak from the *inside*.)"

  Walt Disney Company President and Chief Operating Officer Franklin G. Wells died in a helicopter crash in 1994 while returning from a ski trip in Nevada. When he was made a Disney Legend, he was described as a "born adventurer." He was an avid mountain climber and came close to achieving his goal of climbing the Seven Summits, the highest mountains on each of the seven continents. Only Everest eluded him.

Secrets of the Members

Armitage Campbell was an aviator from the Royal Air Force who spent time in the club attempting to auction off artifacts obtained on his last expedition to help finance his next adventure. Craig McNair Wilson renamed the character "Hamilton Beach" but because of copyright concerns, eventually the character evolved into Hathaway Browne. Hathaway Brown is the name of an exclusive all-girls school in Cleveland, Ohio which seemed appropriate for a notorious Casanova.

Professor Otis Wren was originally supposed to be a burly "rampager" with an eye patch and a petrified piranha clamped onto the side of his infantry lace up boots. Those boots and piranha were hung just above the Zeus statue in the Main Salon. According to Wilson's description: "Whenever Otis Wren enters the Adventurers Club, he is heard from the outside. If there is a line to the club, he will probably select an attractive woman to pull out of line to enter the club with him. He comes in with great bravado." He later evolved into the white linen clad ichthyologist who was desperate to win the Balderdash Cup.

Colonel Crumb was an Audio-Animatronics bust that evolved into the famous Colonel Suchbench puppet who was desperately in love with Babylonia. From one early script, the Colonel revealed how he discovered Babs. "It was my final adventure…I was transversing Polynesia in search of rare tribal icons, when I saw the rarest of all on the peak of a dormant volcano. Babylonia.

"I was smitten by her visage. I went to retrieve her but as luck would have it, the volcano came to life, and I was able only to save her head and the rest of her rare form disappeared into the molten lava. You should have seen the rest of her!

"She was one hot piece of igneous rock! I had myself nailed to the floor just so I could be close to her." Some of the improvisational comedy sketches from this time revolved around the Colonel's jealousy when Babylonia flirted with male guests and indicated that she had dated Zeus. Babylonia was originally going to be called "Kia" ("Know It All").

Fletcher Hodges' name came from the very real Fletcher Hodges Junior who for over five decades was the curator in charge of preserving the memory of composer Stephen Foster. The collection eventually ended up at the University of Pittsburgh. AC show writer Roger Cox attended the University of Pittsburgh.

Pamelia Perkins was named after a classmate of Imagineer Roger Cox. The very first actress to perform the role was Emmy Award-winning actress Paula Pell, who became a writer on the television show *Saturday Night Live* among other credits.

Arnie and Claude were originally to be named "Ned and Fred" and at one time "Comedia" and "Tragedia". Their official WDI biography lists them as "lifetime partners." What that means I don't know. I never asked and no one ever told.

The Yakoose was originally called the "Nauga" (as in "nauga-hyde", a brand of artificial leather). WDI wanted a stuffed animal head on the wall (since many explorer clubs had stuffed animal heads on the walls) but didn't like the possible negative reaction of guests to seeing a "big, old grungy head of a dead animal," according to Rohde.

To get a few laughs, the head was "upholstered" instead of stuffed and was just hanging around. The yakoose is a distant cousin of Melvin the Moose ("I'm only part moose as it is.") who was hanging around on the wall of the Country Bear Jamboree in Frontierland at the Magic Kingdom. It is the same audio-animatronics framework. It was hoped that guests might assume other heads might spring to life unexpectedly at any moment as well.

According to the official history of Pleasure Island, there was an Upholstery Shop that opened in 1923 (and in 1989 became Changing Attitudes, a trendy clothing and accessories shop that closed in 2006 and taken over by Harley-Davidson), six full-time seamstresses worked on the interiors of the custom yachts that M.A. Pleasure was building.

However, the rest of the story written in 1988, and generally unknown to both cast and guests, was that the business "shut down in 1932. In 1934, this space was leased to Guiseppe ("Joe") Rohde, Furniture Re-Upholsterer and part-time Taxidermist (also an expert on Italian opera, and protégé of Isabella Pleasure, M.A. Pleasure's wife who loved opera).

"Merriweather allowed Giuseppe to work on one of his trophies, the head of a Mongolian Yakoose and the results of his (dubious) efforts can be seen on the wall of the Adventurers Club Main Salon. A war time shortage of kapok put Rohde out of business, and this space was abandoned in 1943."

When the final plaque was installed on the building in 1989, it eliminated the name of Guiseppe Rohde.

The First Performers

One of the original performers at the Adventurers Club was Donna Charles. However, most Walt Disney World guests would know her better as Rosie, the cleaning lady who did the incredible one woman pre-show warm-up for the Indiana Jones Epic Stunt Show at Disney's Hollywood Studios for many years.

Show writer and director Roger Cox went to Boardwalk and Baseball (a once-popular entertainment venue in Central Florida) and saw Michael Branson (singer/pianist) and Donna Charles do an act and loved them and wanted them for the Adventurers Club.

Michael immediately took the offer, but Donna was going through some family issues and didn't want to make the move. So Roger went to the head of entertainment at Boardwalk and Baseball and begged him to let them borrow Donna for an afternoon. He took her to the site with both of them wearing hard hats where the Adventurers Club was being built and convinced her she wanted to be a part of all of this.

After him passionately explaining the concept, she eventually agreed.

A week before the Adventurers Club was to open Disney management saw the three planned library shows at the time. They hated the third show and told Roger, "We don't care what you do for the third show but you can't do this."

So Roger told Michael and Donna they had to do their cabaret act that they had done at Boardwalk and Baseball. The difficulty was that since Michael played the keyboard he had to be where the Fingers Zambezi pianist was which was being hidden offstage stage so Donna was all alone on the stage and they had to eliminate the banter that they did.

Donna did a bit similar to Jim Nabors where when she talked in a high, irritating Brooklynese accent, but when she sang it was smooth and professional occasionally stopping the song to say in the annoying accent, "How do you like it so far?".

The original Adventurers Club was not going to have music in the shows and this was the first time that concept was introduced.

Before opening, Roger came to Donna and said, "You have more talent in your little finger, but your hair is a disaster."

So he took her down to a local hairdresser and spent a $100 having her hair done for the opening. She took the first official photo with Marcel the Missing Link and it was used on the pamphlet handed out to guests in the early days of the club.

Disney leadership considered the Adventurers Club was like an attraction and that guests would come in, see a show and leave, so there would be about three different cycles during an evening. So it was not uncommon for a performer to be scheduled for three different roles during the evening, playing a different character during each cycle.

However, it only took about three weeks for management to realize that it was a bar and that guests might stay all night.

Donna told me that she was the first Pamelia and the first maid. Her maid's name was "Gladys" as in "Glad to see ya" and then would flip up her skirt and laugh. Eventually, the maids were all named "Doreen" for a period of time but that stopped when repeat guests would come in and go "you're not Doreen".

So it was determined that each maid would have their own individual name. The original maid's costume was low cut, which proved to be a problem during one Hoopla event where one of the maids, who was very well-endowed, bent over and when she sprang back up, her breasts popped out making it the "Best Hoopla Ever" joked actor Tim Goodwin who worked with Donna Charles as one of the original members.

Tim developed the hand wiggle and lifting the hand that goes with the Kungaloosh Salute. He remained with the show until the very final performance.

The maid's dress was changed so that it went right up to the neck to give the performer more freedom of movement without surprise exposure. One maid had a costume that was a long black dress with a white apron looking a lot like the cartoon character Hazel.

However, that costume, only worn by one actress disappeared as did other original costume items. For instance, Emil originally wore a plaid jacket. Later, when he was shifted into the pseudo Boy Scout outfit, the plaid jacket was sometimes worn by a short lived character called The Plaid Monkey, which was a combination of the jacket and the old Marcel the Monkey mask.

Pamelia Perkins outfit changed many times over the years. Some of the actresses didn't like wearing the Samantha Sterling pants if it was a time of the month when they felt bloated. One actress playing Samantha in a library show wearing new pants, actually burst out of them when she struck a pose and one of the other cast members quickly found electric tape to patch her up in front of the audience.

Originally the club allowed smoking—and had ashtrays—and it was rough on the performers' voices. Speaking of which, the role of Otis Wren was so rough on an actor's voice and energy that usually an actor was scheduled to do it only once a week.

At one point, the performers were typed into a "preferred role" meaning that was the role that management saw as ideal for them based on body image. For instance, Otis was considered a "large" person. That scheduling eventually went away but some performers could only perform one or two roles or only felt comfortable doing those roles.

It was determined what the characteristics were for each character (eg. Otis was grumpy, Emil was endearing, etc.) but each actor was given leeway in how they achieved that stereotypical characteristic. Actress Sheila Smith Ward actually wore a different perfume for each of the characters she played which occasionally caused some discomfort when she would show up for work and find that she had to do a different role because someone had called in sick.

The actors tried to monitor each other to walk the line of appropriateness without stepping over it. It was determined that if they could say something as a double entendre (so that it could be interpreted different ways) that Disney Legal would back them because they could always say to a disgruntled guest, "We are sorry you interpreted it that way because it was meant this way."

To the best of most performers' knowledge there was never an incident where they were "coached" about something inappropriate that happened on stage.

Over the years, there were many different directors and if a director took something out that the actors wanted in, they just waited until a new director came on board and slipped it back in.

Madame Zenobia

When early publicity about the Adventurers Club was published, the only character that was mentioned was Madame Zenobia.

In fact, later articles also connect that name with the club. "A giant stone face, known as Miss Zenobia, tells fortunes and spins tales from the past" claimed the Disney-approved Hyperion-published book *Since the World Began* in 1996. Of course, Disney fans know that giant stone face is Babylonia not Zenobia but there is a legitimate reason for the confusion with the names.

Originally, there was going to be a club on Pleasure Island that would be themed to magic, very much like the famous Magic Castle in Hollywood that was frequented by Imagineers working on the Pleasure Island project. Just like the Magic Castle that had "Irma", an invisible piano player, the club would also have an invisible piano player. An outside special effects firm, Technifex, run by two former Imagineers began to develop effects for that Pleasure Island club.

Madame Zenobia would have been a mysterious gypsy woman who wandered the club and told fortunes, accompanied by other performers like close-up magicians.

However, CEO Michael Eisner stopped by Church Street Station in downtown Orlando and saw the extreme popularity of a Country Western club called the Cheyenne Saloon. Eisner insisted there be a similar experience on Pleasure Island and so the magic club quickly became the Country Western club called Neon Armadillo.

The concept of close-up magicians and Madame Zenobia and some of the special effects that had been developed moved next door into the Adventurers Club.

Before Imagineer Roger Cox helped develop the characters that most Disney fans remember as being connected to the Adventurers Club, Imagineer Craig McNair Wilson wrote some brief character sketches to be used to help inspire some performing possibilities within the club.

The performers at the Adventurers Club were going to use the Orlando SAK theater method of improvisation of taking a character sketch and using it to develop scenes and dialog. Wilson had been one of the founders and directors of SAK theater that did "trunk shows" at two Epcot World Showcase pavilions and for conventions.

Among those characters that Wilson described was Professor Otis Wren who was an explorer and a "rampager."

Wilson wrote: "Whenever Otis Wren enters the Adventurers Club, he is heard from the outside. If there is a line to the club, he will probably select an attractive woman to pull out of line to enter the club with him. He comes in with great bravado and a sack full of goodies. If Madame Zenobia is a room-filling presence, Otis Wren is a building shaking presence. He is so much bigger than life and so much louder than any one would like him to be."

Certainly, this was a much different interpretation that the scholarly Wren who eventually inhabited the club and was club treasurer and an Ichthyologist. Although a piranha permanently attached to his boot hints at the ichthyologist background in the eye-patched, unshaven, python-holding professor described by Wilson.

In addition, Wren "has a great love and respect for Madame Zenobia and apparently had a deeper relationship with her in the past than is completely evident in the present, though there are hints to a previous dalliance."

Then there was Armitage Campbell, an aviator and auctioneer.

Wilson wrote: "He is tan and youthful and needing a shave. His one goal in life is to circumnavigate the planet in his plane. In order to do this, he will auction off small bobbles he has found along the way or simply pull something from the wall of the Adventurers Club and sell it to the highest bidder. He'll sell anything to anyone to accomplish his selfish ends. Smuggler, gambler, soldier of fortune."

Of course, with input from other writers, this aviator evolved into the more familiar and less greedy but still very much a ladies' man, Hathaway Browne.

Interestingly, Wilson's notes hint that "Campbell is obviously younger than Otis Wren and Campbell's relationship is somewhat different with Madame Zenobia. If one pays close enough attention to their dialog, an understanding is reached that apparently she raised him or perhaps even found him somewhere on one of her many travels and then raised him. His sense of adventure and spirit of wanderlust grow as much out of his having been raised ('mothered') by Madame Zenobia."

Also, there was a huge bearded, fez wearing Turk known as Abdul who would have been the doorman as well as club security, but had a servant relationship with Madame Zenobia. At one point in the evening, he might bring her a mysterious bag and she would respond testily, "I will deal with that *later.*"

So who was this colorful Madame Zenobia who was to be the centerpiece and driving force for the original concept of the Adventurers Club?

From June 1987, here is Craig McNair Wilson's description of Madame Zenobia:

"Although the complete and specific details of her past remain shrouded in mystery, rumor and innuendo, it is known that she is the current proprietess of the Adventurers Club: a position she has held as long as any member of the current staff can remember.

"Whereas her direct links with the Pleasure family and the allegations that she is in fact the long-lost daughter of Merriweather Adam Pleasure cannot be substantiated by any hard evidence, she seems to have more than a passing familiarity with the Pleasure legacy.

"She is a woman of great presence and style. She fills any room she is in and her presence spills over into adjoining rooms. If she is not in the back room smoking a Turkish Clove cigarette or English Oval, her bigger than life personality does not permit her to sit quietly in a corner enjoying a cordial unobserved.

"Physically, Madame Zenobia may be a tall woman. She certainly has a powerful voice. If she were cast in a movie, she would undoubtedly be portrayed by Bea Arthur. And, though she is no knock-out, she certainly is alluring as well as being, not so much a flirt, as she is a woman capable of making any person proud of who they are.

"With a look, a smile, a laugh, a gesture, a touch, she can make you glad to be in the Adventurers Club. She brings out the adventurer in all of us. She is at once eternally youthful and timeless.

"She would probably be better portrayed by an actress in her 30s or even early 40s than an actress in her 20s trying to come off as something that she really isn't. I would like to think that in casting Madame Zenobia, we could find an actress who would be available to us five nights a week and on the other two nights that she is not there, we would cast another actress of similar qualities we would give a different name who is probably an old friend.

"She is a little bit gypsy, a little bit fortune teller and she resembles, but is not limited to, the qualities of Maude (Bea Arthur), Dulcinea from *Man of La Mancha* (Sophia Loren), and Madame Roza (Mercedes McCambridge). She will make you laugh one minute, be listening to a sad story you may tell her and offer a shoulder or a handkerchief to cry on the next minute, and just as quickly get you on your feet and dancing.

"The next time you come to the Adventurers Club and approach the maitre d's podium, you will ask, 'Is Madame Zenobia here?' and then think to yourself, 'Oh, I hope she remembers me'."

The rough costume sketches for the character show a gypsy like character with a large flat hat ("a sun hat transformed into a Huichol Indian shaman hat") and dress and shawl both "pulled from South America. The old hiking boots hint at a past as an adventurer."

She wore bracelets and charms and other exotic trinkets. She carried a beat up old saddlebag or a shoulder bag inlaid with beads, teeth, animal fur and more. Her appearance was to be very much a patchwork affair with international influences.

She would greet guests to the Adventurers Club with "Hello, everyone. Are we drinking? Are we in love?"

As the hostess and emcee of the club, she would interact in the Mask Room and there would a mystical Chinese lantern (later to evolve into Beezle the genie head in the floating lamp) that would talk to Zenobia.

She would gather items from the guests and put them in a black bag and then the lamp would tell what the objects were and from their "vibrations" tell about the dark corners of the guest's life.

The lamp would also tell stories of the life and times of Merriweather Pleasure. If the guests doubted the lantern's tales, it would respond, "Believe it or... Leave!" to parody the famous Ripley phrase "Believe it or Not!"

Madame Zenobia only made one physical appearance. At a press conference aboard the Empress Lilly on July 21, 1986, Michael Eisner introduced to the press the concept of Pleasure Island that was to open in 1988.

Nash the Bartender

Why was the Adventurers Club entire staff of mixologists all called by the name of "Nash" in the early years of operation? *The Adventurers Almanac* newsletter revealed the reason.

In early April of 1919, while probing the upper reaches of the Amazon, Merriweather Adam Pleasure, founder and original owner of Pleasure Island, came upon and befriended the well-known yachtsman and adventurer Gilbert ("The Rambler") Nash. Gilbert, or "Gremlin," as he preferred to be called, had spent most of his adult life (and several fortunes) pursuing the formulas of the world's greatest elixirs.

(Nash Rambler was a 1950s American Motors Company compact car. AMC also produced a subcompact car in the 1970s called the Gremlin.)

Gilbert introduced Merriweather to several enticing mixtures, but none as wonderful or noteworthy as the native concoction that we now call simply "Jungle Juice". After Merriweather returned to his beloved isle in Florida, he introduced the marvelous drink to his yachting cronies and fellow adventurers.

The original formula for "Jungle Juice" was quite potent and known only to Merriweather himself. Properly mixed, this elixir was widely accepted to increase strength and intelligence. However, improperly calibrated, the compound was known to become volatile, causing the recipient to become feeble-minded and clumsy.

This side-effect was demonstrated by young Stewart Pleasure in the great Library fire of '29 which subsequently destroyed the only existing copy of the recipe and several of Merriweather's prized journals.

After surveying the damage to his beloved club and realizing that no man could ever hope to match the talents of Gilbert, Merriweather vowed that "from this day forth, no one but NASH will tend this bar."

And so the tradition began; first with Ogden Nash, the bookish son of Gilbert, and later with Laurence Nash, credited with the first electric lemonade, to the club's present staff of mixologists, all descendants of the admirable Gilbert Nash himself.

ORIGINAL KUNGALOOSH RECIPE

Kungaloosh is the Official Drink for all Adventurers.

1 1/4 ounce vodka

1 1/4 ounce Malibu Rum

3/4 ounce Midori (melon liqueur)

2 tablespoons pineapple juice

1 splash cranberry juice

NEW KUNGALOOSH RECIPE—INTRODUCED AROUND 2000

1 cup Daily's Strawberry Daiquiri Mix

1/4 cup orange juice

1/4 cup Captain Morgan's Spiced Rum

1/4 cup blackberry brandy

Toss it in a blender with enough ice to make it slushy.

ADVENTURERS CLUB DRINK MENU

Hot Chocolate Yakoose Mousse

This tattered recipe of dark creme de cacao, Bailey's Irish Cream and hot chocolate was found stitched to the bottom of our own Yakoose, back fresh from the upholsterers.

Pamelia's Punch

This wild mix of Cruzan orange, pineapple and coconut_rums mixed with pineapple, cranberry, orange and sour.

Bongo's Jungle Juice

Enough to make any sane man go ape! The tongue tingling flavors of Captain Morgan Original Spiced Rum, Bacardi151, Banana liqueur, Strawbery Daiquiri Mix, orange, pineapple and cranberry juice. Bongo, the Man-Ape, appears in *Tales of the Adventurers Club* radio serial.

The Hoopla

This concoction of Bacardi CoCo, vodka, melon liqueur and pineapple juice is sure to curl the toes of the most hearty adventurers.

Samantha's Passion Potion

Samantha cooked up this potion while in the rain forests of South America. The tropical flavors of Absolut Citron, melon liqueur, raspberry liqueur, pineapple and cranberry are sure to stir the animal inside!

Baldersmash

Bacardi Big Apple, Bacardi O, Bacardi Razz, Cranberry Juice, Sour Mix and a splash of Sprite

Gypsy Moth

Bacardi O, Blue Curacao, Melon Liqueur, Sour Mix and Pineapple Juice

NON-ALCOHOLIC DRINKS

Emil's Strawberry Colada

From deepest, darkest...Sandusky, Ohio! Emil brought us his grandmother's recipe for this delicious frozen confection! This frozen blend of Strawberry Daiquiri and Pina Colada.

Babylonia's Brew

A refreshing mixture of pineapple juice, orange juice, Sprite and a splash of sour mix.

Over the years, a variety of different drinks and collectible drinking glasses were sold in the club including a canteen, a variety of colorful tiki mugs, a monkey nut cup, a mug in the shape of a Yakoose head, shot glasses, glasses with images of Arnie and Claude, Colonel Suchbench and just the word "Kungaloosh".

Raoul Manzanera

The back story of Pleasure Island and its many characters was originally much more elaborate than many people realize.

A character who was strongly promoted in the early planning but disappeared completely when Pleasure Island officially opened was Raoul Manzanera.

From the official Imagineering storyline for Pleasure Island from 1989: "An elaborate wedding worthy of royalty is held when Pleasure's daughter Merriam, on her 22 birthday, marries an ambitious tango composer from Argentina, Raoul Manzanera on July 4, 1933."

Of course, it never occurred to any of the show writers to indicate whether Merriam met Manzanera on one of her many journeys with her father or if he was a special invited guest to the Island or what it was about this fellow that charmed the independent and adventuresome daughter of Merriweather Adam Pleasure.

By the way, Merriam, along with her father, founded the infamous Adventurers Club the year before she was married so Manzanera might have had some connection with that location as well. Or was it the Argentine tango which includes a close embrace that thrilled Merriam?

There are a lot of unanswered questions that might exist elsewhere or may be lost forever after the decades. Manzanera was directly involved with two of the buildings on Pleasure Island.

Did you ever wonder why Mannequins had a huge turntable on the floor? Well, it was because it assisted Manzanera in his work to create a new locomotive that was dubbed "Maxwell's Demon" so it was a turn around for a train.

According to legend, the building was where Pleasure originally made the canvas that made him famous throughout the world. In 1922, he moved the Canvas Works to a much larger new facility at the other end of the Island, in a facility that would become the AMC Movie Theater complex in 1989.

The Mannequins building re-dubbed Warehouse No. 3 was leased out to Invincible Pictures in 1931 for use as a soundstage.

Two early talkies were supposedly filmed there: *Fighting Devil Dogs of Orlando* (based on the life of Pleasure's poker pal and Adventurers Club regular, Hathaway Browne who was portrayed by Warner Oland) and *The Blushing Bridegroom* (a musical, starring Rod LaRoque, Conrad Nagel and Helen Twelvetrees, with M.A. Pleasure in a bit part as "The Train Conductor").

The film company moved to Hollywood in 1932 and the place was once again used for storage. That was supposed to help explain why mannequins dressed in theatrical costumes hung throughout the building, since they were left-overs from the film company. Oh, and that Upholstery Shop that shut down in 1932 closed that year because it had been making costumes for the films in order to stay in business.

The official plaque was going to include the following information: "In 1935, Pleasure remodeled the warehouse into a massive design studio for his son-in-law Raoul Manzanera, who was obsessed with a new system of locomotive propulsion combining thermodynamics and magnetism in what he called 'Thermomagnetics'.

"A colossal turntable was installed to facilitate his work on 'Maxwell's Demon', a gargantuan locomotive that would revolutionize world transportation. This project (funded by a secret government contract worth millions) became so huge in scope that Raoul had to move it to an even larger facility, in what is now the AMC Theater complex."

Manzanera believed, according to other documentation about the original building that now houses the AMC Theaters, that the project would "restore the steam-powered locomotive to its rightful place in the forefront of American transportation. With a colossal government subsidy, he began the development of a mammoth train locomotive that utilized his controversial process of 'Thermomagnetics'—a process that reduced coal use to one-20th of the average steam engine.

"When the construction of this project became so massive it outgrew its island birthplace, Manzanera had to re-model this building (the largest in the area) to pursue his dream. In October 1940, just as he was getting ready to test the four-pipe magneto engine in his prototype, 'Maxwell's Demon,' disaster struck.

"The government canceled his contract and the Securities and Exchange Commission sued him for fraud. They had discovered that Manzanera's train wouldn't be able to run on normal gauge train tracks. His locomotive would require an entirely *new* system of rails, three feet farther apart, to be constructed throughout America.

"When he heard about this treachery, Manzanera flew into a rage. He invited his former benefactors down from Washington to see the 'Demon', but instead of taking them inside the building, Raoul, laughing hysterically, rammed down a nearby plunger and blew the facility sky high.

"All that remained was the super-structure in the middle of the factory, and some of the outer buildings. Re-built in 1988-89 by a joint effort of AMC Theaters and the Disney Company."

Manzanera then disappears from the Pleasure Island storyline and chronology. Since this dynamite explosion of "Prototype Design Center" happened at the end of 1940, we might assume that Manzanera—to escape the consequences of his actions— joined his wife Merriam on the ill-fated *Dominoe* yacht. That ship, during an Antarctica Circumnavigation, was lost at sea with Merriam, her father and the entire crew in 1941.

If Raoul's "Maxwell's Demon" sounds familiar, it is a reference to Scottish physicist James Clerk Maxwell's concept of an imaginary creature who is able to sort hot molecules from cold molecules without expending energy, thus bringing about a general decrease in entropy and violating the second law of thermodynamics.

Interior of the Adventurers Club

The Zebra Mezzanine. The top floor of the club. It is called the Zebra Mezzanine due to the Zebra Bar (a full zebra figure split in half with a bar in the middle) that was designed by Joe Rohde. It was a circular balcony area overlooking the Main Salon. The walls feature many artifacts, and a framed parchment of the Club Creed. "All the framed photos, throughout AC are 90% from a huge historic photo library in NYC. I brought in my old, portable, Royal manual typewriter. I still have it. We sat around WDI for days coming up with captions for them. They were typed on newsprint that we had soaked in tea and left in the sun to dry. I think everyone got their name—or some version of it—in at least one of those captions. It is an old WDI gag," AC Show Writer Craig McNair Wilson told me.

The Main Salon. The central room of the club filled with artifacts, the Yakoose, the Colonel, Babylonia and a statue of the famous Artemision Bronze. The bar in the Main Salon was originally to be an "Illusion Bar".

Rock Hall of Technifex who installed the effects in the club told me the original plans for the room included "bar stools that lower with each round of drinks (this was installed and used in the early years frequently), beautiful patrons who appear in the mirror behind the bar when the stool is empty (this would have been the Pepper's Ghost effect used in the Haunted Mansion attraction), bottles behind the bar that pour by themselves (based on a concept by Imagineer Yale Gracey), overhead effects, etc. Close up magic at tables provided by strolling magicians."

The Mask Room. A small room off the Main Salon that featured masks gathered by Joe Rohde from garage sales and swap meets in the Southern California area. Technifex installed all the mechanics in the masks. Technifex had to carve out the wooden, ethnic masks to put in mechanisms for the mouth action, eyebrows, etc. In retrospect, they realized it would have been easier to work with custom-made masks because it was time consuming and delicate to modify the masks to house the mechanics. Arnie (Mask of Comedy) and Claude (Mask of Tragedy) were named as a reference to "Bonnie and Clyde" and were built from scratch.

The Treasure Room. Another small room off the Main Salon, the Treasure Room contained additional artifacts gathered by the club, and a cabinet that houses a lamp with the head of Beezle the Genie. This illusion was designed and built by Rock Hall of Technifex. The room was meant to suggest the interior of an Arabian tent filled with exotic treasures which is why it is the home to a genie.

The Library. This room is the largest in the club with a bar and a raised stage where shows were presented including the Balderdash competition. It also housed the famous sinking ship in a bottle illusion (inspired by a concept by Imagineer Yale Gracey) and the organ possessed by the spirit of Fingers Zambezi (inspired by a concept of a piano being played by an invisible spirit at the Magic Castle in Hollywood, California).

One secret of the Adventurers Club that most fans never knew was on the outside wall of the library. Merriweather Pleasure claimed to have won the plans for the Adventurers Club in a game of dominoes. In addition, the yacht that Pleasure was sailing when he disappeared was also named the *Dominoe*. Facing the exterior of the club, walking to the left down the rampway for guests in wheelchairs, it is apparent that the wall is decorated in a domino pattern.

The Library Shows

"Some days you eat the bear, some days the bear eats you... But always dress for the hunt."

The Library doors would open at 8:15pm every night and could only seat 150 guests. According to the handout flyer: "Serial Thriller Radio Broadcast 8:15pm. Balderdash Cup Competition 8:50pm. Curator's New Discovery 9:30pm. RadioThon Show 10:05pm. Mandora's Cabaret 11:00pm. Maid's Sing-a-long 12:00am. Fingers Takes Requests 12:45am." Later, Chris Oyen would eliminate some shows and include Samantha Sterling's Cabaret and the Hoopla that would end the evening.

Mask Room Events: "Where our mystical menagerie of masks come to life: 7:40pm, 8:30pm, 10:00pm, 11:10pm."

Treasure Room Events: "Featuring priceless antiquities, rare artifacts and the floating head of a genie. 8:00pm, 9:20pm, 10:40pm, 12:30am."

"Other Club activities and events occur every ten minutes!"

Show writer and director Chris Oyen was brought on in January 1990 to create a structure for the Adventurers Club experience. As a result, over his first years at the Club, he developed a performing matrix that included three different shows in the Mask Room, three different shows in the Treasure Room as well as a beginning, middle and an end experience for the shows in the Library.

Additional shows including a séance with an appearance by Houdini, specialty Hooplas, different Halloween and Christmas celebrations were created and performed over the years to refresh the experience.

Oyen eventually came up with a midnight exorcism. The show titled *Fletcher's New Discovery* revolved around curator Fletcher Hodges opening an artifact and poor Emil Bleehall being possessed by the spirit of Goatha, Warrior Queen of Assyria. Eventually, the spirit then inhabits the Fingers Zambeii organ for a little supernatural hanky panky: "Sometimes the spirit consumes you. Sometimes you consume the spirit." Reportedly, Disney executive Frank Wells did not care for this show.

Welcome Party. Samantha Sterling and Fletcher Hodges throw a welcome party to start the "Open House" festivities.

Radio Broadcast. Otis T. Wren and Pamelia Perkins direct and perform a version of their weekly old-style radio serial, *Tales of the Adventurers Club* sponsored by *Jinkies*. ("We love 'em!") However, half the cast is missing and must be replaced by audience members with comic results.

Jinkies is the "perfect cereal for adventuring...high in protein, high in fiber...and when hurled at a high velocity, Jinkies can render an opponent unconscious. Jinkies is the only cereal aerodynamically designed with beveled edges and when combined with its amazing laxative properties...it's always an adventure when you jump up for Jinkies!" Inside the cereal box were lima beans that were sometimes spilled on the stage. On the back of the box was a picture of Hathaway Browne.

The Balderdash Competition. Hathaway Browne, Otis T. Wren and Emil Bleehall compete to be "Adventurer of the Year" by relating the most outrageous stories that have supposedly happened to them and demonstrate their skills. Of course, these tall tales are all balderdash (exaggerated nonsense).

Bleehall always won with his demonstration of tap dancing pigeons that could be heard on the roof of the building. Only club members or relatives of past and current club members may compete.

1. Each competing member shall tell or actually demonstrate one true to life adventure.

2. Upon completion of the tales, the audience shall determine the winner through their applause.

3. All members must be present inside the library to compete.

4. Each permanent member of the Adventurers Club shall be eligible to compete for the Balderdash Cup provided that he, or she, arrives before midnight of the contest date.

The RadioThon. An amateur talent show performed by various members to attempt to raise $2,000 using a radio telethon to save the club from losing its lease. Unfortunately, the phone lines are crossed with an Asian restaurant, the House of Wong, that is a particular favorite dining location of Club President Pamelia Perkins who shares with the audience her passion for their mustard sauce and duck sauce.

At the end of the skit, the club is rescued by a last-minute oversized check from the House of Wong except for the final performance when the check never arrived. For several years, WDW Entertainment leased offices at 7680 Republic Drive (now renamed Universal) in a building that is now available for lease near a shopping mall that didn't have a Chinese restaurant but did have a Flippers Pizza. By the way, there are several House of Wong restaurants scattered throughout North America—but not in Florida.

Check# 2659 from the House of Wong:

Harry and Seymour Wong
7680 Republic Drive
Orlando, Florida 32819

Pay To the Order of "The Adventurers Club" $2,000.

Memo: Official Egg Roll

Samantha's Cabaret. A show featuring Samantha Sterling singing.

The Maid's Sing-Along. A show featuring the Maid and audience participation.

The Rhythm Ritual. A show centered in the Main Salon that leads into the Hoopla. The Ritual usually features all the Adventurers looking down from the balconies of the mezzanine as they take turns performing humorous solos on percussive instruments. The ritual usually builds to a crescendo as they come downstairs into the Main Salon, all playing their instruments together. Then the Colonel responds to the sound by coming off duty and shouting out rhythmic but often nonsensical phrases for the patrons to repeat, finalizing in the announcement of the Hoopla.

The Hoopla - The Adventurers Club evening finale hosted by Samantha Sterling, and always begins with a sing-along of *The Happy Wanderer*. There are usually two or three other numbers performed by other Adventurers, then the show is always concluded with Samantha leading everyone in "When the Saints Go Marching In", with each remaining Adventurer creating an original verse. The actors either invent a new verse on the spur of the moment or reuse one they've previously found to be effective.

The Physical Magic of the Club

It has been said that the best special effect is the one that takes place in an audience's mind where they imagine what the monster in the darkness really looks like. Imagination can create a much more effective image than a small budget.

According to the plaque and the empty stand in the Zebra Mezzanine of the Adventurers Club, one of those unseen monsters is the "Bronze Durubashna Weasel Bat Spirit of Kharshati Nomads. Once the pride of the club this statuette turned out to be cursed and came to life on October 12, 1937 a night described by Merriweather A. Pleasure as 'that monumental unpleasantness'. The Weasel-Bat is still loose in the club, and occasionally roosts in the upper inseam of mens' cotton trousers, hence the 'unpleasantness'."

Fortunately, other special effects in the Adventurer's Club can be seen and enjoyed by the guests.

Rock Hall and Monty Lunde started their amusement industry careers as special effects designers for WED (later known as Walt Disney Imagineering). Hall was hired as a consultant in 1979 and then became a full-time employee in 1981. Lunde was hired that same year.

Hall worked on the New Fantasyland project (specifically the dark rides including Snow White's Scary Adventures, Pinocchio's Daring Journey, Mr. Toad's Wild Ride and Peter Pan's Flight) and Lunde was assigned to work on Epcot. During this time, they worked with second generation Imagineers who would become legends including Tony Baxter and Joe Rohde.

Eventually, Hall and Lunde became "sort of drinking buddies" working on some of the same projects. When both were laid off by WED, they formed their own company, Technifex, in 1984. Six Flags gave the company its first major project by hiring them to work on the Power Plant in Baltimore, Maryland.

For decades, the company has created special effects (visual illusions, 4-D theater effects, lighting, water, fire effects) for theme parks, water parks, casinos, trade shows, retail centers and many other industries.

One of their early projects was the special effects for the Adventurers Club. Many people, myself included, mistakenly believed that the legendary Jim Steinmeyer was involved with the illusions for the Club especially since he was working with Imagineering at the time.

Steinmeyer was kind enough to write to me and included this statement:

"I had very little to do with the Adventurer's Club. In fact, the illusions weren't mine, but were developed at Imagineering. I think that, over the course of the project, I was called in for a meeting or two on the illusions, but I wasn't responsible for them. I was working in the Entertainment Centers group at the time, and my office was across from the office of all the fellows who were developing Adventurers Club. (My project was something called Disney Island, which didn't happen.)

"So, I heard a lot about it, and saw various presentations. But I think I can safely say that I never worked directly on Adventurers Club…. As for the illusions, I believe that they were developed from Roger's [show writer Roger Cox] basic script concepts and developed at Disney special effects. Technifex was involved in building them. I seem to recall going out there to see the ship in the bottle."

In the library of the Adventurers Club during the competition for the Balderdash Cup, Otis T. Wren tells a tall tale that culminates in a huge ship in a bottle behind the bar experiencing a severe storm and literally sinking out of site. Hall and one of his employees first saw that effect being developed by legendary Disney special effects expert Imagineer Yale Gracey who intended it to be added to the Haunted Mansion.

Hall shared space at WED with Gracey for a period of time and Gracey was also developing the illusion of a bottle pouring itself that was later going to be incorporated into the Adventurers Club.

Since Power Plant in Baltimore was a harbor-themed entertainment environment, Technifex built the sinking ship in a bottle illusion for that venue, but soon the company was involved with Pleasure Island.

The Neon Armadillo was originally going to be a magic club and then evolved into a Country Western club. Several of the original proposed Pleasure Island nightclubs never developed. Technifex worked on some stuff for the magic club and was also going to help out as well with Madison's Dive.

Madison's Dive, according to the original Imagineering pitch, was a "Crab house/saloon themed as a waterfront dive complete with concrete floors and brown paper covered tables where guests crack fresh cooked crabs. Features an 'old salt' owner who entertains guests with sea chanteys and tales of his lost love ... Madison the mermaid."

That "old salt" was later named "Captain Spike" and he appeared in person at Michael Eisner's announcement of the Pleasure Island project in 1986.

Imagineering also pitched "Nemo's—Enter the Victorian elegance of Captain Nemo's Nautilus submarine lounge. Undersea effects and live fish tanks seen through view ports. Stage features torch singers performing tunes from the '20s and '30s."

Technifex pitched the idea of a sinking ship in a bottle similar to the one they created for the Power Plant. Originally, it would have been in Madison's Dive when the magic club disappeared but then when that club was cancelled as well, the bottle floated over to the library of the Adventurers Club.

After the Adventurers Club closed, the bottle was warehoused and then relocated to Trader Sam's Enchanted Tiki Bar at the Disneyland Hotel. That bottle is the original bottle with the projection effects but Kevin Kidney and Jody Daily built a new ship for it to resemble The *Wicked Wench* that was attacking the fort in Pirates of the Caribbean attraction.

Technifex also built the Zebra Bar (from Joe Rohde's sketch that specifically indicated that the zebra tail had to be on the top portion of the spilt and not the bottom) and there was some paint on that bar that never did set correctly.

In those days, vendors working for Disney had a lot more flexibility and didn't have to do a lot of drawings for pre-approval but followed the sketches they were given.

The bar in the Main Salon was originally according to Hall to be an "Illusion Bar where bar stools that lower with each round of drinks (this was installed and used in the early years frequently) to make guests think they were drunk, beautiful young women who appear in the mirror next to you when the stool is empty (this would have been the Pepper's Ghost effect used in the Haunted Mansion), bottles behind the bar that pour by themselves (based on a concept by Yale Gracey), overhead effects, etc. Close up magic at tables provided by strolling magicians."

The masks in the Mask Room were all obtained by Joe Rohde. Many people I interviewed all told me that Rohde would laugh that he traveled the world looking for artifacts for the club but couldn't find any that he felt would work so that all the artifacts were obtained at swap meets in the Pasadena, California area.

Writer Craig McNair Wilson told me: "Joe [Rohde] went around the world once a year, with his wife Melody "Mel" Malmberg, WDI show writer [author of the book *The Making of Animal Kingdom*] on vacation to Borneo, Nepal, etc. Joe Rohde had a Sunday afternoon soirée in his backyard in Pasadena themed as 'The Last Days of the Raj' where we would make up tall tales.

"And every second Sunday for *years* we went to the Rose Bowl swap meet and bought stuff: rugs, masks, statues…. He'd bring back a new earring and a couple other odd curios from his trips that would inspire our next trip to the Rose Bowl swap meet, Hollywood and Pasadena estate sales, etc. He also designed, drew and oversaw the manufacture of items like the first floor zebra bar, javelin thrower statue, etc."

The "javelin thrower statue" is based on a famous Greek statue called the Artemision Bronze that was recovered from the sea off Cape Artemsion. The statue's throwing hand was empty so there continues to this day some controversy whether it is Zeus (throwing a missing thunderbolt as in similar statues) or Posedion (throwing a missing trident). The statue was discovered in 1926 and excavated in 1928 so it logically fits within the mythical time frame of the Adventurers Club.

The task was given to Technifex to make those masks in the Mask Room actually work. They had to carve out the wooden, ethnic masks to put in mechanisms for the mouth action, eyebrows, etc. In retrospect, they realized it would have been easier to work with custom-made masks. It was time consuming and delicate to modify the masks to house the mechanics.

Arnie (Mask of Comedy) and Claude (Mask of Tragedy) were custom made and originally going to be called "Ned and Fred." It has been said that the names were to be a cute reference to the names "Bonnie and Clyde".

Monty Lunde, President of Technifex recalled, "We had some initial meetings with Joe Rohde and Rick Rothschild over at Walt Disney Imagineering about what the club was going to look like.

They'd send us sketches and we would then create nearly every effect you saw in the Adventurers Club.

"As an example, we created all the masks for the Mask Room. The ones on the wall were all automated and triggered by the actors for certain parts of the show. However, the two main puppets were being controlled by actors on the other side of the walls. There was one operator/actor per mask that had a series of actuators and cables. Those made the mouth move, the eyes look in various directions and the eyebrows to raise up and down."

"Fingers" Zambezi, paranormal piano protégé, and the organ in the library were inspired by a similar effect at the popular Magic Castle in Hollywood. At the Magic Castle, the spirit of 'Irma' magically plays the piano and takes musical requests from guests who little suspect that another piano and speaker are directly below and connected to the piano up above that is mirroring the playing."

In the Adventurers Club, the keyboardist is hidden behind the crooked picture (actually a one way mirror) on the side of the stage.

"The Magic Castle in Hollywood was a regular hang out for the team as it was old, mysterious, goofy, and full of odd people," Wilson remembered. "You never know who is staff, who the magicians are, and who the weird old guy in the dark corner doing one-handed shuffles is.

"In fact, we always wanted AC to have a restaurant attached. The space that might have been the AC dining room became a magic club, then jazz club, then a country western club [Neon Armadillo] after Michael [Eisner] visited the Cheyenne Saloon at Church Street Station, downtown Orlando, and was stunned by the vastness of it *and* it was packed."

Susie Cowan who was a WDI Production Designer recalled in an interview with me: "I remember showing up at the Adventurers Club on Pleasure Island, assuming I was about to be shown a mock-up of one of the club's gag elements—the organ that crashed through the ceiling from the floor up above. Instead of a mock-up, I saw this fanciful thing that had nothing to do with the realistic look we were attempting to create.

"So we had it taken out, and we started work all over again. For two weeks we tried all different kinds of materials and techniques to make this thing look right. Finally, we came up with what we thought was the right look. In the meantime, the rest of the club had been finished, and the cleaning crews had been coming in everyday to keep the place tidy.

"We knew we had exactly the right look when one of the cleaning crew leaned over and tapped me on the shoulder and said, 'Honey, when is someone gonna clean that mess up in there, so we can get on with our cleaning?'"

Technifex also built the huge Babylonia head (that at one time was going to named "KIA" for "Know-It-All") and the cable controlled Colonel puppet.

Babylonia was built with the help of John Shadow., Shadow had experience making large puppets for Hollywood films. On the back side of the mask, an actor had access to move her foot up and down, and roll her eyes in a circle. As well as hit a button where they could make smoke appear from her mouth.

All of these things were built at Technifex in Valencia, California, and then shipped out to Florida.

Connie Orfanos, administrative assistant, remembered: "Once while we were in Florida we needed a puppeteer to work on a puppet for the Adventurers Club. Normally, this would be no big deal, but [executive show producer] Rick Rothschild came to me at 7pm Florida time, and said that we had to fly this guy in from California by the next day.

"I called the puppeteer to see if he was available. He was, so I called Ask Mr. Foster to make the arrangements. It was already around 5pm California time when we worked out the guy's travel plans. I called the puppeteer back to let him know when his plane left and he said, 'By the way, did I tell you that I weigh 350 pounds and I need two seats on the plane?' Thank goodness the people at Ask Mr. Foster were still there and we got everything taken care of."

The rare Mongolian Yakoose is part yak and part moose and WDI wanted a stuffed animal head on the wall (since many explorer clubs had stuffed animal heads on the walls) but didn't like the possible negative reaction to seeing a "big, old grungy head of a dead animal." So to get a few laughs, the head was "upholstered" instead of stuffed and was just hanging around.

The yakoose is a distant cousin of Melvin the Moose ("I'm only part moose as it is.") who is hanging around on the wall of the Country Bear Jamboree.

The voice of the Audio-Animatronics Yakoose was supplied by Tom Sherohman, who had a background in improvisation and was a writer and theatre guy from way back. He had worked a good bit with Pat Proft who created *Police Academy* among other projects. Sherohman became the first director of the Comedy Warehouse.

The difficulty of the Yakoose was that it would go off at any time, in order to add to the chaos and spontaneity of the club. When Chris Oyen came in as show director in January 1990, he begged WDI to either put the head on a timer or install an "on/off switch" because the Yakoose would go off unexpectedly in the middle of scenes that the actors were performing in the Main Salon. Eventually, a switch was installed.

The Yakoose was popular enough that it inspired a specialty mug that was sold at the club. Over the years, other specialty glasses from a monkey head to a tiki head to one featuring Arnie and Claude were sold.

SPOILER WARNING. In the next few paragraphs I am going to reveal the secret behind one of the most amazing illusions at the Adventurers Club, the floating head in the cabinet. This is an illusion that was built into the wall itself so it can't be saved and relocated but would have to be rebuilt from scratch.

Beezle is the name of the head of a genie imprisoned in a lamp in the Treasure Room. He wants nothing more than a body and a date with the lovely maid who dusts his cabinet. In the performance matrix, usually the actor who portrays Hathaway Browne also performs as the genie head.

This impressive effect was designed and built by Rock Hall of Technifex. He took a mirror weighing more than 200 pounds and cut a square in it for an actor to put in his head. On either side of the square are grips so the actor with the help of rollers and counter balances can move the mirror up and down and back and forth. Since it is a mirror, the audience just sees the illusion of the lantern with the head floating up and down. It is heavy to start but glides easily once it starts to move.

On the side of the cut square there are handles on each side to not only control the movement but push buttons on the side of the handles that control the effects like lighting. The toughest part about creating the illusion is that WDI supplied the already built cabinet so once again, the mechanics had to be adjusted to adapt to an existing piece.

It is a fairly simple illusion but over the years it has amazed countless guests, including myself, and what is even more amazing to me is that this effect has never been duplicated anywhere else. Guests who sat close to the cabinet sometimes felt the movement in the wall.

Rock Hall remembered that working on the Adventurers Club was "Great fun-much better than I thought" and that "Joe [Rohde] knew exactly what he wanted.

New Year's Eve Every Night

While Pleasure Island officially opened May 1989, it went through some changes almost immediately as the Walt Disney Company adjusted to running a club district for the first time.

It was felt there needed to be something to catch the audience's attention that this was going to be a new experience. At one point, it was suggested that a spaceship land on Pleasure Island each night that would lead into a nightly celebration of Christmas.

Part of the Merriweather Pleasure legend was his attempts to contact life in outer space and in fact, the West End Plaza had a plaque stating that Pleasure had originally intended it to be a landing platform for extraterrestrial craft.

That plaque stated: "West End Plaza. Island founder and star-gazer Merriweather Adam Pleasure was convinced during the sole flight of his 'X-Thing' aircraft that he could make contact with alien beings. Working feverishly, Pleasure completed the world's first and only Alien Landing Platform on July 4, 1941. His wife Isabella immediately laid claim to it for her beloved Pleasure Island Philharmonic Concert Band. Much to Merriweather's disgust ('How can 'they' land when that blasted band is playing?') this became home base for the P.I.P.C.B."

Fortunately, wiser Disney marketing people realized that Christmas and outer space visitors didn't seem to be a good fit for the Island but that suggestion did spark the idea of celebrating New Year's Eve, a time traditionally known for partying and drinking and fireworks.

So, in 1990, the Island welcomed in the New Year every night (sometimes on weekdays as early as 11pm) with fireworks, lots of confetti, music, professional dancers and more until New Year's Eve 2005.

The animated series *The Simpsons* parodied the concept in its October 1994 episode *Itchy and Scratchy Land* where Homer and Marge spend time on Parent's Island and visit the restaurant T.G.I. McScratchy's Goodtime Foodrinkery where they wear party hats and dance. The location celebrates New Year's Eve all the time. Marge tells a waiter, "It must be wonderful to ring in the New Year over and over." The waiter responds, "Please kill me."

Guests staying at the nearby Disney Institute complained about the noise since it traveled across the water so was not muffled at all. The original concept was that New Year's would also be celebrated inside the clubs, as well. It was a captive audience.

Club owners tried to push to the powers-that-be that guests needed to be outside to celebrate since they didn't gain added revenue by having a celebration inside the club.

The promotional flyer proclaimed: "Join an incredible island-wide, nightly New Year's Eve Party! The fun spills from six fabulous nightclubs into the street—the "seventh club". Fireworks and searchlights light a blizzard of confetti as dancers catch the beat on the street. It's a Street Party like you've never seen! After 7pm, you must be 18 or older for admission to Pleasure Island unless accompanied by a parent."

The show was written by Lynn Hart who wrote lyrics and music for the Comedy Warehouse and the Adventurers Club. Hart told me, "In 1992 (I think it was) I wrote and directed the West End New Year's Eve show ("In With the New") at PI. I revised it when the new West End stage opened the next year. Overall, it ran for three years."

There was an attempt to revise the Merriweather Pleasure story to more closely come in line with this new entertainment directive of celebrating New Year's every evening. Chris Oyen, who was the show writer and director for both the Comedy Warehouse and the Adventurers Club, came up with this back story revision in June 1991.

However, like the original story, it was never fully understood nor adopted by the regular cast members or shared with the guests and no attempt was made to readjust the plaques that were already on the island nor add new plaques to explain the change.

At best, this revision is an interesting historical footnote and oddity, as well as an example of the imagination and writing skill of Oyen, who during his time with the Adventurers Club was sorely underappreciated for his contributions in creating a perfor-mance structure that allowed the club to survive for decades while other venues changed significantly or completely disappeared.

It was Oyen who battled the original "club mentality" that insisted that the lights be turned up full when a show was on so that guests could more clearly see the servers and the request that performers stop periodically during their scenes to do commercials for the drink specials.

It was Oyen who came up with the "Open House" concept to explain why guests were allowed into a private club. It was Oyen who created the character of Samantha Sterling.

Oyen's initial three-month contract kept getting extended for five years until Oyen left to work on other Disney shows including the *Diamond Horseshoe* and *Galaxy Search* both at the Magic Kingdom as well as directing the *Sword in the Stone* show with Merlin, although he did also remain the show director of the Comedy Warehouse for many years.

Here is the story that Oyen devised to explain why every night was New Year's Eve at Pleasure Island. Oyen made some changes to the original mythology. For instance, Merriweather is not lost at sea and it is Hurricane Charlotte and not Hurricane Connie that devastates the island. He also included the introduction of the I-4 Indians (a reference to Interstate 4 freeway that was near Walt Disney World). Some of Oyen's ideas did become incorporated in sketches and printed material that were released in later years.

When Merriweather Adam Pleasure steamed through the Florida Barge Canal System on his mighty paddle wheeler, he knew immediately upon entering the peaceful waters of Lake Buena Vista that he had found his destiny.

The years he had spent in the steel business, back in Pittsburgh, had taught him that he was not meant for the conventions and restraints of "society". He had set out to create a home far from civilization, and further still from the skeptics, naysayers and those who would stifle the dreamers and men of imagination, such as himself.

There, in the wilds of semi-tropical Central Florida, on the northern bank of an uncharted lake, Pleasure saw the primitive totem of a half moon, with a smiling face.

"The Funmeister! I've found the Funmeister! This shall be where we will build Pleasure Island," Pleasure proclaimed to a travel weary family and crew.

Pleasure had read about this ancient half-moon icon, whose roots go back to the Barbarians after the sack of Rome.

It symbolized individuality, the celebration of life, and the sharing of laughter. The ancient Germanic name for this idol translated to "Funmeister," as close as historical linguists could approximate. On every continent, in every civilization that Pleasure had studied, he had found a Funmeister counterpart.

Now, purely by coincidence, he had stumbled upon a link to those ancient times and our own.

Rushing ashore, he found the descendants of the I-4 Indians, who had held the land on this lake as their sacred ceremonial territory. Clad in their traditional attire, the Indians carried themselves in a regal, almost other worldly manner. These natives told Mr. Pleasure the island was imbued with the spirit of one of their deities, the one they called the "Funmeister".

Excitedly, Pleasure begged the Indians to allow him to settle and build on their land and he would make the island a living monument to the spirit of the Funmeister. They told him that he would have their answer in the morning.

Pleasure returned to his ship with the sense that fate had led him to this spot. In the morning when he returned, the village that he had seen only hours before had vanished completely and without a trace—with the exception of a giant image of the Funmeister on a totem pole. The Indians he had met the day before were actually the spirits of the Island's former inhabitants who, by their disappearance, were now granting him permission to settle there.

The next week, an excited Merriweather Adam Pleasure officially purchased the land on the shore of Lake Buena Vista from the Seminole Land Agency. He knew, however, that the land would always truly belong to the Funmeister. That is why Pleasure island has always been dedicated to individuality, the celebration of life, and the sharing of laughter.

Pleasure never forgot his vow to those ghostly Indians. While his sail making and canvas fabrication business was quickly amassing him a fortune by day, by night the little factor district was turned into a nightly New Year's Eve Party. His guest list to these every evening events put the drinking and eating side by side with poets, artists, adventurers, and the elite of the upper classes. In fact, a trip to Pleasure Island was a social "must," as anybody who was "anybody" simply had to stop at least once a year.

Pleasure welcomed them all.

All these nightly celebrations did not quell Pleasure's ambitions for progress. He moved the bulk of the business concerns into custom yachts during the 1920s and made that a successful endeavor. There were inventions, innovations, and bold new ideas constantly being developed, as well as upgrades to the technologies, such as the communication center.

There were many expeditions to the far-flung corners of the globe, which brought back not only intriguing artifacts but unique new acquaintances. So many, in fact, that in 1932 The Adventurers Club was formed in order to accommodate both artifact and eccentric alike.

Aided by the transportation link provided by the Avigators, a group of wild barnstormers organized by Pleasure in 1924 to carry the mail and run an import/export business, visitors from all over the world had access to Pleasure Island—if they knew the right people.

Mixed in with the interesting people and successful enterprises were some projects that did not quite work out. The Pleasure Distilleries went to the dogs—actually the armadillos.

The XZFR floated away in five even but slightly different shaped pieces. Merriweather Pleasure's son Stewart destroyed the bridges while attempting to navigate blindfolded, trying to see only with his "second sight".

The most interesting was the disappearance of the Pleasure family and the Island itself.

By 1944 Pleasure Island was famous among the "in the know." A corrupt syndicate of developers attempted to capitalize on this by turning the Island into a spa and retreat for the rich and famous.

The only problem was that Merriweather would not sell his land as he was not about to compromise his obligation to the spirit of the Funmeister. Through a series of bribes, the developers had a court declare the title to the land null and void and were granted the ability to take possession as of the first of the year, 1945.

On New Year's Eve, 1944, Hurricane Charlotte headed across Florida toward Pleasure Island. Merriweather Adam Pleasure evacuated everyone but his family from the property. Once the storm had passed, there was no trace of the Island or its inhabitants left. The topography was so drastically altered, creating an uninhabitable marshland worthless to the developers.

The power of the hurricane's destruction was so great, it was even impossible for them to determine the former site of the Island.

In 1971, Pleasure's paddlewheler mysteriously floated into an inlet where a Disney surveying team was camped. It was renovated and re-commissioned as the Empress Lily.

This event caused further exploration of Disney's undeveloped property. It wasn't until 1987, however, while on a routine helicopter fly over, that a group of Disney construction engineers claimed they saw a man dressed like a ship's captain waving to them from the banks of Lake Buena Vista.

When they circled back and landed, they found only a captain's hat with the name "Merriweather Adam Pleasure" written on the inside, alongside the crescent moon totem of the Funmeister. Disney archaeologists then undertook the excavation and reclamation of Pleasure Island where every night is New Year's Eve, once again.

On New Year's Eve in 1873, Merriweather Adam Pleasure was born. He would say later that he had been born on that day deliberately, so everyone in the world would have a reason to celebrate with him.

As fate would have it, on New Year's Eve 1901, his eldest son, Stewart, was born. A plucky Merriweather claimed he had planned it that way all along. When a second son, Henry, was born on New Year's Eve, 1905, people began to believe there might be something to Merriweather's claim of orchestrating the date of his offspring's birth.

On New Year's Eve, 1911, when Pleasure steamed into Lake Buena Vista, a new chapter was opened in his life and Pleasure Island was born. When his last child, Miriam, was born on Feb. 17, 1912, Merriweather said that it was a sign.

A family tradition of landmark events occurring on New Year's Eve had been broken, and the only way to correct this chronological indiscretion was to correct time itself. Pleasure said that since it was his island, he could say it was any day he wanted it to be.

He claimed that the birth of Miriam on a date so far out of Pleasure family tradition was clearly a sign from the Funmeister that every day should be New Year's Eve on Pleasure Island.

This, of course, meant that every night there was a New Year's Eve party on Pleasure Island. At the end of each work day, every day of the year, the laborers, artisans, inventors, and globe-trotting millionaire visitors alike, would dance in the streets as the entire Island community kicked back with wild abandon. The buildings that provided industrial functions during the daytime were reset to be dancehalls, concert or theatrical venues, or locations for dining or refreshments.

Every night there was a fireworks display, choreographed by Merriweather Pleasure himself.

Pleasure had brought his daughter's birthday back in line with the family lineage and created a reason for nightly merriment with one fabulously whimsical decree. It is in honor of this spirit of unabated whimsy and dedication to unrelenting fun that the tradition of a nightly New Year's Eve Party had been restored to Pleasure Island.

Letters

In the earliest days of the Adventurers Club, the butler Graves might approach a guest with a silver tray bearing one of four pre-typed letters. These letters would give the guest a persona so the performers of the club might interact with that guest as that identity during their time in the Club.

In later years, it was not used as a springboard for improvisation but as a cute little extra touch especially for frequent visitors. They were kept in a drawer in a desk on the Zebra Mezzanine.

As director Chris Oyen explained to me: "We moved on from that sort of 'endowment' as the performers became better trained at improvisation and as we better defined our central purpose and them, making more specific choices in order to support our overall show."

The exterior of the envelope would have the character name written in a clear and pleasing cursive and the address was always the Adventurers Club.

There was an exotic foreign stamp and the postmark (in either black or red ink) was a round circle with a unicorn in it and no date.

Letter One:

From Pamelia Perkins, President of the Library Committee
To Alston Golf, The Adventurers Club

My Dear Mr. Golf:

Your behavior at last Tuesday's Tea and Supper was contemptible. Perhaps grammar school boys find it entertaining to dance on the bar with lampshades on their heads but I assure you the Library Committee does not.

What little laughter there was merely confirmed everyone's embarrassment. As for the money that was thrown at you—I think it only fair that it be given to the Library Committee to pay for having the bar refinished.

I am sure nothing like this will ever occur again. Please see that you are as sure as I am. See you next Tuesday night.

Sincerely, Pamelia Perkins

Letter Two:

From: Sedgewick, Somewhere East of Jakarta, Sometime after Christmas

To: Dr. Gaberdine (although the outer envelope spells it "Gabardine"), The Adventurers Club

Dear Doctor,

May this letter find you well. Personally, I've seen better days. As you know, the expedition turned a difficult corner once we left Jakarta. Seems someone tied Cobby's boot laces together and then cried "Fire!" he's been in a nose brace for several days now and I feel for him every time he sneezes.

We've all been tested by pain and aggravation. Poor Cranfield has suffered the worst: his athlete's foot has now merged with his chapped lips so that he currently resembles a glazed doughnut that's been left out in the rain. Still, the men have not lost Hope. Hope left on his own accord with a Naguri priestess that wanted to see Rio. We never should have brought those travel broucheres.

I remain undaunted. With fresh supplies we stand a good chance of reaching our destination which, as you know, will bring us all the attention we richly deserve.

Plainly, the immediate need is financial. Your generosity at this point would not only ensure the success of the expedition but would guarantee you a Christmas card every year for the rest of your natural life. Make arrangements with Hathaway Browne. He's an idiot but knows how to fly a plane. I knew I could count on you.

Desperately yours, Sedgewick

Letter Three:

From: Hathaway Browne, Cleveland, Ohio (July 23, 1933
To: Miss Weggie Wishmeyer, The Adventurers Club

My Dearest Weggie,

I hope this finds you at the Club. Graves has always been good about getting my mail out. I would have written sooner, but I cracked the wing spars on the Gypsy Moth when I ran into a freight train.

You'll probably laugh, but I'm going to tell a little story on myself: I had run out of fuel at 15,000 feet. Normally, I'd just glide until I found a clearing, but not this time! I decided to try and make Cleveland (another 800 miles). Well, the joke was on me! First, I hit a fog bank, then I hit the train. But I only missed Cleveland by 1,500 feet! I'll be fine when the hand heals.

My only disappointment is that in an effort to gain altitude, I threw out all my food, water, and cologne overboard, but I refused to let go of the kimono I bought you in Hong Kong. I guess the additional weight was just too much. Sorry, I don't think the bloodstains will come out.

Anyways, I'll have the Moth back in shape as soon as I do a little welding with my lighter.

Remember—pookie bear needs cuddlewinkes.

Higher and faster, Hathaway

Letter Four:

From Alston Golf, MBKEMBE, August 2, 1933

To: Mr. Henshaw, The Adventurers Club

My Dear Mr. Henshaw:

After several lengthy confabulations with my solicitors, I have decided to release this epistle rather than encircle you with noxious litigation. Suffice it to say that I am not a happy chappy.

I would draw your attention, if at all possible, to the phantasmatic incident alleged to have transpired during the recent fortnight's stay I endured in that tar pit which you insist on advertising as your "marina". I arrived to find my yacht, MBKEMBE, translated literally from the Swahili to mean "King of the Earth, ruler of the Sea, Lord of all mankind", was indeed berthed proximate to the type of overly pretentious yachties which I had presumed were excluded from your little club. Not so.

To wit: the spurious allegations to which my vessel was subjected regarding the overboard discharge of the entire contents of MBKEMBE's on-board sanitation system. I find absolutely no foundation to this slander. Quite simply, it is an egregious lie constructed for the purpose of defaming myself and my honorable craft. Should this absurd hallucination be mentioned again, I shall have no other choice other than buying the marina outright and reduce it to bits of charred wood floating on the surface. Idle threat? Think again!

Yours in pique, Alston Golf

At Disney's Aulani Resort in Hawaii on the island of Oahu is Aunty's Beach House, the Kids Club, that includes a painting accompanied by the following letter. Imagineer Joe Rohde was the creative director of the project.

Pamelia Perkins
The Adventurers Club
Lake Buena Vista, Florida
Dreamy Ka'imi
Whichever's the Best Fishing spot Nowadays
O'ahu, Hawai'i

My Dear Ka'imi,

I do hope this letter finds you in good health and high spirits—and if it finds you back in your home islands, why shouldn't you be? Everyone here at the club misses you something dreadful and send many kungalooshes your way....well everyone except for Hathaway. He's become the lady's man of the group ever since you vacated the position, and between you and me, I do believe he prefers the lack of competition. After all, it's not as though Fletcher and Otis offer up much sport!

But I digress. Fletcher and I were rummaging through the storage room when we came across this portrait of the Adventurers Club's less-than-honorable ancestor The Pillagers Brigade. This particular expedition was led by the Pillaging Prince himself, the late Harrison Hightower III. It was on this very journey that Hightower learned of the ghastly Shiriki Utundu idol he became so intent on possessing. Can you imagine? To spend years searching an entire continent for a certain artifact, finally finding it, only to go missing in a freak elevator accident soon afterwards? A woman less sophisticated than myself might be inclined to say the idol really took Hightower for a ride.

At any rate, I thought you might like to add this painting to your ever-expanding collection. I must be off, as we're preparing for tonight's Open House and if I don't start weaning the Colonel off his giggle juice now, he's liable to scare away yet another roomful of potential recruits.

Me Ke Aloha

(Bet you thought I forgot my Hawaiian, hmmm?)

Pamelia Perkins

At Trader Sam's Enchanted Tiki Bar at the Disneyland Hotel is a letter from Pamelia leaving Sam a ventriloquist dummy called Slappy and that Colonel Suchbench had great affection for the doll and to feed it sandwiches. She mentions having to leave several items in Sam's possession due to her going on a new Adventurers Club adventure.

If they didn't return, they wanted them to be in good hands. She said that Professor Hodges would be on the lookout for any artifacts that he could display at the bar.

Also at Trader Sam's Enchanted Tiki Bar is a short letter and photo from Hathaway Browne: "Sam, Thanks for keeping the tiki torches lit! Would have made for a rough landing that night without them. Until we meet again. Higher and Faster, Hathaway Browne."

Additionally, there is a photo of Colonel Suchbench on a wall and underneath is a note to Sam from the Colonel reading: "Sam, remember that time in Burma? Good heavens, I think I need a G&T just thinking about it. Until the next time we two great explorers are paired...Kungaloosh! -Colonel Critchlow Suchbench".

At Trader Sam's Grog Grotto at the Polynesian Village Resort is the following postcard: "There is a man, a handsome man. As adventurous as he can be. And our friend Trader Sam, actually knows this man... it's me." (Signed with a big "H" for Hathaway Browne.)

Adventurers Almanac

Guests loved the characters at the Adventurers Club and frequently wrote to them at the club. The performers would write back "in character". Eventually, this became so overwhelming that show writer and director Chris Oyen created a four-page newsletter called *Adventurers Almanac* actually modeled after a turn-of-the-century newsletter from an Explorers Club called *Adventurers Newsletter.*

While some articles had the by-lines credited to the fictional Pamelia Perkins or Hathaway Browne, Oyen wrote much of the material with the help of everyone from Stage Manager Reed Jones (who later was the show director) to the performers themselves including Paula Pell, Kristian Truelsen, and Phil Card.

The first issue was Volume No. 54, Issue No. 1. Oyen told me that he chose "Volume No. 54" to make it seem as if the almanac had been published forever. Two other issues were published labeled "Volume 55 No. 9" and "Volume 56 No. 8" in order to make guests assume there were missing issues.

The *Adventurers Almanac* was distributed at the club itself but was also available through the mail. Its purpose was not just to enlarge and perpetuate the stories behind the club but to attract new visitors. It also served the purpose of avoiding legal issues of having Disney cast members responding to guests and helped eliminate the possibility of stalkers.

Oyen also created the pseudonym "Bernice Smythe-Fenton, personal assistant to Miss Pamelia Perkins" (in actuality a rotating cast member from WDW Guest Communications department) to answer letters to guests. Oyen was often brought in to help with the more difficult answers.

Correspondence Committee member Bernice Smythe-Fenton explained the newsletter process in Volume No. 56, Issue No. 8:

Greetings and Salutations, fellow Members!

I cannot tell you how rewarding it is to be able to personally correspond with you clever, creative, and daring Adventurers from all over the globe. Over the past several months, we have received many fabulous updates on your expeditions. I encourage you to keep up the good work!

It is your communiques back here to the Club that keep the Permanent Members, and those of us who don't get out much, abreast of the latest news. I very much enjoy my challenging and exciting task of trying to keep up with all of you. It is to that end that I feel it would be prudent to remind you of Membership Policy #7-29565.32 which explains how the *Adventurers Almanac* is distributed.

According to the Policy, at the point in time you go through the New Member Induction Ceremony (held twice nightly in the Main Salon), you shall receive a current copy of the *Adventurers Almanac*, if it is available. Your membership is valid for ONE YEAR, and you will be sent any additional issues of the Almanac printed in that one year time period. (I must confide that we have a very random publishing schedule due to the fact that Prof. Wren speculates on ink futures).

Once that one year time period has passed, however, you must renew your Membership. This, of course, entails participating in the New Member Induction Ceremony, paying your annual dues, and once again filling out a mailing address card for the Records Committee.

If there is anyone out there within the sound of my typewriter whose Membership is delinquent, or if your membership is about to expire, please take this notice as a gentle reminder to come in to the Club so we may keep you on our memership rolls.

Yours in Postage,

Bernice Smythe-Fenton
Correspondence Committee

The *Almanac* disappeared because it was time consuming (this was in the days before computers and everything had to be done by hand, including the paste-ups of articles and screening the photos), expensive and, more importantly, was not generating new attendance but was primarily used by regulars who would rip out the coupon for a complimentary buffet, drink special and free admission to Pleasure Island on "General Membership Meeting" nights.

"Membership meetings" did take place for guests to come and bring artifacts and share stories. That stopped for several reasons including the fact that Disney Legal was "troubled" about accepting artifacts from guests as well as the fact that the club manager felt the club was losing too much money on the free appetizers and drinks.

Members were either Associate Level (which came with a drink coupon and official Club membership badge) or Presidential Level (which came with the canteen or mug and official Club membership badge).

The public domain photos that appeared in the *Almanac* were drawn from the coffee table book: *America's Yesterdays: Images of our Lost Past Discovered in the Photographic Archives of the Library of Congress* by Oliver Ormerod Jensen (Scribner 1978) and depicted photos of family life, Americans at work, people relaxing and much, much more.

The *Almanacs* are an interesting source of information. Two articles in Volume No. 56, Issue No. 8 in particular give some insight into the exterior of the Club. One article reveals that apparently thirsty adventurers—who were in a hurry to visit with Nash, the Club's bartender—left items stacked, piled or stuck in the ground outside the club that they were loaning or donating to the Permanent Collection from their recent expeditions.

"A general announcement has been made on behalf of both the Landscaping Committee and the Artifact Committee. To put it simply, these Committees request that Members do not leave artifacts unattended in front of the Club.

"Recent visitors to the Club could not help but notice many 'new additions' to the Club entrance. There is, evidently, a new custom being practiced by our Members who have items they wish to submit as loans or donations to the Permanent Collection.

"Upon arrival at the Club, Adventurers appear to be simply leaving the trophies and acquisitions from recent expeditions on the front lawn and front stoop. While some of these are tagged or registered with Club curator, Fletcher Hodges, others are merely stacked, piled, or stuck in the ground.

"The aesthetic offense being taken by our more staid and traditional members, however, is nothing compared to the real danger created by this random manner of artifact warehousing.

"A recent lecture scheduled on 'Central African Tribal Feuds' turned into a minor tragedy as a result of our haphazard entry way décor. Lecture Committee chairman, Comdr. (Retired) Alan Glassman had the nearly impossible task of calming down our hysterical guest lecturer, Mishanti tribal chieftain named Oshubu. Apparently, a cluster of spears casually stuck in the front lawn by a thirsty Adventurer was unknowingly placed in a configuration that symbolized a curse on Oshubu's livestock.

"Only after protracted apologies, pleas of ignorance, and lengthy financial negotiations was Comdr. Glassman able to convince our Mishanti vistior not to cut off the right thumb of everyone in the Club at that moment (evidently the only way to counteract the curse, according to their traditions). Needless to say, the lecture was canceled as a simple precautionary measure.

"The delay and altering of the evenings activities caused further mayhem, however. Dame Mildred had come dressed for the lecture in an authentic Mishanti costume, quite fetchingly fashioned entirely out of porcupine quills. She consumed several chilled adult beverages while waiting for the evening's events and then several more than her usually liberal limit. She caused a great deal of alarm by inadvertently inflicting several nasty puncture wounds upon fellow attendees when the lecture was hastily replaced by a square dance competition.

"In order to avoid further complications, we ask that no more artifacts are added to the front of the Club without first obtaining permission from Club curator, Fletcher Hodges."

That issue also sheds some light on the column to the left of the entrance where plaster has fallen away to reveal Egyptian hieroglyphs. According to Fletcher Hodges:

"I was having the pre-Columbian statue (donated anonymously by Wainwright Smithfield) hoisted to its current resting place, immediately to the left of our front door.

"Hans, our diligent but near-sighted hoist operator, accidentally bumped the wall of the watchtower with the statue several times. No damage was done to the statue, but this wrecking ball technique of moving it dislodged several layers of exterior plaster from the tower wall. A closer inspection showed that the plaster had hidden ancient hieroglyphs.

"I quickly researched the building plans for the Club and found that the three architects who Mr. Pleasure commissioned to design our building had given specific instructions to construct the watchtower to the exact dimensions of a particular tower they had visited in Egypt. They were so set on it that they left directions to this tower as a point of reference, right on the blue prints.

"After further research, I discovered receipts and shipping invoices proving that the building contractor, overwrought from the pressures of satisfying the artistic vision of three very temperamental architectural visionaries, purchased the actual tower, had it moved here in sections and reassembled it as our watchtower.

"This Machiavellian masterstroke apparently worked because I found a memo from the architects complimenting the contractor for his design accuracy. I am currently in the process of deciphering the glyphs, and from what I am able to determine, this obelisk was originally used as hurling place, from which people were thrown when they did not laugh at the Pharaoh's jokes.

"I have not, as yet been able to find the full name of the Pharaoh in question, but I have been able to decipher that his reign was short but loud. If there are any Egyptologists who can help provide insight or information, kindly contact me c/o the Club. I am off to scrape more bits of plaster."

(Editor's Note: Since this column was submitted, Fletcher has determined there are symbols that represent some of this Pharaoh's actual jokes. Mr. Hodges can be seen working on this wall in front of the Club, scraping, deciphering and chuckling, 'just in case', as he puts it.)

From Volume No. 55, Issue No. 9. Club Curator Fletcher Hodges relates the story of the Belsky Bass:

Greetings Adventurers; Hodges here. My topic for this "Curator's Corner" is the Belsky Bass. Now, I'm sure when you have visited the Club, you have had the dubious honor of having a conversation with the loquacious Professor Otis T. Wren. In addition to the many self-aggrandizing events he may have recounted for you, he has probably taken your valuable time to tell you of that glorious day he landed the magnificent fish that perches (pardon the pun) on the wall high above the Treasure Room.

I feel duty-bound to inform you of the accurate version of how this particular, and often overlooked specimen, came to be a part of the Adventurers Club.

In 1910, Merriweather Pleasure was floating around Lake Buena Vista assessing the possible purchase of the Ferderber Peninsula. Without warning, a Belsky flung itself into his dinghy! It, of course, began doing its characteristic 'Belsky Gyrations', unique to a Belsky out of water. Mr. Pleasure took the sighting of the rare Belsky Bass as such a good omen that he promptly bought the land he had been surveying and renamed it Pleasure Island. He took the fish as a pet - naming it 'Sue'.

There was an uncommon attachment between the two, which ultimately led to tragedy. One afternoon during the construction of the Adventurers Club, before the patio doors were installed, while Merriweather was surveying the design of the Main Salon, 'Sue' spied him from the lake.

Apparently longing for its master's company, the fish did a 'Belsky Leap' out of the water, ricocheted off of Zeus, and landed smack dab on a freshly painted wall towering above the Treasure Room. There she remains to this day. Thankfully, Mr. Pleasure immortalized Sue's exuberant spirit with 'Forever Fish' -a natural preservative of his creation. This has prevented the summer heat from taking its toll, if you nose what I mean.

Yours in authenticity,

Fletcher Hodges, Club Curator

From Volume No. 54, Issue No. 1, Club President Pamelia Perkins provides a bit of fashion-related advice:

PAMELIA PERKINS MANNER MINDERS

The Club motto states, 'Always dress for the hunt!' I am continuously looking for ways to combine the heart-thumping excitement of adventure with the toe-tingling rush of a well designed pump. This issue I share with you, my beloved readers (and supporters in the next election), a few tips on wearing fashionable skirts in the wild, while participating in seated tribal rituals.

In layman's terms: 'How to squat down into a sits, without showing your private bits'. Learn this simple technique and you'll never have to sacrifice modesty or appearance!

Step 1: Tuck skirt between knees

Step 2: Cross legs securely

Step 3: Rotate one full circle

Step 4: Point up and scream, 'What is that large pointed object pummeling through the clouds?'

Step 5: When the tribe is distracted, drop quickly and assume a relaxed pose.

Most importantly, be sure to avoid sandy areas where burrowing chiggers may be as adventurous as you are. Don't let pain become your fashion statement.

From Volume 54 Issue No. 1, Club butler Graves shares a tradition of the Club:

FROM THE DESK OF GRAVES

Greetings, fellow Adventurers!

In future issues, as part of my duties as Club butler, I will be discussing the etiquette involved in many of the Adventurers Club functions (Manure Diving Competition, Gator Grappling Olympics, etc.), however, it has come to my attention that many of the present membership, particularly the newer members, are avoiding, if not totally ignoring, one of our most time honored traditions, the 'Teddy Toast'.

As the ritual indicates, upon returning to the Club after a hard day of adventuring, one should move as speedily as possible to the nearest bar or watering hole and purchase the beverage of one's choice. Moving without delay, one should wend one's way back up to the 'Founders' Corner' and stand before the portrait of Teddy Roosevelt, the ultimate adventurer. You are to raise your untouched drink high to the heavens, shout "Charge!" at the top of your lungs, and drain your glass completely. This tradition dates back to the time Bart Biffbay was stopped in that particular spot by Nashy. Nash inquired how 'Bilge-Water Bart' planned to settle his extremely large and extremely delinquent bar tab. Bart replied he would charge it, to which a rather angry and red-faced Nash screamed, 'Charge!?!?' 'Exactly!,' said Bart, downing a gin and tonic, after which Nash downed Bart. In these simple times, we need to be true to our simple traditions.

Yours ever loyally — Graves

Oyen was kind enough to share with me the material he still had that was intended for the never published fourth issue:

ANGLING WITH OTIS. (Picture of woman between two fish, page 310, *America's Yesterdays*) Adventurer Dame Veronica Schnorr sends us this picture from a recent deep sea fishing expedition. She claims that she corralled these two denizens of the deep with the greatest of ease. "They were traveling as a couple, so I merely stuck my pole in one's mouth and, while the other wasn't looking, I beat him senseless with my hat." Dame Schnorr claims that it won't end here. "I'm going after really big ones next, and these will do nicely as bait."

QUIMBY SAFE FOR NOW (Picture of man in rowboat, surrounded by women, page 207) "Dear Fellow Members, Don't despair, old Quimby still survives! I have been taken captive by a tribe of crazed affection-starved females, while I was on fishing expedition in the Everglades. I have a plan and hope to be escaping soon. Keep the home-fires burning! Yours Truly, Quimby Farmith III."

Although this does explain his sudden, mysterious disappearance, we can only hope that it puts an end to all those nasty rumors about Quimby and the apparent embezzlement from the Farmith family's trust fund. Chin up, Quimby! We'll keep a candle in the window.

PUT ON A HAPPY FACE. (Picture of four people, with titles, page 64) To be a true Adventurer sometimes requires guile and deception. The Chairman of the Disguise Committee, Count Alex Wirth-Mordanue, sends us a composite of some of his most resourceful regalia. Adventurers the world over have always admired Wirth-Mordanue's vast array of identities. Writes the crafty Count, "It's not the disguise; it's how you put it on."

IT'S A LITTLE DRAFTY. (Picture of man in front of a collapsed building, page 86) member of the Club's Experimental Engineering Committee, Brad "Boom-Boom" Birkholz remains undaunted. Shown here, in front of a failed experiment for his upcoming treatise, "Remodeling Through Creative Pyrotechnics", the plucky Brad was overheard saying merely, "What can I say? Oops?" A model of resolve we can all take to heart.

CAMP GRUMP (Picture of surveyors, page 53) The Society of Unsmiling Men send us this photo of their recent wilderness outing. "To keep from smiling," says Society president, Clive

Pilesmoore, "all you need is an extremely uncomfortable place to sit, an unsmiling pet, and some long, sharp sticks to keep away the occasional prankster." The group holds the current world's record by not smiling for three years, two months and five days. We are unsure whether this constitutes an adventure or, simply a very bad attitude.

INTERNAL COMBUSTION (Picture of car with broken axle, page 93). Our encouragement should go out to Transportation Committee member Alfonso Laslo. We all know how convinced he was that he could develop a motor completely powered exclusively by refried beans. Shown here is the aftermath of the first, and possibly last, attempt at harnessing that elusive power source. As you can see in the background, "Axle Al" is walking away from the scene. He was heard muttering, "I tried. Somebody else can clean it up." A kind word or two, the next time Alfonso is in the Club, wouldn't hurt.

Roger Cox (1945 -2007)

Imagineer Roger Cox was deeply involved in the Adventurers Club project beginning in 1988. He was brought in by Larry Hitchcock, an old college friend, who worked at Disney at the time. Cox became concept designer, character creator, head show writer, and show producer for the Adventurers Club. His original script with writer Mel Green for the Balderdash Competition remained almost exactly the same decades later.

"I came to Disney in September of 1987 and began working on leading a concept team for a 40-acre location in Burbank that was mixed use, entertainment, retail, dining and commercial. Disney took a pass on the land option and I moved on to working with the Pleasure Island team. I brought Roger in as a writer. He was perfect for the Adventurers Club and many other zany twists that our program for the island called for," Hitchcock recalled in an interview with me in October 2008.

One of the inspirations for the Adventurers Club was the Explorers Club in New York founded in 1905 to "promote exploration by all possible means." It was home for "gentleman adventurers" like Charles Lindbergh, Edmund Hillary, Robert Peary and Roald Amundsen.

"The Explorers Club in New York was an obvious model," Hitchcock told me. "Roger had first hand experience with the club and the kind of collegial fraternity that existed among members and other similar clubs around the world."

When in 2008 I interviewed Cox's widow, Sybil, she told me, "Roger was not a member of the Explorers Club. His club was Squadron A. Perhaps they had reciprocal arrangements. I know they did with many clubs around the world. In my eyes, it [Squadron A] was a stuffy, old-fashioned men's club. Roger was into the tradition of these places. He also liked to shake them up.

"There is a famous incident of Roger and a buddy inciting the staff to revolt against the powers-that-be at the New York Club. That particular buddy, from high school in Cleveland, was another close friend who died young. I was looking for his name around the club but didn't see it. Maybe you have. It must be there somewhere.

"His name was Doug Kenney. He was one of the founders of *National Lampoon* and writer of the movies *Animal House* and *Caddyshack*. He and Roger must have been a hoot at that old club causing trouble."

Also in 2008, I interviewed world-renowned illusionist and former Disney cast member Jim Steinmeyer now of JHS Productions, Inc. Theatrical Illusion Design. He was an Imagineer who worked during this time with Cox.

Steinmeyer told me, "I really think that the Adventurers Club is a perfect blend of two personalities, Joe Rohde and Roger Cox. You see Joe's sense of visual fun and old-fashioned adventure, and you experience Roger's offbeat humor and loving evocation of these old-fashioned, bigger-than-life personalities.

"Unfortunately, we lost Roger last year to cancer. Roger was a very good friend over the years, and I think that the Adventurers Club was one of his proudest achievements. It certainly 'felt' like Roger, from start to finish. One certainly feels a kind of eccentric personality pulling you through the experience, and Roger was the embodiment of that.

"Phrases like 'Sometimes you eat the bear...' All of that is vintage Roger, and always sounded exactly like him. He was, truly, the kind of person who could have walked into that club and instantly fit right in. In many ways, I think, the characters in the club were 'doing' Roger or Joe, without even knowing it.

"I had a number of opportunities to work with Roger. He was really a wonderful free spirit, who had been an experienced actor, director and writer. The Adventurers Club should have been doomed to fail, like many of the difficult projects on Pleasure Island.

"It was a project that 'fell outside' of the usual Disney formula, and worried everyone before it opened. Roger was very 'un-Disney' in his thinking, and Joe was always deliberately pushing the envelope.

"I'm not really sure that the Disney brass 'got it,' but they saw that it worked. And maybe they were just a little scared of it, or mystified by it. It worked because it had such enormous personality, permeating through the whole place. That was, to me, the charm of The Adventurers Club. It was eccentric and unexpected.

"The humor was unpredictable and offbeat. But it all seemed to make perfect sense, unto itself. You believed that those fellows had been there for years, that they'd figured out their own systems and stories. And I really think that the 'personality' that permeated it all was Roger's.

"That's the comfort of the Adventurers Club, really. You've gone to someone else's party. They've been throwing that party for a long time. They're experts at it. But over the years, it's taken on all of their personalities and quirks. When audiences felt they'd fallen into a rabbit hole and experienced another world, it was really Roger's insight into the entire concept."

When I showed Hitchcock Steinmeyer's tribute, he responded, "I agree. Roger delivered the 'text' and Joe the 'visuals.' But they 'pushed' and 'fulfilled' each other. Roger's prose painted a picture; Joe's art suggested a story."

Sybil Cox who only saw the show for the first time on its last night of performance, September 27, 2008 told me:

"The Adventurers Club's unlikely hero, Emil Bleehall, is based on a long-standing semi-autobiographical character Roger created. He is the funny little guy from Ohio who wins over the higher authorities and gains their respect and admiration with his seemingly awkward modest but ultimately unique crowd-pleasing talents.

"A docu-dramatic version of Cox's journey at Disney by Sandra Tsing Loh called, *It Happened in Glendale* from her book, *Depth Takes a Holiday* was performed on the radio show, *This American Life*. Roger felt Emil's struggle at the Adventurers Club paralleled his own story at Disney getting his Adventurers Club ideas off the ground and accepted there."

Emil says he is from Sandusky, Ohio. Cox was actually from Shaker Heights, Ohio, but felt the name "Sandusky" was funnier. There is a fifteen minute video of Roger telling how he pitched the story of the Balderdash Cup to Michael Eisner, Dick Nunis and other Disney executives who Cox referred to as "cling-ons" because they seemed to cling on to Eisner and his opinions.

Cox said he realized very quickly that despite all the laughter that he was really only pitching to "an audience of one." Michael Eisner. Everyone looked at Eisner for his reaction.

The Balderdash Cup Competition featured Hathaway Browne, Otis T. Wren and Emil Bleehall competing for "Adventurer of the

Year" as signified by the awarding of the Balderdash Cup. The word "balderdash" means "nonsense" and first appeared as early as 1674. Cox referred to an Explorer Club as a "liar's club."

Otis T. Wren tells a harrowing fish tale accompanied by a sinking ship in a bottle while Hathaway Browne enthralls the audience with his aviating adventure where he ends up in Atlantis. Actually, it is the Atlantis Bar and Grill where he has his napkin autographed with "Bon Voyage, Amelia Earhart" and "Good Luck! Will Rogers."

Wren has tricked other adventurers like Sutter Bestwick and Chilton Thompson from not being there to compete but failed in his attempt to distract Hathaway Browne.

Junior Adventurer Emil wins with his demonstration of trained tap dancing pigeons on the roof of the Club to the song *Me and My Shadow*.

In the pitch, Cox revealed that Emil's job in Sandusky was as the "Artistic Director of the School of Modern Dance" and that helps explain why Emil trained 500 one-pound pigeons to tap dance, as well at the one 500 pound pigeon, "Rodan" named after the colossal Japanese Pteranodon kaiju.

At the end of the pitch, Eisner said, "That's too absurd."

Cox pleaded that it was funny and a great idea and that everyone laughed. "Roger never feared authority or even recognized it and always poked fun at people who did," his wife told me.

Finally, Eisner relented and told Cox that if he was so glued to the idea, Eisner would give it a chance. When the Balderdash Cup skit was performed at the Adventurers Club, guests howled with laughter and just stayed and refused to leave.

Eisner came up to Cox and whispered in his ear, "You were right. I was wrong." He always laughed that he never heard Eisner say that to anyone else, including himself, ever again.

In the library, on the stage, there were two paintings and the crooked one (hiding the keyboardist who performs as "Fingers Zambezi") has a caricature of Joe Rohde standing in the right of the picture. Roger Cox is in the picture as well.

Sybil told me, "Yes, Roger is in that painting, the little guy in the middle."

It's too late to see now, but on the wall of the Main Salon bar facing the Mask Room is the name "Joe" in hieroglyphics and backward as another Rohde tribute.

"I saw lots of other photos with captions with our friends' names on them. But essentially I heard Roger's voice come through all the characters voices and actions," Sybil said, "Roger's personality is well distributed among the characters in the Club in their sense of Fun, Absurdity, Charm and Warmth.

"He was always the life of the party when he walked into a room and at the same time included everyone 'in on the giggle' as he liked to say. Everyone around him was drawn in and became part of the Roger Party. He was a great storyteller.

"Each time he told his stories he added more and more 'Balderdash.' So what if it didn't resemble the truth anymore? What was more important: the truth or a good performance making the crowd laugh? Of course, Roger always opted for the latter. He loved to be racy in his remarks and see how far he could push the limits of the language, beyond the acceptable."

As with many Imagineers, Cox incorporated the names of some of his friends in the names of some of the characters referenced in the club.

On the Membership Plaque in the Main Salon under "Members Owing Dues" there is the name "Eben Cockley."

Sybil shared with me, "Roger's 'sandbox' buddy was David Cockley, Eben may have been a family member of his. Pamelia Perkins is the exact name of a classmate of Roger's and mine from the Carnegie-Mellon University Drama Department circa 1980. Roger was a grad student, stage director. Pamelia was also in the department as a grad stage director.

"Roger was always a collector of names that he would pull out and mold into characters. Some other references in the Club that I recognize are on the captions on the photos upstairs in the (Zebra) Bar (Mezzanine) area. The names such as, David Holzheimer, Alexis Conroy and Charley, Gregory Lehane and L. Klatcher, Hugh O'Neil III, Hugh O'Neil IV, Stanley Jaros were all dear friends of Roger's.

"Hugh Davey was a close friend of Roger's (of the Davey tree company family) who died young in college. As a tribute to him, a caption mentions him, it reads, 'Hugh Speer Davey, 1890-1940 Essayist and Forester snatched from this mortal coil in a freak gardening accident.' I noticed that this Hugh Davey lived quite a bit longer than Roger's friend. Roger gave him extra life. I also noticed the 1940 date post dates the Adventurers Club 1937 itself."

In fact, in the Zebra Mezzanine are several pictures of members who passed the mortal coil after 1937. Perhaps these were merely predictions by Madame Zenobia who looked into the future and saw their terrible fates. More likely, it is just another example of the confusing and often contradictory material about the Adventurers Club.

On the walls to the right when you entered the club, you would have seen pictures with these captions:

"C.K. Dexter Haven Jr. 1859-1938 Squandered "Jinkies" cereal fortune". C.K. Dexter Haven is the name of the Cary Grant character in the movie *Philadelphia Story* (1940) and its musical remake *High Society.*

"Wadill Catchings 1890-1940 Climbing accident, Himalayas 'He Never Bounced Once'.

"Burlwood Carruthers Jr. 1891-1940 Led 1st, 3rd and 4th Baltistan-Hunza Trans-Himalayan treks. 1912-23 (not shown: pet leopard, 'Bucky').

"SR. 'Bob" Bobenmeyer' 1878-1938 Introduced the 'conga line' to North America. Buried with Xavar Cugat record collection. 'I am a dancing fool.' (How true! How true!)"

Writer Craig McNair Wilson told me when I interviewed him, "All the framed photos, throughout Adventurers Club are 90 percent from a huge historic photo library in New York City. I brought in my old, portable, Royal manual typewriter. I still have it.

"We sat around WDI for days coming up with captions for them. They were typed on newsprint that we had soaked in tea and left in the sun to dry. I think everyone got their name-or some version of it-in at least one of those captions. It is an old WDI trick dating back to the opening days of Disneyland."

After Cox left, Wilson and others including Chris Oyen wrote and through improvisation exercises with the actors created material that the characters used in the Club.

When asked about the Merriweather Pleasure legend, Hitchcock said, "I loved it. Totally plausible in a land of Flagler and Charles Foster Kane's Xanadu. Well, my vision was always that Pleasure Island was Disney's Bourbon Street.

"Social lubricants like alcohol made it better and much more realistic. Like the fictional Mr. Pleasure, the fabulous Roger Cox, and preposterous Joe Rohde are all larger-than-life characters who realized some of their dreams and shared those with everyone."

Roger Cox was not just the real life version of Emil Bleehall. As Sybil was quick to point out, "At the same time Roger was also a heroic romantic like Hathaway Browne going to extreme lengths against the odds carrying out brave acts."

Artist William Stout with writer Jim Steinmeyer produced two limited edition volumes of a comic strip about an aging Mickey Mouse who was sixty years old and behaved like an overweight, grumpy old Hollywood movie star past his prime to amuse their friends in Imagineering.

Stout remembered he started writing a one-man play to feature the character. Stout said, "I was originally writing it for our mutual friend, Roger Cox. Roger would have been ideal to portray Mickey on stage but he sadly passed away."

Interview: Joe Rohde

On April 3, 2006, I got to attend a special Walt Disney World cast member only presentation by Imagineer Joe Rohde who was talking about the new addition of the Expedition Everest attraction to Disney's Animal Kingdom. During the question-and-answer session that followed the presentation, I got to ask him about his memories of the Adventurers Club.

JOE ROHDE: I'll tell you the *whole* story. Rick Rothschild was in charge of Pleasure Island, as the chief show producer of Pleasure Island. And I had had a party at my house and he had come over to this party and my house is full of stuff like that. Not, at the time, as much stuff as now 'cause it's many years later. But it was full of stuff like that.

Masks, and carvings and weird things. And so he called me in Monday morning and goes, "I have a project you should work on. You should work on this Adventurers Club concept."

Fortunately, this whole concept of a type of business that was other than theme parks and theme park attractions was something that very few people were very interested in. Very few people had opinions on it and so, we few of us who were working on it had tremendous freedom to do what we thought was cool.

To call people up. Make deals. Go places. See things. Make things happen. The Adventurers Club happened under those circumstances. My two projects, Animal Kingdom and Adventurers Club, both of them have this oppositional kind of point of view. Like we're gonna deliberately do something that is not the thing that you commonly see around you.

The Adventurers Club idea was: People have been in the parks all day long. And they have been programmed, by being in these parks, to expect certain things to be true.

For example: If an inanimate object does something, it's gonna do that same thing again later. Right? This environment is on a loop. It will stay. It will stay like this. It will stay like this for an hour, for a day and for a year it will retain its sameness. It's built to do that. Right?

Everything in this environment was designed and made by designers out of fiberglass and plastic and things. So nothing in this environment is made of real things. Everything in this environment is made, designed and built. And I don't mean this in a negative way. You're walking around in this environment and the environment tells you all these things.

So we wanted to mess with all of that with the Adventurers Club and create an environment where you'd walk into the environment and first you'd think, "Wait a minute. This stuff is like real. That…that's like really a <u>real</u> thing. Is that fake? I think that's real!"

There's incredible junk in the Adventurers Club but the real stuff is where you can get right up to here on it and go, "I swear that is real." Right? So, number one, it's like real stuff.

Then the second thing was that things would not repeat the same way. Like it would know that you were there. The Adventurers Club would know that you were there and things would change based on the fact that you were there. And if it didn't talk to you, it would talk to somebody. And you'd know, "Wait. That thing's talkin' to the guy in the red shirt." So, you know, inanimate things would come to life but they would not be on cycles, other than the Yakoose, which was the only thing that had to be that way.

It was how tightly we could keep the theatrical envelope. Think back to the early, early Adventurers Club to where the performers' outfits were as close as we could get them to every day clothes.

And their performances were as close as we could get them to kinda ordinary behaviors. So, when Hathaway Browne would come sit at the bar with somebody, it would be like a minute before you'd go, "Wait a minute. This guy is like not real. I thought this guy was real." Like that, right?

And so all of those things then, they take on a disproportionate sort of thrill. Because…if you built it in New York City, like whatshisname did with the other thing (Jekyll and Hyde Club), whatever…it's not the same. It's the same because of where it is and how it plays against expectations that have been set up by other experiences.

And that's kind of how it was meant to be. How it was meant to work. And then the other kinda cool thing is because it's not on a cycle, because it can respond, it can develop a relationship and it is nice that it has developed a kind of a human relationship through the performers with the people. And, you know, people just go and sit there and they are in an entirely different experience.

I don't go very often, because you wanna mess with it and tweak with it and change...and you just need to forget about it and move on. But I check in on it every so often and I think it has endured fairly well, really.

You think about it, it's a theatrical performance running for I don't know what—almost twenty years. A long time. But it was deliberately constructed to be the counterpoint to the more pro-grammed kinds of behaviors given to Disney theme park guests.

Interview: Craig McNair Wilson

In October 2008, I interviewed Craig McNair Wilson who was the artistic director of an Orlando improvisational theater group known as SAK. Wilson was responsible for the commedia dell'arte shows at Epcot's Italy and United Kingdom pavilions, where actors came out with a trunk of props and costumes and recruited guests to help in their presentation.

Later, Wilson was also involved with the training of the original actors who comprised the "Streetmosphere" performers at the Disney-MGM Studios. Currently, he is a consultant specializing in creativity.

He was involved in the early days of the Adventurers Club.

Jim Korkis: How did you get started at the Walt Disney World theme parks?

Craig McNair Wilson: I was artistic director at SAK theater, an improvisational theater company in Orlando that created all the street theater at Epcot. Initially we had a three-month contract just for Italy from Opening Day (October 1, 1982 through the end of the year).

Our immediate popularity led to Disney "Creative Entertainment" asking if we had enough additional "Saktors" to add a troupe to the United Kingdom. Since SAK had been in existence since August 17, 1977, we had a roster of almost 60 trained street performers and had been sending SAK troupes to more than 30 Renaissance Festivals and other street fairs every year.

We doubled our strength and had our UK troupe in place before Thanksgiving of EPCOT's opening year (1982). Eventually SAK was producing five different projects in EPCOT—[in World Showcase:] Italy's Il Teatro di Bologna ("Boloney Theatre"), UK's Renaissance Street Theatre Co., and, in Future World: Robot Show, Mr. Intelligence (aka Miss Intelligence), and the enormously popular Gutfred & Myrtle (a senior citizen couple that were lost in Future World and got separated in line at various major attractions).

SAK remained at Epcot for eight years and produced 42,000 EPCOT shows, hundreds of convention shows and developed numerous other proposals for others, including: *Disney Story Talers for the Magic Kingdom*.

Audiences loved it, but the Magic Kingdom management didn't want to "copy" Epcot. The two shows we created—*The Adventurers of Pinocchio* and *Snow White and a Couple of Dwarfs* ("Budget cut!") were picked up by the Disney Travel Company and used all over North America at big travel shows.

JK: How did you become involved with the Pleasure Island project?

CMW: I became involved in the Pleasure Island project in1985 after a few meetings at Epcot with various WDI [Walt Disney Imagineering] guys [Bob Weis, Randy Bright, Rick Rothchild]. My SAK Theatre partner, Herb Hansen, and I were invited to come out to WDI [Glendale, California] for "a few days" to "take a look at some projects we're playing with" and see if we had any ideas about "adding live actors to them."

One of the very first questions was what it's like to work in a Disney theme park, given our free-spirited ways. I said that park management was very rigid, formulaic, and strict! "I think their ideal theme park attraction would be an empty building (requiring no maintenance) with a turnstile and a long line."

The entire room screamed with laughter and applause. I had just stepped into a long-time tension between WDI and many of the key folks who run the parks. WDI loved us.

JK: What information were you given on the project?

CMW: We were briefed on (very little other than a few early ideas existed) "Disney Studios Florida" (just a working movie studio, no attractions, but a small public behind-the-scenes-tour), Typhoon Lagoon (with no name or theme yet), and the big idea to transform the WDW Shopping Village into a restaurant and nightclub district with a few shops and one huge Disney stuff store.

The "nightclub district" got its own team: Rick Rothchild (show producer), Chris Carradine (architect), Joe Rohde (designer), John Kavelin (was designer for the jazz club and Neon Armadillo), myself and then later Tony Anselmo (designed and directed the interior effort for Mannequins), and one or two others like Tom

Sherohman (voice of the Yakoose) who was an improv whiz who was the original director at the Comedy Warehouse and of course, Roger Cox, director and writer for Adventurers Club.

Roger Cox was brought on to be the day-to-day show director of the Adventurers Club and he brought me in at night to work with his theatrically experienced cast on audience interaction. Roger Cox was enamored of SAK at Epcot and what I was inventing with "Streetmosphere" (my word combining "atmosphere people" which is what they called extras in the Hollywood movies who created the atmosphere of the scene with the street) at Disney-MGM Studios.

He wanted that same texture in the Adventurers Club, especially in interaction with guests. I wish I could dig back twenty years to recall all the artisans and craftsmen and women at WDI who built, designed, fabricated, remodeled, and decorated props, furnishings, and finishes for the Club. It was a small army of unsung geniuses.

JK: Where did the concept of an island come from as the location for this nightclub district?

CMW: One day Chris Carradine asked, "Has anyone ever been to Vancouver? Have you been to Granville Island?" I had been there and knew where Chris was going. An industrial/fishing/sailing (light manufacturing) island under a huge bridge that was being transformed into shops, theatres, restaurants, cafes, galleries, and still several boat repair and other light industry.

Chris set us on a course to concoct our very own old industrial area — fallen on hard times — and do a Disney reuse, a la Ghirardelli Square here in San Francisco.

At some point we dug out an aerial photo of WDW Shopping Village and noticed a little peninsula at the far end, adjacent to the Lilly Belle restaurant and how easy it would be to make it an island. We began to riff and created the mythology and back story of Merriweather Adam Pleasure.

We all improvised it and it grew and grew. Mostly it was the minds of Carradine, Rohde, and me. Rothchild threw in a lot, too. At one point the full mythology was way too long and Marty Sklar called me into his office and asked me to rewrite it in one "voice" and make it pithy, brief, and fun. The now-famous Pleasure Island plaques were excerpted from that document: "The Final, Ultimate, Semi-Official History of Pleasure Island."

JK: So where did the concept of the Adventurers Club originate?

CMW: It came out of our collective, shared love of the world of the pith helmet and all that circled around it. It was the place we always wanted to go, but it didn't exist.

Joe Rohde had a Sunday afternoon soirée in his backyard in Pasadena themed as "The Last Days of the Raj" where we would tell tall tales and celebrate. And every second Sunday for *years* we went to the Rose Bowl swap meet and bought stuff: rugs, masks, statues. There's also more than a pinch of Rick's Cafe (*Casablanca*).

We all went to see and experience *Tamara*, a live theatrical, multi-room play that debuted in 1981 in Los Angeles. *Tamara* was a major influence in Adventurers Club. Chris Carradine and I saw the show three or four times together and a few times more with others.

About a dozen actors and there were 150 in audience who were allowed to follow the character(s) of their choice throughout eleven rooms in an Italian Villa in the late 1930s and get part of the story.

It took place in an old Elks hall in Los Angeles. At intermission there was a buffet dinner and after the show a no-host bar, with the cast in civilian clothes, out of character.

JK: What inspired the physical design of the Adventurers Club?

CMW: The physical design of the club grew out of Chris Carradine's brilliant and dangerous mind. Chris explained it to me on a series of cocktail napkins, late one night in NYC. It had been Merriweather Pleasure's house. "There are twice as many rooms as Adventurers Club guests will ever see."

I recall telling Chris, at the time, "When the Adventurers Club is a huge hit, we should add a few new rooms in a big PR blitz. New treasures, now arriving from around the globe... Adventurers Club: bigger, wilder, crazier. Kungaloosh!"

JK: So you always thought that the Adventurers Club would be a huge success?

CMW: Almost a full year before Pleasure Island opened I stood in what is now the Mask Room of a concrete block shell of the Adventurers Club. There was Eisner, Rothchild, Carradine, and me.

I said, "Take this place and drop it into Midtown Manhattan, add a 200-seat restaurant—in the same theme— and when there are lines around the block in January, build an Adventurers Club in Chicago, Atlanta, Dallas, San Francisco, Minneapolis, Seattle…"

Adventurers Club was a huge hit. Meanwhile, a stock broker in New York City —who loved all things Disney but especially Pleasure Island and Adventurers Club—built a place called Jekyll & Hyde Club (with restaurant, walk-around characters, animatronics, secret entrance like Magic Castle)… and I stood in line in January to get in. They even hired away several of the actors I had trained from Streetmosphere at Disney-MGM and Adventurers Club.

When I met the manager, he said, "It is based on and totally inspired by the Adventurers Club at WDW."

The Adventurers Club was like no other entertainment experience anywhere and it was never the same show twice. That was the plan and that was what happened. The club itself is a character in the show. The whole place is a huge surprise to guests. They've never seen, visited, or experienced anything like it. That's why they come back, and back, and back, and…

Instead of closing it, I would expand it to include a restaurant and open it from 11 a.m. to 1 a.m. daily. We'd serve lunch and dinner and in the afternoon a hard ticketed Mystery Meal with food, cast, clues, and prizes.

I always wished there was a deck, pier and boat launch to do Adventurers Cruises on Lake Buena Vista, every hour on the half hour. Short, 30-minute cruises with a special on board bar, snacks and a high-seas adventure (mini show that is only performed on the boat—the *SS Merriweather*).

The Adventurers Club gift shop with adventure gear and souvenirs: passport to get stamped through out the club, boat, etc… pith helmets, khaki jacket with emblem, canvas adventure bags, totes, rucksacks, etc. (some of the gear that was in the original "Avigators" shop when PI opened). I still have my great leather bag from there.

JK: Outside the Adventurers Club, why are there three ape skulls and three human skulls on poles?

CMW: The county building code limit on displaying skulls outdoors in Florida is six.

JK: Of course, I should have realized. It is so obvious. Thank you for sharing your memories.

Interview: Lynn Hart

I had the opportunity in July 2009 to interview composer Lynn Hart who wrote the music and lyrics for the *Adventurers Club All-Purpose Theme Song* and the *Jump Up for Jinkies* jingle.

Hart has several Disney credits including writing additional lyrics to the *Golden Dreams* song when the American Adventure was updated at Epcot. He also designed the Fantasy Waters show that was performed at the Disneyland Hotel (which were supposed to be updated every two years, but never was), and designed several years of the "Fantasy in the Sky" fireworks show at Disneyland.

Like many people, Hart also did a great deal of non-Disney shows including writing and directing the main stage show at the Atlantis Resort in the Bahamas that ran for four years until they turned the showroom into more casino space; and global events such as Goodwill Games, Special Olympics, and a show celebrating the 100th anniversary of Saudi Arabia.

I have eliminated my questions and just retained Hart's memories:

Lynn Hart: "I'm really glad and grateful that you are documenting PI's history. It was a fascinating project, and one that changed a lot of mindsets within Disney. As to feelings about the Adventurers Club and PI, I have a great fondness for both.

"I used to love to go to the Club and just hang out whenever I was in Orlando. When I went back to PI to stage the West End show, someone had just discovered the verses of the theme song, and they had put them back in the radio show.

"The last two times I went, no one there knew me, or that I had worked on the club. It was interesting to see what had changed, and what had endured. It's really fun when they sing the theme song, although I always wished that they would occasionally review the melody.

"In 1992 (I think it was) I wrote and directed the West End New Year's Eve show ("In With the New") at PI. I revised it when the new West End stage opened the next year. Overall, it ran for several years.

"I was working as a stage manager at Disneyland at the time, then freelancing as a writer, designer, and creative consultant for various entities (including Universal.) I had been recommended to be on the team by Brian Gale, one of WDI's leading lighting designers.

"I was in Texas doing the lighting design for a ballet (freelance, not Disney) when I got a call asking if I could be in Orlando as soon as I finished. I made arrangements with Disneyland to be away a little longer, and went to Orlando.

"That first week, I was just a temporary consultant. I had been brought in as a concept writer and music programming consultant. Although I was encouraged to give thought to all of the clubs, my main focus seemed to be consulting on the overall programming and concept for Mannequins and Videopolis East.

"We had meetings at Pleasure Island, which at the time was a bunch of concrete slabs and shells under construction. Chris Carradine—who had the uncanny ability to draw things freehand on the white board *to scale*—took us through the overall project, and Rick Rothschild was in charge of entertainment development.

"I guess that I did well enough in the brainstorming meetings to get offered an ongoing consulting job. I gave Disneyland two-weeks notice.

"Back in Glendale, I was encouraged to sit in on any meeting I wanted, although Mannequins and Videopolis remained my main thrust. Since I have a legit theater background (and had written a musical a few years earlier that had received several productions) I was very interested in both Comedy Warehouse and Adventurers Club, both of which had strong elements of musical theater.

"I was invited by both Roger Cox and Tom Sherohman to attend their story and brainstorming sessions. These were an absolute hoot. The entire creative team for both projects was filled with terrifically funny people.

"Roger in particular was stream-of-consciousness funny and extremely unpredictable—especially when 'the suits' were in the room. I remember him using the phrase 'squeaky white sphincter muscles' in a presentation for Disney brass that had the same effect as if he had mooned them.

"I remember meeting Craig Wilson and liking him a lot, although once Roger and Tom were officially made show/project directors, his involvement became more that of a consultant, if I remember correctly. At any rate, I don't remember him being involved day-to-day at that point, at least not in the circle of people I was with every day.

"At some point in the creative process, Roger said in a meeting that he wanted a theme song for the club. Since I was officially on the project as a music programming consultant, he asked if I knew of a composer who might be good for this kind of thing.

"His concept was to have a song with a short chorus that could be taught to the audience. He also wanted something for the Radio Show that was a musical telling of some tall tales.

"His first concept was to use Gilbert and Sullivan's *I Am the Very Model of a Modern Major General* and change it to *I Am the Very Model of a Modern-Day Adventurer*.

"He knew I had written a musical, so he thought maybe I could take a stab at lyrics to fit the music. I worked on it for several days, and didn't come up with anything I liked. So I asked him if the whole thing might be original music.

"He said that would be fine, so we again tossed around some names of potential composers. He was reluctant to have me do it, because I was officially attached to the other clubs, and he didn't want to cause problems by taking too much of my time away from them.

"Over the next weekend, I wrote the theme song. I took in a tape of me playing a synthesized organ (since it was well established by then that Fingers would be playing it.) Not wanting to put Roger on the spot, I told him that a friend of mine had written it.

"I gave him a lyric sheet and sang live as the tape played. Roger was noncommittal, except to go get Rich Proctor, who was the principal writer besides himself, to listen. They both listened.

"They whispered to themselves, and then told me that they thought it was exactly what they wanted. They wanted me to bring my friend in to talk to Rick Rothschild, so they could hire him to write all of the Club's music.

"I told them it was really me, so they went to talk to Rick, who gave his okay for me to add the Adventurers Club to my work load.

"This is so far an unnecessarily long answer to how I came to write the song, but I think it's a nice demonstration on how WDI worked in those days. Anyone could contribute their ideas to anything, and they would be respected.

"This was a concept fostered by both Chris and Rick, and it seemed to flow down through the various project directors. It was a terrific creative environment.

"Anyway, I then started work on the Radio Show, which was an ongoing musical bed that was supposed to help establish Fingers' character. It also included the musical jingle for Jinkies.

"The Adventurers Club music was virtually all first draft. There were no substantial changes made to the theme song, the Radio Show soundtrack, or any of the other original music that Fingers played.

"I wrote the jingle for Jinkies. Rich Proctor told me the cereal's name, and its tag line ('Jump Up for Jinkies!'). He said 'make the song as asinine as possible, while still being absolutely plausible as a cereal jingle.' It, too, was a first draft. Only after I had turned it in did I realize that I inadvertently had made it similar to the Club Theme [rhyming "west" and "best"].

"When I pointed this out and offered to change it, Roger said he liked it just the way it was, so it stayed. I did, however, provide a few variations to the third line, and those were mixed in sporadically by the cast."

Here are the lyrics written by Lynn Hart. According to the script for the *Tales of Adventurers Club Radio Broadcast* written by Roger Cox and Mel Green, "Jinkies" is the "perfect cereal for adventuring...high in protein, high in fiber...and when hurled at a high velocity, Jinkies can render an opponent unconscious.

"Jinkies is the only cereal aerodynamically designed with beveled edges and when combined with its amazing laxative properties...it's always an adventure when you jump up for Jinkies!"

> *J-I-N-K-I-E-S,*
> *Make your mouth say "yes, yes, yes"!*
> *From the East Coast to the West,*
> *Jinkies is the best (Yes sir!)*
> *So ju.....mp up*
> *For Jinkies! (We love 'em!)*

(Alternate third lines written by Lynn: "Don't think I would ever jest," "Swallowing this treasure chest," and "Lots more flavor than the rest".)

I asked Hart to give me some impressions of the people he worked with on the Adventurers Club.

"Mel Green—terrific writer, and a heavy influence on the style of Adventurers Club—used to love to riff on the back stories of the characters. In his mind, they were mostly aberrant and abnormal.

"We would be sitting in the Club, and he would go off on whichever character happened to be around. My favorite 'back-story' concerned Pamelia Perkins, who, according to Mel, had an 'unusually friendly relationship with her Great Dane. It started as just a Good Dane, but became Great after a few drinks.'

"He also loved to go in the club as just a regular tourist, and get into verbal sparring with the characters. They knew who he was, of course, but they had to go along with it. He would treat them as if they were absolutely real, and then take them to task for one thing or another.

"A great exchange was once had between him and Tim Goodwin, which went on for about 30 minutes, to the great amusement of all around. When Emil finally had to go, a lady who had been watching came up to Mel and said 'You know, they're really only actors.'

"I was told by Joe Rohde several years ago that he and a group of friends were hiking in some forgotten corner of the world, and sang the Adventurers Club theme song as they made their trek up the side of a mountain. He was such a major part of the Club. I don't think he particularly approved of some of the changes that were made over the years.

"I have one particular memory of Joe during the rehearsal period of the Club. We were sitting at a table in the library while the cast was rehearsing the radio show. He had thought of a prop for the maid—a '30s version of a 'dust buster.' He drew the thing out as we sat there. It was really clever. I said to him "How the hell do you *do* that?" And he motioned to the cast as they were singing the full version of the theme song, and said 'I don't know. How do you do *that*?'

"A favorite anecdote. One day during opening week, I was in the Club, going over some music changes with one of the key-board players who did Fingers. I don't remember their names, but they were both great. We were in his booth behind the painting off stage. A family came in the library to look around. This was in the afternoon before the Club opened. Someone in the family worked at WDW or something.

"Anyway, the mother, who had seen the show, was telling her family about it. She told them that a ghost played the organ, and that it was a real ghost. Her son (about 9 or so) wanted to hear him play. The mother, thinking that no one was there, was making excuses for the ghost not being there, when the key-boardist suddenly brought Fingers to life.

"He played for them, then took a couple of requests. When they left, I think the mother was thinking that there might really be a ghost.

"You asked about the word 'Kungaloosh'. It was not a part of the original show, but I think it got added in the second or third year. I'm betting it originated with Rich Proctor, but I don't know for sure. (He loved making up words.)"

Hart was also involved in the legendary first show produced for the Comedy Warehouse when it opened in 1989. The infamous "Forbidden Disney" is another part of Pleasure Island that has never been documented.

Fun Facts

The maximum posted capacity for the Adventurers Club was 504 people. When the Club closed, *Starlog* magazine declared it the worst decision of the month.

Abby Cadabby: Leslie Carrara, best known today for manipulating the Abby Cadabby Muppet on Sesame Street television series was one of the first maids at the Adventurers Club under the name Dusty Cabinets.

Television Series: In Fall 1993 the Disney Channel considered a television series to be filmed in Florida and take place in the Adventurers Club. The pilot script was written by Jim Hill, Sheila Greenberg, Darin De Paul and Kristian Truelsen.

Official Address: The official address of the Adventurers Club is 5189 Hill Street, Lake, Buena Vista, Fl. 32830 and it first appeared on a tag on a crate in the queue line of the Jungle Cruise at the Magic Kingdom.

That crate has the following address: "Ship to: The Mary Henrietta Kingsley Collection, The Adventurers Club, 5189 Hill St., Lake Buena Vista, FL. 32830." When Imagineering repaved the street in front of the club, they discovered that the blueprints did indeed list the street as "Hill Street."

Various other artifacts are in the queue line at the Jungle Cruise destined for the Adventurers Club. At one time, the FastPass machines had tags for Pamelia Perkins and Emil Bleehall but they disappeared.

Merriweather's Nighttime Fireworks Show: One early concept in 1987 by independent consultant Michael Kennedy was a nighttime fireworks show on the water surrounding Pleasure Island to be called "Pleasure Island Pyrotechnical Exposition." Supposedly, Merriweather Pleasure built another steamboat, the Pleasure Island Princess.

This ship was blown up by greedy cousins who set alight fireworks (stolen supposedly from the Fireworks Factory) in the belief that Pleasure was misusing their eventual inheritance on such folly. The phantom ship piloted by a ghostly Merriweather Pleasure would re-appear each evening (or at least the sound of the steamship) and would vanish in a final flurry of showering fireworks.

The Flying Carpet: "Authentic Flying Carpet of Abu Dhabi. Acquired by Lord and Lady Reed and donated to the Club's permanent collection following an unfortunate camel collision. Fortunately, Lord and Lady Reed walked away from the incident unscathed. 'It pays to buckle up.'"

There are two seat belts on the carpet that was displayed on the wall of the Zebra Mezzanine by the bar. This was the last artifact donation that was accepted from guests by the club.

In the early years, the club would host "Membership Parties" and as part of the celebration, the club would accept submissions of artifacts: "Please bring any artifacts that you wish considered and be prepared to deliver an explanation of their origin, function, and how it came into your possession. For the purpose of this Club event, it must be an artifact that fits our aviation motif.

"It may be anything that is associated with flight, has flown, or is intricately connected to mankind's attempt to conquer the skies. Remember, all artifacts are non-refundable." After accepting two or three such artifacts, the practice was stopped by Disney Legal who had misgivings about taking and displaying such treasures from guests in fear of possible future litigation of some kind.

Mandora: The character of Samantha Sterling (based on Amelia Earhart) was created specifically for the charming actress and talented singer Sheila Smith Ward who continued to play the role until the Club's closing. Previously, she had played the part of Mandora who was named that by one Imagineer who hoped that guests might sense that it could be a man impersonating a woman, basically Dora was a man or a "Mandora". This concept was never explored in reality.

Collectible Pins: The talented Karl Anthony who performed at the Adventurers Club (and I always liked him as Hathaway Browne) had an equally talented wife who used to work for the Disney Design Group.

She was the one who designed the limited Artists Collection pin set in March 2007 (in an edition of 750 that sold out quickly) with Mickey as Hathaway, Donald as Otis Wren, Daisy Duck as Pamelia Perkins, Minnie as Samatha Sterling, Goofy as Fletcher Hodges, Pete as Graves and Pluto as Emil.

For the hat that Donald wears Karl's wife, Dawn Ockstadt, did not use the fez that most performers wore as Otis. When Karl played the role, he used a different style hat and that is the one that adorns Donald on the pin. Dawn claimed she did not include the maid because "she was last seen dusting the Colonel."

The club pin that was a replica of its logo, most frequently given free to a guest who participated in a show or ceremony, changed several times throughout the years. Size and materials have ranged from large plastic, to small metal, to the final pin being made of a stiff rubber to prevent conflict with the popular pin trading practice in the parks. At least seven different variations exist.

Merriam Pleasure: Merriam Pleasure, Merriweather's only daughter and youngest child, was born in 1911 after he discovered Pleasure Island. One of the reasons we know this is because on the Zebra Mezzanine was a glassed in model of a Turkish Galley with a plaque stating "Built by M. A. Pleasure as a gift for daughter Merriam's 16th birthday. 1927." So that means that she was 30 years old when she was lost at sea with her father in 1941.

On the plaque in the Main Salon, Merriam is listed as one of the "Founder's Circle" of the Adventurers Club. Since the Club was founded in 1932, Merriam was 21 years old when she helped found the club. Interestingly, there were no photos of any member of the Pleasure family in the Club nor were they portrayed by any performers over the years.

Hidden Mickeys: On every banner proclaiming the "Open House for 1937", look directly above the word "Open" and just under the word "Club" and you will see a bluish vertical line. Dotting that line is the familiar three circles in proper proportion of Mickey Mouse's silhouetted head.

Another Hidden Mickey was in a picture frame at eye level to the left of the Main Salon bar, near the Mask Room, there was a framed artifact labeled "1,001 Puns for All Occasions" filled with several lines of hieroglyphics. Towards the bottom in the middle of a line was the old Disney Channel logo of a white silhouette of Mickey's three-circled head inside a rectangular black box screen. Imagineer Joe Rohde placed a shrunken head of Mickey Mouse as a hidden Mickey behind the bar in the Main Salon but it was discovered and removed before the Club opened to the public.

Hidden Imagineers: Both of those paintings hanging on stage in the Library were painted by Joe Rohde and feature caricatures of the original Adventurers Club Imagineering team including Rohde himself, Susan Cowan, Roger Cox, Rick Rotschild and Chris Carradine.

Celebrities: Many celebrities attended the Adventurers Club over the years, including Bob Hope, Robin Williams, George Lucas, Neil Patrick Harris, John Lithgow, Jim Henson, Gilbert Gottfried, David Ogden Stiers, Leslie Nielsen, Liza Minelli, and a host of others.

South Park: The popular Comedy Central animated series *South Park* ran an episode titled *The Return of Chef* (March 22, 2006) where Chef had been brainwashed by a club called the "Super Adventurers Club" composed of explorers who molested children around the world.

The interior of the club includes many items familiar to those who visited the P.I. Adventurers Club, including the Main Salon with Babylonia on the wall and the Artemision Bronze ("Zeus with a Fishing Rod"). One of the co-creators and writers of the show, Trey Parker, spent his honeymoon at Walt Disney World and visited the Adventurers Club.

The Sneaker: One character for the Club that never made it off the drawing board was a creation of Craig McNair Wilson's. The character was only identified as "The Sneaker". According to the description from 1987: "During the evening in rooms throughout the club various characters show up quietly in a corner, or a great outburst running through the club stealing one of the items in the club.

"It might be a masked Turk or a pert little gentleman with a monocle, cutaway coat, bow tie and a little mustache. Another time it might be someone just back from the Arctic, or an English lieutenant with pith helmet, knee socks, Bermudas and riding crop, or a commando with length of rope thrown over his shoulder, flashlight and articles preparing him to be able to break into the top floor of an ancient museum."

Pleasure's Grandchildren: Merriweather Pleasure had a granddaughter, Katie, who converted the island's Machine Shop (Doodles which became the Island Depot) into Katie's Kustom Kars, the first female owned and operated auto customizing shop in the southeastern United States. Katie, aka "Doodles," closed the shop in 1954 to join the Air Force as a test pilot for the only customized X-1 ever built.

Gideon Adam Pleasure (the son of Henry), born on the island in 1925, opened the Pleasure Island Publishing Headquarters (Front Page Magazine Portraits) in 1951 to publish *Rutabagas*, a magazine dedicated to "vibrancy through vegetables." The magazine ceased publication after seven issues.

Avigators: The Avigators were a group of native Floridian stunt pilots organized by Merriweather Adam Pleasure in 1939 to carry the mail to and from Pleasure Island. Eventually, they also transported visitors from all over the world to Pleasure Island—"if they knew the right people".

In addition, they operated a short-lived import/export business that lasted until 1951, four years before the Pleasure family declared bankruptcy.

Avigators Supply was originally known as the Pleasure Shipping and Receiving building, constructed in 1924 by Pleasure to facilitate his business refurbishing ships and yachts. Pleasure began using the building as a "clearinghouse and depot for the booty from his global adventures," which led to him repurposing the building for the Avigators. The building was right next door to the Adventurers Club.

The mascot of the Avigators was a Florida alligator attired with flight goggles and wings. It has always been assumed that the character helped inspire Blizzard Beach's Ice Gator and Typhoon Lagoon's Lagoona Gator that first appeared in the 1990s.

Avigators Supply had a brand label designed exclusively for Pleasure Island. The whimsical winged alligator was emblazoned on a wide variety of merchandise, including T-shirts, sweatshirts, magnets, and tote bags. There was also a broad selection of aviation-related gifts, clothing, and accessories. Leather bomber jackets, heavy-duty duffle bags, airplane clocks and sculptures, and a variety of collectibles rounded out the offerings. There was also merchandise with the Adventurers Club logo.

The crashed plane in the front of the Adventurers Club was an Avigator who crashed but ejected his cargo in a net and it hung, attached to a parachute on the obelisk outside the Adventurers Club, for many years.

Originally, there was also a skeleton in a flight suit hanging just above the cargo, but it was removed because it communicated the wrong story about the festivities inside the Club and it received a few guest complaints. Most of the logo is missing from the tail of the plane but it originally said: "Explore the Unknown. Discover the Impossible."

At the time, Church Street Station had the themed Lili Marlene's Aviator's Pub and Restaurant that featured authentic aviation memorabilia from both World Wars and that may have been an inspiration for the Avigators since CEO Eisner wanted to capture the tourists who visited that downtown Orlando location.

Pleasure Island Plaques

The Pleasure Island Histerical Society placed quasi-historical plaques at the entrances to Pleasure Island and on several buildings to share the illustrious and illusionary past of Merriweather Adam Pleasure. The original proposed signage was quite elaborate but was eventually edited down to these descriptions that were finally installed.

PLEASURE ISLAND (entrance plaque near bridge by the ticket booths) Founded 1911

An unverifiable, anecdotal, purely subjective, theoretical alleged purported history. Also, ersatz. A living monument to "the wise fool, the mad visionary, the scoundrel, the scalawag, and the seeker of enjoyment." Merriweather Adam Pleasure, who purchased the island in 1911. Pleasure's profitable canvas manufacturing/sail fabricating empire, founded on this site, provided him with the capital to indulge his lifelong interest in the exotic, the experimental, and the unexplainable. Known as the Grand Funmeister, Pleasure disappeared during his 1941 circumnavigation of the Antarctic. His sons, Henry and Stewart, took over the island and the Pleasure enterprises. Their mismanagement led to bankruptcy in 1955; Hurricane Connie hit that same year, and Pleasure Island was abandoned. In 1987, Archaeologists uncovered the site and its remains, and a large scale reclamation project was begun. In 1989, the new Pleasure Island was re-opened and dedicated to the legacy of Merriweather Adam Pleasure: "Fun for all, and All for fun!"

THE EMPRESS LILLY
The Floating Arts Palace 1886

Originally christened The Floating Arts Palace, this vessel plied the mighty Mississippi River for 25 years. Boat fancier Merriweather Pleasure purchased it in 1911 to use as a home, guest house, and entertainment center while he began construction on Pleasure Island. In 1918, the former showboat was unmoored and transformed into a summer houseboat for steaming down the tree-lined waterways of Central Florida. In 1971 the boat was restored to her original glory and re-commissioned The Empress Lilly in honor of Mrs. Lillian Disney.

LILLY PLAZA
1922

Originally a turnaround for the limousines of guests visiting the Pleasure family houseboat. The plaza was remodeled for the July 4, 1937, debut of the 118-member Pleasure Island Philharmonic Concert Band conducted by Maestro Don G. O'Vanni. The P.I.P.C.B. concerts on this site ended with a piece Mrs. Isabella Pleasure commissioned, the haunting "Fugue for Triangle, Piccolo and Steampowered Riverboat Whistle."

PORTOBELLO YACHT CLUB
Pleasure Family Home 1918

Island Founder Merriweather Pleasure built this home for his family who lived on their beloved island for 20 years. Here, Mrs. Isabella Pleasure hosted hundreds of tea socials, garden parties and croquet tournaments, featuring fine food and uninhibited conversation. As she often said, "If you don't have something nice to say, come sit next to me!" Restored in 1989 as a joint effort of the Walt Disney Company and the Levy Restaurants.

PORTOBELLO ROSE GARDEN

Mrs. Isabella Pleasure, wife of Island founder Merriweather Pleasure, spent 20 years and several-hundred-thousand dollars attempting to crossbreed a "true blue" rose. Like others before her, she had to be content with variations on the color lavender. Mrs. Pleasure's garden, first planted in 1919, was recreated in 1989 from notes in her journals and diaries.

BRIDGE
Originally constructed 1914

This bridge stood until 1943, when young Stewart Pleasure, son of Island founder Merriweather Pleasure, piloted the family showboat directly into the graceful span connecting Pleasure Island with the mainland. Stewart supervised the rebuilding of the bridge in 1944, but destroyed it again on September 2, 1954.

The current bridge was built from the 1914 plans by the Walt Disney Company.

MERRIWEATHER'S MARKET
M. A. Pleasure's Original Sailmaking Factory 1912

Foundation and wellspring of the considerable fortune of Island founder Merriweather Adam Pleasure. Once a month during the full moon, Pleasure could be seen on the roof of this building, chanting to the goddess of the tides to keep his various enterprises afloat. Pleasure Island's first sail was completed here December 18, 1912. After the assembly of the last sail on June 4, 1931, perfectionist Merriweather Pleasure insisted that the factory be preserved intact. The building was devastated by Hurricane Connie in 1955. Restored in 1989.

MANNEQUINS
Pleasure Island Canvas Works Fabrication Plant 1912

Second building erected on the island, this actually housed Merriweather Pleasure's famous canvas fabrication works. In the 1930s, it was converted to a soundstage for Invincible Pictures, then into a design studio and workshop for various Pleasure projects. Most notable of these was a huge locomotive powered by a combination of steam and magnetic power. A colossal turntable was installed to facilitate the work on this revolutionary product, called "Maxwell's Demon" that was intended to revolutionize world transportation. It didn't.

THE ISLAND DEPOT
Pleasure Island Administration Building 1913

Originally a wooden shack housing Pleasure Island's paymaster/accountant/bookkeeper, telegraphy office, mailroom, first aid station, and social center, the first building on this site (constructed in 1913) burned to the ground in 1933 during a party celebrating the repeal of Prohibition. A subsequent building erected on the site was blown apart by a savage 1944 typhoon. Refurbished 1988-1989.

FIREWORKS FACTORY
Fireworks Laboratory and Storage Bunker 1922

Island founder Merriweather Pleasure had a passion for pyrotechnics. In 1922, he persuaded China's premier fireworks inventor, The Bang Master, to immigrate to Orlando. The Master's lab and storage bunker were built on this spot, and for the next four years Orlando's citizens enjoyed stupendous Independence Day aerial displays. On July 3, 1927, a stray spark from Pleasure's pipe set off an explosion that was heard in Tampa, 82 miles away. Mrs. Pleasure insisted that the wreckage of the factory be preserved as a reminder of "Pleasure's Folly." Renovated as a joint venture by the Walt Disney Company and the Levy World Company.

CHANGING ATTITUDES
Pleasure Perfect Upholstery 1923

Six full-time seamstresses worked here to refurbish the interiors of the custom yachts in the Pleasure Island Dry Dock. In 1934, the shop was responsible for stuffing the head of a rare Mongolian Yakoose for the Adventurers Club. This profitable sideline ended in 1943 when a war time shortage of kapok put taxidermy on the endangered species list.

DOODLES
The Machine Shop 1937

Built as a custom tool-and-die shop for fearless flyer and Island founder Merriweather Pleasure's "X-Thing" project. His granddaughter, Katie, converted it into Katie's Kustom Kars, the first female owned and operated auto customizing shop in the Southeastern United States. Katie, a.k.a. Doodles, closed the shop in 1954 to join the Air Force as a test pilot for the only customized X-1 ever built.

ROCK AND ROLL BEACH CLUB
(XZFR Rockin' Rollerdome-a roller skating dance club) Building X 1937

Island founder and UFO enthusiast Merriweather Pleasure built his experimental "X-thing" here. Pleasure himself designed this super amphibious aircraft that could harness the power of the wind. The "X-Thing" flew only once—Sept. 1, 1940—with Pleasure himself at the controls. The test flight is shrouded in mystery, but upon landing Pleasure began broadcasts to outer space. Beamed from the roof of this building, the international Morse Code messages repeated "W-E-L-C-O-M-E."

REEL FINDS
(Hammer and Fire - shop that featured titanium jewelry, stoneware, and wall hangings)
Fittings Foundry 1923

The bronze foundry for Pleasure Island Yacht Refurbishing Inc. was built in 1923. Unique custom fittings, individually cast at great expense, were required to achieve the "pleasure principle" of lavish but functional ornamentation of sailing vessels.

YESTEREARS
Remains of Pleasure Island Ltd. Chandlery and Tool Crib 1924

One of the many support facilities for the cornerstone of Island founder Merriweather Pleasure's commercial empire, Pleasure Canvas and Sailmakers, Ltd. A 1944 hurricane sheared off the front of the building, sending a million (more of less) bolts, screws, linchpins, lugnuts, and spanner wrenches into the depths of Lake Buena Vista.

SUSPENDED ANIMATION
Navigational Pleasure Graphics Ltd. 1924

Island founder and graphics connoisseur Merriweather Adam Pleasure rocked the art world when he lured R. North Camilpoter, America's premier gold leaf stylist, to Orlando. Camilpoter spent his days peacefully hand-painting the bows of the yachts Pleasure refurbished. When Hurricane Charlotte damaged the building in 1944, only three years after his patron's demise, the graphic artist was too dispirited to rebuild.

AVIGATORS SUPPLY
Pleasure Shipping and Receiving 1924

Island founder Merriweather Pleasure had this building constructed to facilitate his business refurbishing ships and yachts. It later became a clearing house and depot for the booty from his global adventures. In 1939, Pleasure befriended a group of native Floridian stunt pilots, the "Avigators" who operated a short-lived import/export business here from 1949-1951.

SUPERSTAR STUDIOS
Mrs. Pleasure's Music Parlor Composed 1929

Built to store island matriarch Isabella Pleasure's gargantuan collection of 78 rpm Italian opera records. Immediately upon her passing in 1949, her two sons sold her collection (valued at $475,000) to an Orlando junk dealer for $150. Refurbished by the Walt Disney Company and Star Trax Enterprises in 1989.

VIDEOPOLIS EAST/CAGE
Artificial Intelligence Lab 1929

Built for Island founder Merriweather Pleasure's son Henry, the "mad genius of Lake Buena Vista" and Henry's life work, the Pleasure Cellular Automaton. Henry died thinking his experiments in artificial intelligence had failed. But when the building was reopened in 1987, the automaton was alive and thriving. In fact, it directed the refurbishing of its home and designed the sophisticated computer hardware that shows itself to best advantage.

LOMBARD PROMENADE
1929

Designed by Island founder and incurable romantic Merriweather Adam Pleasure after a trip he and wife Isabella took to San Francisco. They both fell in love with the city's back-and-forth boulevard, Lombard Street. Isabella wanted a photograph as a souvenir, but Merriweather insisted on recreating the street itself. It later became a favorite site for the legendary, day-long hide-and-seek tournaments organized by the Pleasure grandchildren.

COMEDY WAREHOUSE
Power Station 1912

This building became a storage facility when Pleasure Island was electrified in 1928. Six years later, the power station became home to the Pleasure Island Thespian Players, founded by and featuring Isabella Pleasure, wife of island founder and drama enthusiast Merriweather Pleasure. The players specialized in elaborate Central Florida Historical Pageants, including the seminal "Song of the Seminole." After Mrs. Pleasure's death in 1949, the building was closed and the players disbanded. Since its restoration by the Walt Disney Company, this site is a warehouse, storing strange notions, again attractions and ideas slightly ahead of their time.

NEON ARMADILLO
The Greenhouse 1927

Constructed to house the vast array of exotic desert plants collected by Island founder, a globe-trotter and amateur cactogogist Merriweather Pleasure. Pleasure regarded the Greenhouse as his personal Eden. He nurtured his "prickly pals," as he called them, with fanatical devotion. After Pleasure's disappearance in 1941, his Greenhouse was sealed off. When it was reopened in 1989, scientists discovered a huge and happy family of armadillos. The inhabitants were immortalized in neon by the Island renovators.

ADVENTURERS CLUB
Founded 1932

This imposing building was designed to house the huge personal library and archeological trophy collection of island founder and compulsive explorer Merriweather Adam Pleasure. Pleasure won the plans in a game of dominoes and attributed them throughout his life to noted architects Sir Edwin Luytens, Charles Rennie Mackintosh, and Eliel Saarinen. The building became the headquarters for the Adventurers Club, Pleasure's zany band of globe-trotting friends. Exotic souvenirs of the members' outlandish expeditions and riotous adventures were displayed on the walls. After Pleasure vanished at sea in 1941, the Club was sealed until it was opened to the public for the first time in 1989.

WEST END PLAZA
1941

Island founder and stargazer Merriweather Adam Pleasure was convinced during the sole flight of his "X-Thing" aircraft that he could make contact with alien beings. Working feverishly, Pleasure completed the world's first and only Alien Landing Platform on July 4, 1941. His wife Isabella immediately laid claim to it for her beloved Pleasure Island Philharmonic Concert Band. Much to Merriweather's disgust ("How can 'they' land when that blasted band is playing?'") this became home base for the P.I.P.C.B.

THE PLEASURE ISLAND AMC 10 THEATERS
Pleasure Canvas Works Fabrication Plant No. 12 1922

Originally constructed to house Island founder Merriweather Pleasure's burgeoning canvas fabrication business. Hoping to discover and patent a cheap, clean, abundant, renewable source of power, Pleasure had the building refitted in 1938 as a laboratory for testing "thermomagnetics"—a process designed to harness the earth's magnetic force. The success of the experiment was proven in 1940 when the facility blew sky high with no visible, provable use of combustibles. Pleasure commanded that the ruined super structure and outbuildings remain as testimony to "the awesome power of the planet". Rebuilt jointly by American Multi-Cinemas, Inc. and the Walt Disney Company. Opened in 1988.

LOOKOUT POINT, PLEASURE ISLAND
Defense League 1941-44

Son of Island founder Merriweather Pleasure, "Paranoid Henry" Pleasure camped up here every single night from December 8, 1941, to V-J Day. He was convinced that the Axis powers were plotting an assault on America by coming ashore at Pleasure Island, which was then—and remains—80 miles from the Atlantic Ocean. In his nearly four years of vigilance, Henry fired his musket only once. He mistook a family of herons for the leading edge of an invasion force. The herons escaped unharmed.

About the Author

Jim Korkis is an internationally respected Disney historian who has written hundreds of articles and thirty books about all things Disney over the last forty years. Jim grew up in Glendale, California where starting at the young age of fifteen, he was able to interview some of Walt's original team of animators and Imagineers.

In 1995, he relocated to Orlando, where he worked for Walt Disney World in a variety of capacities including Entertainment, Animation, Disney Institute, Disney University, College and International Programs, Disney Cruise Line, Disney Design Group, Disney Vacation Club, Disney Learning Center, and Yellow Shoes Marketing.

He grew up watching Tarzan movies and on television episodes of *Sheena Queen of the Jungle*, *Ramar of the Jungle*, and *Jungle Jim*. He had a collection of *Tarzan*, *The Phantom*, *Ka-zar* and similar comic books as well as watching several versions of The Jungle Book so he felt he was well prepared when he got a job at the Los Angeles Zoo. He was sorely mistaken.

His original research on Disney history has been used often by the Walt Disney Company as well as other organizations including the Disney Family Museum.

Several websites currently frequently feature Jim's articles about Disney history:

- MousePlanet.com
- AllEars.net
- Yesterland.com
- CartoonResearch.com
- YourFirstVisit.net

Jim is a frequent guest on multiple podcasts as well as a consultant and keynote speaker to various businesses, schools and groups.

Jim is not currently an employee of the Disney Company.

To read more stories by Jim Korkis about Disney history, please check out his other books, all available from ThemeParkPress.com:

- *Secret Stories of Extinct Walt Disney World* (2020)
- *Hidden Treasures of the Disney Cruise Line* (2020)
- *The Vault of Walt, Volume 9, Halloween Edition* (2020)
- *The Vault of Walt, Volume 8, Outer Space Edition* (2019)
- *Disney Never Lands* (2019)
- *Secret Stories of Extinct Disneyland* (2019)
- *The Unofficial Walt Disney World 1971 Companion* (2019)
- *The Vault of Walt: Volume 7, Christmas Edition* (2018)
- *Secret Stories of Mickey Mouse* (2018)
- *More Secret Stories of Disneyland* (2018)
- *Extra Secret Stories of Walt Disney World* (2018)
- *Call Me Walt* (2017)
- *Walt's Words* (2017)
- *Other Secret Stories of Walt Disney World* (2017)
- *Secret Stories of Disneyland* (2017)
- *The Vault of Walt: Volume 6* (2017)
- *Gremlin Trouble* (2017)
- *Donald Duck's Daddy* (2017)
- *More Secret Stories of Walt Disney World* (2016)
- *The Vault of Walt: Volume 5* (2016)
- *The Unofficial Disneyland 1955 Companion* (2016)
- *How to Be a Disney Historian* (2016)
- *Secret Stories of Walt Disney World* (2015)
- *The Vault of Walt: Volume 4* (2015)
- *Everything I Know I Learned from Disney Animated Features* (2015)
- *The Vault of Walt: Volume 3* (2014)
- *Animation Anecdotes* (2014)
- *Who's the Leader of the Club? Walt Disney's Leadership Lessons* (2014)
- *The Book of Mouse* (2013)
- *The Vault of Walt: Volume 2* (2013)
- *Who's Afraid of the Song of the South?* (2012)
- *The Revised Vault of Walt* (2012)

About Theme Park Press

Theme Park Press publishes books primarily about the Disney company, its history, culture, films, animation, and theme parks, as well as theme parks in general.

Our authors include noted historians, animators, Imagineers, and experts in the theme park industry.

We also publish many books by first-time authors, with topics ranging from fiction to theme park guides.

And we're always looking for new talent. If you'd like to write for us, or if you're interested in the many other titles in our catalog, please visit:

www.ThemeParkPress.com

Theme Park Press Newsletter

Subscribe to our free email newsletter and enjoy:

- Free book downloads and giveaways
- Access to excerpts from our many books
- Announcements of forthcoming releases
- Exclusive additional content and chapters
- And more good stuff available nowhere else

To subscribe, visit www.ThemeParkPress.com, or send email to newsletter@themeparkpress.com.

Read more about these books
and our many other titles at:

www.ThemeParkPress.com